# TEXT BOOK OF PATHOPHYSIOLOGY FOR MEDICAL GRADUATES

[According to latest syllabus of M. Pharm of Pharmacy Council of India]

**Prof. (Dr.) Syed Hussain**

Professor

Clinical Medical Sciences &

Pharmacotherapy

AGA Academy, Calgary, Canada

**Mohseen**

Research Scholar

Department of Pharmacology at

NIMS Institute of Pharmacy

University

Jaipur, Rajasthan

**Bushra Choudhary**

Assistant Professor

Aryan college of Pharmacy

Ghaziabad (U. P.)

**Vidya Kakad**

Assistant Professor

(Pharmaceutics)

CSMU School of Pharmacy

Panvel

**NOTION PRESS**

# TEXT BOOK OF PATHOPHYSIOLOGY FOR MEDICAL GRADUATES
## NOTION PRESS
### PREFACE

---

The authors feel great pleasure in presenting the first edition of the book **"Text Book of Pathophysiology for Medical Graduates"** for graduate and post graduate students. The present book on **Text Book of Pathophysiology for Medical Graduates** has been written according to the syllabus of M. Pharm of Pharmacy Council of India and covers full course of the subject.

**THE SALIENT FEATURES OF THE BOOK ARE: -**

- *Easy to understand style of writing* which makes the book a self-study material.

- *Each new concept has been introduced through day-today problem of interest* to the students which makes the subject matter interesting.

- *The language of the book, on the whole, is lucid and easy to understand.*

- Wherever needed *neatly labeled figures have been drawn.*

The authors hope that the students, teachers and other readers will find the book interesting and to the point covering the course. We hope that the students will receive the book warmly.

I express a sincere thank you to the Management of Clinical Medical Sciences & Pharmacotherapy, Department of Pharmacology and Toxicology, Institute of Industrial Research and Toxicology, Aryan college of Pharmacy, AGA Academy and CSMU School of Pharmacy, for their support during the writing of this book.

Every effort is made to keep the book error free. The author will gratefully acknowledge the suggestions to improve the book to make it more useful.

Wishing our readers success in examination and life ahead. The authors feel that their efforts will be fully rewarded if the book serves the purpose for which it is written.

TEXT BOOK OF

PATHOPHYSIOLOGY FOR MEDICAL GRADUATES

**First Edition 2024**

**Published by:**

**NOTION PRESS**

Publisher and distributor

Head office: Notion press Media Pvt. Ltd.

# 7, Red cross Road,

Egmore, Chennai, Tamil Nadu 60008

# TEXT BOOK OF PATHOPHYSIOLOGY FOR MEDICAL GRADUATE

## CONTENTS

Introduction, Pathophysiology, Epidemiology, Symptoms and Complications, Diagnosis, Treatment, Complications, Prevention:

- **Nervous system**
  - Epilepsy
  - Parkinson's disease
  - Stroke
  - Psychiatric disorders
  - Depression
  - schizophrenia
  - Alzheimer's disease.
- **Gastrointestinal system:**
  - Peptic Ulcer
  - Inflammatory bowel diseases
  - Jaundice, hepatitis (A, B, C, D, E, F)
  - Alcoholic liver disease.



Introduction, Pathophysiology, Epidemiology, Symptoms and Complications, Diagnosis, Treatment, Complications, Prevention:

- **Disease of bones and joints:**
  - Rheumatoid arthritis
  - Osteoporosis
  - Gout
- **Principles of cancer:**
  - Classification of cancer
  - Etiology of cancer
  - Pathogenesis of cancer



Introduction, Pathophysiology, Epidemiology, Symptoms and

Complications, Diagnosis, Treatment, Complications, Pre00vention:

- **Infectious diseases:**
  - Meningitis
  - Typhoid
  - Leprosy
  - Tuberculosis
  - Urinary tract infections
- **Sexually transmitted diseases**
  - AIDS
  - Syphilis
  - Gonorrhea

# CHAPTER – 1

## BASIC PRINCIPLES OF CELL INJURY AND ADAPTATION

**INTRODUCTION:**

Cell injury and adaptation are fundamental concepts in understanding how cells respond to various types of stress and damage. Here's a detailed introduction to these principles:

**Basic Principles of Cell Injury**

1. **Definition**:
    a. **Cell Injury**: Refers to the damage that occurs to a cell due to adverse conditions, leading to a loss of cell function or structure. If the injury is severe or prolonged, it can lead to cell death.

2. **Causes of Cell Injury**:
    a. **Physical Agents**: Trauma, temperature extremes, radiation, and mechanical injury.
    b. **Chemical Agents**: Drugs, toxins, heavy metals, and pollutants.
    c. **Biological Agents**: Bacteria, viruses, fungi, and parasites.
    d. **Nutritional Imbalances**: Deficiencies or excesses of nutrients.
    e. **Hypoxia and Ischemia**: Lack of oxygen and reduced blood flow, respectively.
    f. **Immune Reactions**: Autoimmune responses and hypersensitivity reactions.

3. **Mechanisms of Cell Injury**:
    a. **ATP Depletion**: Decreased production of ATP impairs cellular functions, including ion pumps, leading to cell swelling and dysfunction.
    b. **Oxidative Stress**: Accumulation of reactive oxygen species (ROS) damages proteins, lipids, and DNA.

c. **Membrane Damage**: Injury to cellular membranes can cause leakage of cellular contents and loss of membrane integrity.

d. **Calcium Homeostasis Disruption**: Increased intracellular calcium levels can activate enzymes that damage cellular structures.

e. **Protein Misfolding and Aggregation**: Improperly folded proteins can accumulate and disrupt cellular functions.

4. **Types of Cell Injury**:

a. **Reversible Injury**: Cells can recover if the damaging stimulus is removed; characterized by cellular swelling and fatty change.

b. **Irreversible Injury**: Leads to cell death, often marked by necrosis or apoptosis.

5. **Cell Death**:

a. **Necrosis**: Uncontrolled cell death due to severe injury, often resulting in inflammation.

b. **Apoptosis**: Programmed cell death that occurs in a controlled manner without inflammation.

**Basic Principles of Cell Adaptation**

1. **Definition**:

a. **Cell Adaptation**: The process by which cells adjust to stress and changes in their environment to maintain homeostasis and function.

2. **Types of Adaptations**:

a. **Hypertrophy**: Increase in cell size due to increased workload or stimuli, such as in cardiac muscle cells in response to high blood pressure.

b. **Hyperplasia**: Increase in cell number due to increased cell division, seen in conditions like benign prostatic hyperplasia.

c. **Atrophy**: Decrease in cell size or number due to reduced workload, decreased nutrients, or aging.

d. **Metaplasia**: Replacement of one cell type with another, often seen in chronic irritation or inflammation, such as in the respiratory tract of smokers.

3. **Mechanisms of Adaptation**:

   a. **Stress Response Pathways**: Activation of various cellular pathways, such as heat shock proteins, to manage stress.

   b. **Gene Expression Changes**: Alterations in gene expression to produce proteins that help the cell cope with the stress.

   c. **Autophagy**: Cellular process where cells degrade and recycle damaged organelles and proteins.

4. **Limitations of Adaptation**:

   a. **Thresholds**: Cells can only adapt to a certain extent; beyond this threshold, adaptation fails, leading to injury or death.

   b. **Maladaptive Responses**: Sometimes, adaptive changes can become maladaptive and contribute to disease.

## DEFINITIONS OF CELL INJURY AND ADAPTATION

### Cell Injury

**Definition**: Cell injury refers to the damage sustained by a cell when it is exposed to adverse conditions or harmful stimuli. This damage impairs the cell's normal function and structure and can lead to a range of outcomes depending on the severity and duration of the injury.

**Key Aspects**:

1. **Nature of Injury**: The injury can be physical, chemical, biological, or environmental.

2. **Severity**: The extent of the injury can vary from mild and reversible to severe and irreversible.

3. **Outcomes**: Depending on the injury's severity and the cell's capacity to adapt or recover, outcomes can include reversible injury, cell death, or chronic disease.

**Mechanisms:**

1. **ATP Depletion**: Insufficient energy to power essential cellular functions.
2. **Oxidative Stress**: Damage caused by reactive oxygen species (ROS).
3. **Membrane Damage**: Loss of membrane integrity and function.
4. **Calcium Overload**: Disruption of calcium homeostasis leading to activation of damaging enzymes.
5. **Protein Misfolding**: Accumulation of incorrectly folded proteins.

**Consequences:**

1. **Reversible Injury**: Temporary impairment that resolves once the harmful stimulus is removed (e.g., cell swelling, fatty change).
2. **Irreversible Injury**: Leads to cell death through necrosis or apoptosis when the damage is too severe or prolonged.

## Cell Adaptation

**Definition**: Cell adaptation refers to the cellular processes that enable a cell to adjust to changes in its environment or stressors in order to maintain homeostasis and function effectively. These adaptive responses help cells survive and continue to perform their functions despite adverse conditions.

**Key Aspects:**

1. **Purpose**: To manage stress and prevent cell death by modifying cell structure and function.
2. **Types**: Adaptations can include changes in cell size, number, or type in response to specific stimuli.
3. **Limits**: Adaptations have thresholds beyond which they become ineffective, leading to injury or disease.

**Types of Adaptations:**

1. **Hypertrophy**: Increase in cell size due to increased workload or stimulation (e.g., muscle cells in response to exercise).
2. **Hyperplasia**: Increase in cell number due to increased cell division (e.g., epithelial cells in response to irritation).

3. **Atrophy**: Decrease in cell size or number due to reduced workload, decreased nutrients, or aging (e.g., muscle atrophy from disuse).

4. **Metaplasia**: Replacement of one differentiated cell type with another, usually in response to chronic irritation or inflammation (e.g., squamous metaplasia in the respiratory epithelium of smokers).

**Mechanisms**:

1. **Stress Response Pathways**: Activation of cellular mechanisms like heat shock proteins to protect against stress.

2. **Gene Expression Changes**: Adjustments in gene expression to produce proteins that help the cell cope with stress.

3. **Autophagy**: The process by which cells degrade and recycle damaged organelles and proteins to maintain function.

**Limits of Adaptation**:

1. **Thresholds**: Cells can only adapt to a certain extent; beyond this threshold, adaptation fails and can lead to injury or disease.

2. **Maladaptive Responses**: Some adaptations may become harmful if they persist or are excessive, potentially leading to disease.

## HOMEOSTASIS

Homeostasis is a fundamental concept in cellular physiology and is crucial for understanding cell injury and adaptation. Here's a detailed look at how homeostasis relates to these principles:

**Homeostasis**

**Definition**: Homeostasis refers to the process by which living organisms, including cells, maintain a stable internal environment despite external changes. This stability is crucial for the cell's proper functioning and survival.

**Key Aspects**:

1. **Dynamic Equilibrium**: Homeostasis is not a static state but rather a dynamic process where internal conditions fluctuate within a narrow range around a set point.

2. **Regulatory Mechanisms**: Cells use various feedback mechanisms to adjust their internal environment and maintain balance.

3. **Parameters Controlled**: Includes factors like temperature, pH, ion concentrations, and metabolic processes.

**Role of Homeostasis in Cell Injury and Adaptation**

**1. Homeostatic Mechanisms:**

a. **Feedback Systems**: Cells employ feedback loops to regulate their internal conditions. For example, the regulation of intracellular calcium levels involves feedback mechanisms that adjust calcium influx and efflux.

b. **Stress Response**: Cells activate stress response pathways (e.g., heat shock proteins) to restore homeostasis when exposed to adverse conditions like high temperatures or oxidative stress.

c. **Metabolic Adaptations**: In response to metabolic stress, cells may adjust their metabolic pathways to produce energy more efficiently or protect against damage.

**2. Cell Injury and Disruption of Homeostasis:**

a. **ATP Depletion**: Energy failure impairs homeostatic mechanisms, leading to cellular dysfunction and injury. For instance, decreased ATP affects ion pumps, causing ionic imbalances and cellular swelling.

b. **Oxidative Stress**: Excessive reactive oxygen species (ROS) damage cellular components, disrupting homeostatic processes and leading to cell injury.

c. **Membrane Damage**: Injury to cellular membranes affects their ability to maintain ionic gradients and other homeostatic functions, resulting in cell damage or death.

d. **Calcium Overload**: Increased intracellular calcium disrupts various cellular functions and processes, further compromising homeostasis.

3. **Cellular Adaptation and Homeostasis**:

   a. **Adaptation to Stress**: Cells may undergo hypertrophy, hyperplasia, atrophy, or metaplasia as adaptive responses to stress, aiming to restore or maintain homeostasis.

   b. **Autophagy**: Cells use autophagy to remove damaged organelles and proteins, thereby restoring balance and preventing further injury.

   c. **Gene Expression Changes**: Alterations in gene expression help cells produce protective proteins and adjust their functions to cope with stress and maintain homeostasis.

4. **Limits of Homeostasis and Adaptation**:

   a. **Thresholds**: There are limits to how much a cell can adapt to stress. Once these limits are exceeded, homeostasis cannot be maintained, leading to irreversible injury or cell death.

   b. **Maladaptive Responses**: Sometimes, adaptations meant to restore homeostasis can become maladaptive. For example, chronic inflammation or prolonged hypertrophy can contribute to disease rather than protect the cell.

5. **Disease Implications**:

   a. **Chronic Conditions**: Long-term disruptions in homeostasis can lead to chronic diseases, such as hypertension or diabetes, where cells and tissues fail to maintain proper function.

   b. **Acute Injuries**: In acute settings, such as trauma or infection, the rapid loss of homeostatic control can lead to immediate cell damage or death.

## COMPONENTS AND TYPES OF FEEDBACK SYSTEMS

Feedback systems are crucial for maintaining homeostasis in cells and organisms. They allow for the regulation of various physiological processes and help manage responses to internal and external changes. Here's a detailed look at the components and types of feedback systems in the context of cell injury and adaptation:

**Components of Feedback Systems**

1. **Sensor (Receptor):**

   a. **Function**: Detects changes in the internal or external environment and monitors specific variables (e.g., temperature, pH, ion concentrations).

   b. **Examples**:

      i. In cells, sensors might be proteins or receptors that detect changes in cellular conditions or external signals.

      ii. For instance, ion channels and receptors on the cell membrane can sense changes in ion concentrations.

2. **Control Center:**

   a. **Function**: Receives information from the sensors, processes it, and determines the appropriate response to restore homeostasis.

   b. **Examples**:

      i. In cells, the control center could be a central regulatory molecule or signaling pathway that integrates sensory information.

      ii. For example, the nucleus may play a role by altering gene expression in response to stress signals.

3. **Effector:**

   a. **Function**: Carries out the response dictated by the control center to restore equilibrium.

   b. **Examples**:

      i. Effectors can be various cellular mechanisms such as ion pumps, metabolic pathways, or stress response proteins.

      ii. For example, heat shock proteins help protect cells from damage caused by high temperatures.

**Types of Feedback Systems**

1. **Negative Feedback:**

a. **Definition**: A mechanism where the response to a stimulus reduces or eliminates the original stimulus, helping to bring the system back to its normal state.

b. **Characteristics**:

    i. **Stabilizing**: This type of feedback helps maintain homeostasis by counteracting deviations from a set point.

    ii. **Self-Limiting**: Once the desired change is achieved, the system decreases the response to avoid overcorrection.

c. **Examples in Cells**:

    i. **Temperature Regulation**: Heat shock proteins are produced in response to high temperatures, which helps the cell recover from heat stress. Once temperatures normalize, the production of these proteins decreases.

    ii. **Ion Regulation**: The sodium-potassium pump maintains ion gradients. If ion concentrations deviate, the pump adjusts to restore balance.

2. **Positive Feedback**:

a. **Definition**: A mechanism where the response to a stimulus enhances or increases the original stimulus, leading to a greater deviation from the set point.

b. **Characteristics**:

    i. **Amplifying**: This type of feedback reinforces changes, often leading to a more dramatic response.

    ii. **Non-Self-Limiting**: Positive feedback usually continues until a specific event or endpoint is reached.

c. **Examples in Cells**:

    i. **Blood Clotting**: When a blood vessel is injured, platelets adhere to the site and release chemicals that attract more platelets, amplifying the clotting process until the bleeding stops.

ii. **Inflammatory Response**: During inflammation, cytokines and other signaling molecules are released, which can attract more immune cells and amplify the inflammatory response.

**Role in Cell Injury and Adaptation**

**1. Negative Feedback in Cell Injury and Adaptation**:

a. **Stress Response**: In response to cellular stress, negative feedback mechanisms help to counteract the effects and restore normal function. For example, if oxidative stress increases, cells may activate antioxidant defenses to reduce ROS levels.

b. **Regulation of Protein Expression**: Cells regulate the expression of stress-related proteins to prevent excessive damage and restore homeostasis.

**2. Positive Feedback in Cell Injury and Adaptation**:

a. **Damage Amplification**: In some cases, positive feedback can exacerbate damage. For example, chronic inflammation can lead to a cycle of tissue damage and immune activation.

b. **Adaptive Responses**: Positive feedback mechanisms can also play a role in reinforcing adaptive responses. For instance, during wound healing, the positive feedback loop of clotting and tissue repair can accelerate the healing process.

## CAUSES OF CELLULAR INJURY

Cellular injury occurs when cells are exposed to harmful stimuli or stressors that impair their normal function and structure. Understanding the causes of cellular injury is crucial for diagnosing and managing various diseases. Here's a detailed look at the causes of cellular injury:

**Causes of Cellular Injury**

1. **Physical Agents**:

a. **Trauma**: Physical injury from mechanical forces can disrupt cellular structure and function, leading to cell death. Examples include cuts, bruises, and fractures.

b. **Temperature Extremes**: Extreme temperatures can cause damage through thermal injury. High temperatures (burns) can denature proteins and disrupt cell membranes, while low temperatures (frostbite) can cause ice crystal formation and cellular rupture.

c. **Radiation**: Ionizing radiation (e.g., X-rays, gamma rays) and non-ionizing radiation (e.g., UV light) can cause cellular damage. Ionizing radiation can induce DNA damage and lead to mutations or cell death, while UV light can cause DNA damage leading to skin cancer.

2. **Chemical Agents**:

a. **Toxins**: Various chemical substances can be toxic to cells, including heavy metals (e.g., lead, mercury), industrial chemicals, and environmental pollutants. These chemicals can interfere with cellular processes and cause damage.

b. **Drugs**: Certain medications, particularly when used improperly or in excessive doses, can cause cellular injury. Examples include acetaminophen toxicity and certain chemotherapeutic agents.

c. **Poisons**: Biological poisons such as those produced by bacteria (e.g., botulinum toxin) can interfere with cellular function and lead to cell death.

3. **Biological Agents**:

a. **Infectious Agents**: Bacteria, viruses, fungi, and parasites can cause cellular injury through direct invasion, production of toxins, or triggering immune responses. For example, viruses can integrate their DNA into host genomes, disrupting normal cellular function.

b. **Immune Reactions**: Autoimmune diseases and hypersensitivity reactions occur when the immune system mistakenly targets and damages healthy cells. Examples include rheumatoid arthritis and systemic lupus erythematosus.

4. **Nutritional Imbalances**:

    a. **Deficiencies**: Lack of essential nutrients, such as vitamins and minerals, can impair cellular functions and lead to diseases. For example, vitamin C deficiency can lead to scurvy, while iron deficiency can cause anemia.

    b. **Excesses**: Excessive intake of certain nutrients or substances can also be harmful. For instance, high levels of cholesterol can lead to atherosclerosis and cardiovascular disease.

5. **Hypoxia and Ischemia**:

    a. **Hypoxia**: A deficiency of oxygen at the cellular level can impair cellular respiration and ATP production, leading to cell injury. Common causes of hypoxia include respiratory diseases and anemia.

    b. **Ischemia**: Reduced blood flow to tissues can result in both hypoxia and a lack of essential nutrients. It can lead to cellular injury and necrosis, as seen in conditions like myocardial infarction (heart attack) and stroke.

6. **Mechanical Stress**:

    a. **Pressure**: Excessive mechanical pressure can cause cellular deformation and damage. This can occur in conditions like compartment syndrome, where increased pressure within a confined space impairs blood flow and leads to tissue damage.

    b. **Shear Forces**: High shear forces can disrupt cellular integrity and function, particularly in tissues exposed to mechanical stress.

7. **Chemical and Environmental Stress**:

   a. **Oxidative Stress**: An imbalance between reactive oxygen species (ROS) and the cell's antioxidant defenses can lead to oxidative damage of proteins, lipids, and DNA.

   b. **Environmental Pollutants**: Exposure to pollutants such as cigarette smoke or industrial chemicals can contribute to cellular damage and disease.

8. **Genetic Factors**:

   a. **Inherited Mutations**: Genetic mutations can lead to structural and functional abnormalities in cells. For example, cystic fibrosis and sickle cell anemia are genetic disorders that result from mutations affecting cellular processes.

## PATHOGENESIS

Pathogenesis of cellular injury involves various forms of damage to key cellular structures. Each type of damage affects cellular function and can lead to cell death if severe or prolonged. Here's a detailed examination of how damage to cell membranes, mitochondria, ribosomes, and nuclei contributes to cellular injury:

### 1. Cell Membrane Damage

**Pathogenesis**:

   a. **Disruption of Membrane Integrity**: Damage to the cell membrane impairs its ability to maintain the cellular environment, leading to the leakage of intracellular contents and the entry of harmful substances.

   b. **Causes**: Physical trauma, chemical toxins, oxidative stress, and infections can all cause membrane damage.

   c. **Mechanisms**:

      i. **Lipid Peroxidation**: Oxidative stress leads to the oxidation of membrane lipids, resulting in lipid peroxidation. This causes loss of membrane fluidity and integrity.

ii. **Protein Modification**: Damage to membrane proteins can disrupt their function, including ion channels and transporters.

iii. **Loss of Membrane Potential**: Damage to ion pumps (e.g., Na+/K+ ATPase) leads to loss of membrane potential and ionic imbalances.

**Consequences**:

a. **Cell Swelling**: Disruption of ionic gradients causes water influx and cell swelling.

b. **Cell Death**: Persistent membrane damage can lead to necrosis due to loss of cellular integrity.

## 2. Mitochondrial Damage

**Pathogenesis**:

a. **Disruption of Energy Production**: Mitochondria are responsible for ATP production through oxidative phosphorylation. Damage impairs this process, leading to ATP depletion.

b. **Causes**: Hypoxia, oxidative stress, toxins, and genetic mutations can damage mitochondria.

c. **Mechanisms**:

   i. **Oxidative Stress**: Excessive ROS production damages mitochondrial DNA, proteins, and lipids, leading to dysfunction.

   ii. **Mitochondrial Permeability Transition**: Increased permeability of the mitochondrial membrane allows the release of pro-apoptotic factors (e.g., cytochrome c) into the cytoplasm, which triggers apoptosis.

   iii. **Failure of ATP Production**: Decreased ATP levels impair critical cellular processes, including ion pumps and protein synthesis.

**Consequences**:

a. **Energy Deficiency**: Reduced ATP production affects cellular functions and can lead to cell death.

b. **Apoptosis**: Mitochondrial dysfunction can trigger programmed cell death through apoptosis pathways.

## 3. Ribosome Damage

**Pathogenesis**:

a. **Disruption of Protein Synthesis**: Ribosomes are essential for translating mRNA into proteins. Damage impairs protein synthesis, affecting cellular function and repair.

b. **Causes**: Toxins, oxidative stress, and infections can damage ribosomes.

c. **Mechanisms**:

   i. **Chemical Inhibition**: Certain toxins (e.g., ricin) inhibit ribosomal activity and protein synthesis.

   ii. **Oxidative Damage**: ROS can damage ribosomal RNA (rRNA) and proteins, leading to defective ribosome function.

**Consequences**:

a. **Impaired Protein Synthesis**: Reduced production of essential proteins disrupts cellular processes and repair mechanisms.

b. **Cell Dysfunction**: Accumulation of misfolded or damaged proteins can lead to cellular dysfunction and death.

## 4. Nuclear Damage

**Pathogenesis**:

a. **Disruption of Genetic Material**: The nucleus contains DNA, which is critical for cellular function and replication. Damage to DNA affects cellular integrity and function.

b. **Causes**: Radiation, chemical toxins, oxidative stress, and infections can cause nuclear damage.

c. **Mechanisms**:

   i. **DNA Damage**: DNA breaks, mutations, and cross-linking can disrupt genetic information and affect replication and transcription.

ii. **Nuclear Envelope Damage**: Damage to the nuclear envelope affects nuclear-cytoplasmic transport and can lead to loss of nuclear integrity.

iii. **Chromatin Alterations**: Changes in chromatin structure can affect gene expression and contribute to cell dysfunction.

**Consequences**:

a. **Genetic Instability**: DNA damage can lead to mutations and chromosomal abnormalities, increasing the risk of cancer and other diseases.

b. **Cell Cycle Arrest**: Cells may enter a state of arrest to repair DNA damage, but persistent damage can lead to cell death or senescence.

c. **Apoptosis**: Severe DNA damage can trigger apoptosis through intrinsic pathways, leading to cell death.

## MORPHOLOGY OF CELL INJURY – ADAPTIVE CHANGES

Understanding the morphology of cell injury and the adaptive changes cells undergo is essential for comprehending how they respond to stress and injury. Here's a detailed examination of the adaptive changes in cellular morphology:

### 1. Atrophy

**Definition**: Atrophy refers to a decrease in cell size and function due to a reduction in cellular workload, nutrients, or other stimuli.

**Mechanisms**:

a. **Decreased Protein Synthesis**: Reduced synthesis of cellular components due to diminished cellular activity.

b. **Increased Protein Degradation**: Enhanced breakdown of cellular proteins and organelles through processes like autophagy.

**Causes**:

a. **Disuse**: Reduced activity, such as muscle atrophy from immobilization.

b. **Inadequate Nutrition**: Malnutrition or starvation can lead to generalized atrophy.

c. **Reduced Blood Supply**: Decreased perfusion (ischemia) can cause tissue atrophy.

d. **Aging**: Natural decline in cellular function and size with age.

**Morphological Features**:

a. **Smaller Cell Size**: Cells appear smaller due to reduced cytoplasmic volume and organelle size.

b. **Decreased Organelles**: Reduction in the number of organelles like mitochondria and endoplasmic reticulum.

c. **Increased Autophagic Vacuoles**: Accumulation of vacuoles containing degraded cellular components.

## 2. Hypertrophy

**Definition**: Hypertrophy refers to an increase in cell size and function due to increased workload or stimulation, leading to an enlargement of the organ or tissue.

**Mechanisms**:

a. **Increased Protein Synthesis**: Enhanced synthesis of structural proteins and organelles.

b. **Increased Cellular Demand**: Cells adapt to increased functional demand by enlarging.

**Causes**:

a. **Increased Functional Demand**: For example, cardiac hypertrophy due to increased blood pressure or muscle hypertrophy from exercise.

b. **Hormonal Stimulation**: Growth factors and hormones can induce hypertrophy, such as in the case of breast tissue enlargement during pregnancy.

**Morphological Features**:
   a. **Enlarged Cell Size**: Cells appear larger due to increased cytoplasmic volume and organelle size.
   b. **Increased Organelles**: More mitochondria, endoplasmic reticulum, and other organelles to meet increased energy and functional demands.

## 3. Hyperplasia

**Definition**: Hyperplasia is the increase in the number of cells within a tissue or organ, leading to its enlargement.

**Mechanisms**:
   a. **Increased Cell Division**: Enhanced proliferation of cells due to increased growth signals or stimuli.

**Causes**:
   a. **Physiological Stimuli**: Hormonal changes, such as endometrial hyperplasia during the menstrual cycle.
   b. **Compensatory Responses**: Tissue regeneration after injury or partial removal, such as liver regeneration.
   c. **Pathological Stimuli**: Excessive stimulation, such as in benign prostatic hyperplasia.

**Morphological Features**:
   a. **Increased Cell Number**: More cells within the same tissue area, leading to tissue enlargement.
   b. **Normal Cell Size**: Cells are usually normal in size, but their increased number causes tissue hypertrophy.

## 4. Metaplasia

**Definition**: Metaplasia refers to the replacement of one differentiated cell type with another type, usually in response to chronic irritation or inflammation.

**Mechanisms**:
   a. **Reprogramming of Stem Cells**: Differentiated cells are replaced by a different type through stem cell differentiation.

b. **Adaptive Response**: Cells adapt to stress or injury by altering their phenotype to a more robust type.

**Causes:**

a. **Chronic Irritation**: Such as smoking causing squamous metaplasia in the respiratory epithelium.

b. **Vitamin Deficiencies**: E.g., vitamin A deficiency leading to squamous metaplasia in the eye.

**Morphological Features:**

a. **Change in Cell Type**: The original cell type is replaced by a different, often more robust type that is better suited to the stress.

b. **Altered Tissue Architecture**: Changes in tissue structure due to the new cell type.

## 5. Dysplasia

**Definition**: Dysplasia refers to abnormal changes in cell size, shape, and organization within a tissue, often considered a pre-cancerous condition.

**Mechanisms:**

a. **Disordered Growth**: Abnormal cell proliferation and differentiation, leading to irregular tissue architecture.

**Causes:**

a. **Chronic Irritation or Inflammation**: Persistent damage or stimulation, such as in chronic infections or inflammatory conditions.

b. **Pre-malignant Conditions**: Dysplasia can be a precursor to cancer, seen in conditions like cervical dysplasia associated with human papillomavirus (HPV) infection.

**Morphological Features:**

a. **Abnormal Cell Morphology**: Cells exhibit atypical size, shape, and nuclear characteristics.

b. **Disorganized Tissue Structure**: Loss of normal tissue architecture and cellular arrangement.

**CELL SWELLING**

Cell swelling is a common and early indicator of cellular injury. It occurs when cells are exposed to stress or damage that disrupts their normal homeostatic mechanisms. Here's a detailed look at the causes, mechanisms, and consequences of cell swelling:

**Cell Swelling**

**Definition**: Cell swelling refers to the increase in cell volume due to the accumulation of water within the cell. This condition is also known as **hydropic swelling**.

**Mechanisms of Cell Swelling**

1. **Impaired Sodium-Potassium Pump Function**:
   a. **Sodium-Potassium Pump (Na+/K+ ATPase)**: This pump is essential for maintaining the intracellular concentration of sodium and potassium ions. It actively transports sodium ions out of the cell and potassium ions into the cell, creating a proper ionic gradient.
   b. **Impact of Injury**: Cellular injury or stress can impair the function of this pump, leading to reduced sodium efflux and potassium influx. This causes sodium and water to accumulate inside the cell, resulting in swelling.

2. **Increased Permeability of the Cell Membrane**:
   a. **Membrane Damage**: Physical or chemical damage to the cell membrane increases its permeability. This allows excessive sodium and water to enter the cell while impairing the cell's ability to expel these substances.
   b. **Consequences**: Increased membrane permeability exacerbates cell swelling and disrupts cellular homeostasis.

3. **Failure of Ion Channels**:

a. **Ion Channels**: These are crucial for regulating the movement of ions across the cell membrane. They include channels for sodium, potassium, calcium, and chloride ions.

b. **Impact of Injury**: Damage or malfunction of these ion channels can lead to abnormal ion flux, contributing to cellular swelling.

4. **Disruption of Cellular Metabolism**:

a. **ATP Depletion**: Cellular energy (ATP) is necessary for many processes, including the function of ion pumps and channels. Reduced ATP levels, due to factors like hypoxia or mitochondrial damage, impair the cell's ability to regulate ion concentrations.

b. **Effect on Swelling**: ATP depletion leads to decreased activity of ion pumps and increased intracellular sodium and water, resulting in cell swelling.

**Causes of Cell Swelling**

1. **Hypoxia and Ischemia**:

a. **Hypoxia**: Reduced oxygen levels impair cellular respiration and ATP production, leading to dysfunction of ion pumps and subsequent swelling.

b. **Ischemia**: Reduced blood flow decreases oxygen and nutrient supply, causing ATP depletion and cell swelling.

2. **Toxins and Chemicals**:

a. **Exogenous Toxins**: Chemicals such as heavy metals or drugs can damage cellular membranes and ion channels, leading to swelling.

b. **Endogenous Toxins**: Metabolic by-products or oxidative stress can also contribute to cellular damage and swelling.

3. **Infections**:

a. **Pathogens**: Bacterial or viral infections can damage cell membranes, disrupt ion channels, or cause ATP depletion, leading to cell swelling.

4. **Inflammation**:

   a. **Inflammatory Mediators**: Inflammation can lead to the release of mediators that increase vascular permeability and affect cellular ion balance, contributing to swelling.

5. **Nutritional Deficiencies**:

   a. **Lack of Essential Nutrients**: Deficiencies in nutrients like potassium or magnesium can affect cellular ion balance and contribute to swelling.

**Consequences of Cell Swelling**

1. **Disruption of Cellular Function**:

   a. **Mechanical Damage**: Increased cell volume can cause mechanical stress and damage to cellular organelles, disrupting their function.

   b. **Altered Metabolism**: Changes in cell volume can affect metabolic processes and cellular signaling.

2. **Impaired Cellular Processes**:

   a. **Reduced Functionality**: Cellular swelling can impair processes such as protein synthesis, enzyme activity, and signal transduction.

   b. **Compromised Cellular Integrity**: Prolonged swelling can lead to rupture of the cell membrane and loss of cellular contents.

3. **Precursor to Necrosis**:

   a. **Cell Death**: Persistent or severe swelling can lead to necrosis, a form of cell death characterized by loss of membrane integrity and leakage of cellular contents.

4. **Inflammatory Response**:

   a. **Local Effects**: Swelling often triggers an inflammatory response, which can contribute to further tissue damage and pathology.

## INTRA CELLULAR ACCUMULATION

Intracellular accumulation refers to the build-up of substances within cells that they cannot adequately process or eliminate. This accumulation can disrupt normal cellular function and contribute to cell injury and disease. Here's a detailed look at the types, mechanisms, causes, and consequences of intracellular accumulation:

**Types of Intracellular Accumulation**

1. **Lipids**:
    a. **Types**: Includes triglycerides (steatosis), cholesterol, and phospholipids.
    b. **Mechanisms**:
        i. **Steatosis (Fatty Change)**: Accumulation of triglycerides in cells, often in the liver. Caused by imbalance in the synthesis, export, and degradation of lipids.
        ii. **Cholesterol Accumulation**: Cholesterol and its esters accumulate in cells due to impaired metabolism or excessive intake.
        iii. **Phospholipid Accumulation**: Seen in conditions like Niemann-Pick disease, where there's impaired lysosomal degradation of phospholipids.

2. **Proteins**:
    a. **Types**: Includes abnormal proteins or misfolded proteins, as well as normal proteins that accumulate due to cellular stress or dysfunction.
    b. **Mechanisms**:
        i. **Hypertrophy of the Endoplasmic Reticulum**: Excessive protein production or defective processing leads to accumulation in the endoplasmic reticulum.
        ii. **Inclusion Bodies**: Accumulation of abnormal proteins forming visible aggregates, such as in neurodegenerative diseases like Alzheimer's and Parkinson's.

3. **Carbohydrates**:
   a. **Types**: Includes glycogen and mucopolysaccharides.
   b. **Mechanisms**:
      i. **Glycogen Accumulation**: Results from metabolic disorders like diabetes mellitus or glycogen storage diseases, where there is impaired glycogen metabolism.
      ii. **Mucopolysaccharide Accumulation**: Seen in lysosomal storage disorders like Hurler syndrome, where there is impaired degradation of glycosaminoglycans.
4. **Pigments**:
   a. **Types**: Includes exogenous pigments (e.g., carbon, tattoos) and endogenous pigments (e.g., lipofuscin, hemosiderin).
   b. **Mechanisms**:
      i. **Lipofuscin**: Accumulates as a result of oxidative stress and aging, representing undigested cellular debris.
      ii. **Hemosiderin**: Iron storage complex that accumulates in conditions of iron overload (e.g., hemochromatosis) or hemorrhage.

**Mechanisms of Intracellular Accumulation**

1. **Increased Production**:
   a. **Overproduction**: Excessive synthesis of a substance can lead to its accumulation. For example, increased synthesis of lipids or proteins can overwhelm the cell's ability to process or export them.
2. **Decreased Removal**:
   a. **Impaired Degradation**: Dysfunction in cellular organelles such as lysosomes can impair the degradation of accumulated substances. This is seen in lysosomal storage disorders.

b. **Decreased Export**: Impaired export mechanisms, such as faulty transport proteins, can prevent the removal of substances from the cell.

3. **Altered Metabolism**:

   a. **Metabolic Disorders**: Genetic mutations or enzymatic deficiencies can disrupt normal metabolism, leading to the accumulation of specific substances. For example, glycogen storage diseases result from defects in glycogen metabolism.

4. **Inadequate Cellular Processing**:

   a. **Cellular Stress**: Conditions such as oxidative stress can impair the cell's ability to process and eliminate accumulated substances, leading to their buildup.

**Causes of Intracellular Accumulation**

1. **Genetic Mutations**:

   a. **Inherited Disorders**: Genetic mutations can lead to enzyme deficiencies and metabolic disorders, resulting in the accumulation of specific substances.

2. **Toxins and Chemicals**:

   a. **Exogenous Substances**: Exposure to toxins or drugs can interfere with normal cellular processes, leading to the accumulation of harmful substances.

3. **Chronic Disease**:

   a. **Metabolic and Degenerative Diseases**: Chronic diseases can lead to altered cellular function and accumulation of substances. Examples include diabetes mellitus and neurodegenerative diseases.

4. **Nutritional Imbalances**:

a. **Deficiencies and Excesses**: Imbalances in nutrient intake can affect cellular metabolism and lead to the accumulation of substances like glycogen.

**Consequences of Intracellular Accumulation**

1. **Disruption of Cellular Function**:

    a. **Impaired Processes**: Accumulated substances can disrupt normal cellular processes, including metabolism, signaling, and organelle function.

2. **Cellular Injury**:

    a. **Stress Response**: The accumulation of substances often triggers a stress response, leading to cell injury or death if the stress is prolonged or severe.

3. **Pathological Conditions**:

    a. **Disease Development**: Accumulation can lead to or contribute to disease development, including liver steatosis, neurodegenerative diseases, and various metabolic disorders.

4. **Organ Dysfunction**:

    a. **Tissue Damage**: Persistent accumulation can lead to tissue damage and organ dysfunction, contributing to the overall pathology of diseases.

# CALCIFICATION

Calcification is the accumulation of calcium salts in tissues, which can occur under pathological conditions and lead to various forms of tissue damage. It is classified into two main types: **dystrophic calcification** and **metastatic calcification**. Here's a detailed examination of calcification, including its mechanisms, causes, and consequences:

**Types of Calcification**

**1. Dystrophic Calcification**

**Definition**: Dystrophic calcification refers to the deposition of calcium salts in damaged or necrotic tissues, despite normal serum calcium levels.

**Mechanisms**:

a. **Local Tissue Damage**: Damaged or necrotic tissue releases intracellular calcium and other substances that promote calcification.

b. **Abnormal Calcium Metabolism**: Local alterations in calcium metabolism or pH can facilitate the precipitation of calcium salts.

c. **Calcium Deposition**: Calcium salts, primarily calcium phosphate, are deposited in extracellular matrices, especially in areas of chronic inflammation or tissue injury.

**Causes**:

a. **Chronic Inflammation**: Inflammation can lead to tissue damage and subsequent calcification. Examples include atherosclerotic plaques and chronic granulomatous inflammation.

b. **Necrosis**: Dead or dying tissues can accumulate calcium salts as a result of cellular breakdown. Examples include caseous necrosis in tuberculosis.

c. **Degenerative Diseases**: Diseases such as osteoarthritis and intervertebral disc degeneration may show dystrophic calcification in affected tissues.

**Morphological Features**:

a. **Basophilic Deposits**: Calcium deposits appear basophilic (blue-staining) on histological stains due to their affinity for dyes.

b. **Ectopic Calcification**: Calcium deposits are found in abnormal locations, such as in the walls of blood vessels, heart valves, or damaged tissues.

## 2. Metastatic Calcification

**Definition**: Metastatic calcification involves the deposition of calcium salts in normal tissues due to elevated serum calcium levels (hypercalcemia).

**Mechanisms**:

a. **Increased Serum Calcium**: Elevated levels of calcium in the blood lead to oversaturation of calcium salts, which then deposit in tissues.

b. **Altered Calcium-Phosphate Balance**: Disruption in the balance between calcium and phosphate levels can lead to calcium precipitation in tissues.

**Causes**:

a. **Hyperparathyroidism**: Overproduction of parathyroid hormone (PTH) increases calcium release from bones and absorption from the gut, leading to hypercalcemia.

b. **Vitamin D Intoxication**: Excessive vitamin D increases calcium absorption from the gut, contributing to hypercalcemia.

c. **Malignancies**: Certain cancers can cause hypercalcemia through bone metastasis or paraneoplastic syndromes.

d. **Renal Failure**: Chronic kidney disease can disrupt calcium and phosphate balance, leading to calcification.

**Morphological Features**:

a. **Diffuse Deposits**: Calcium salts are deposited more diffusely throughout normal tissues, such as the lungs, kidneys, and gastrointestinal tract.

b. **Normal Tissue Involvement**: Unlike dystrophic calcification, metastatic calcification occurs in otherwise healthy tissues due to systemic factors.

**Consequences of Calcification**

**1. Tissue Damage**

a. **Mechanical Disruption**: Calcification can alter the structural integrity of tissues, leading to mechanical disruption or loss of function.

b. **Impaired Function**: In organs like the heart, calcification of valves can impair their function, leading to conditions such as stenosis or regurgitation.

**2. Clinical Implications**

a. **Vascular Calcification**: In the cardiovascular system, calcification of blood vessel walls can contribute to arteriosclerosis and increase the risk of cardiovascular events.

b. **Renal Complications**: In the kidneys, calcification can lead to nephrocalcinosis and affect kidney function.

## 3. Diagnostic Value

a. **Imaging**: Calcification can be detected through imaging techniques like X-rays, CT scans, and ultrasounds, which can help diagnose underlying pathological conditions.

b. **Histology**: Tissue samples can be examined with special stains (e.g., Von Kossa stain) to identify calcified areas and assess their extent.

## ENZYME LEAKAGE AND CELL DEATH

Enzyme leakage and cell death are key phenomena in cellular pathology that provide insights into the extent of cellular injury and the processes leading to cell death. Here's a detailed examination of these concepts:

### Enzyme Leakage

**Definition**: Enzyme leakage refers to the release of intracellular enzymes into the extracellular space due to damage or disruption of the cell membrane. This leakage is often used as a diagnostic marker for cellular injury or death.

**Mechanisms**:

a. **Cell Membrane Damage**: Disruption or rupture of the cell membrane allows intracellular enzymes to escape into the surrounding tissues or bloodstream.

b. **Loss of Cellular Integrity**: As cells undergo injury, they lose their ability to maintain compartmentalization, leading to the leakage of cytoplasmic contents, including enzymes.

**Key Enzymes Involved**:

1. **Lactate Dehydrogenase (LDH)**: Often elevated in cases of tissue damage or necrosis, as it is released from damaged cells into the bloodstream.

2. **Alanine Aminotransferase (ALT) and Aspartate Aminotransferase (AST)**: Enzymes found primarily in liver cells; their leakage indicates liver cell damage.

3. **Creatine Kinase (CK)**: Found in muscle cells; elevated levels can indicate muscle damage, such as in myocardial infarction.

4. **Alkaline Phosphatase (ALP)**: Associated with liver and bone tissue; its elevation can suggest liver or bone pathology.

**Clinical Relevance**:

a. **Diagnosis**: Elevated levels of specific enzymes in the blood can help diagnose conditions such as myocardial infarction, liver disease, and muscle disorders.

b. **Monitoring**: Enzyme levels can be used to monitor the progression of diseases and the effectiveness of treatments.

**Cell Death**

**Definition**: Cell death is the irreversible loss of cellular functions and structure, leading to the cessation of cell viability. It can occur through various mechanisms, including apoptosis, necrosis, and autophagy.

**1. Apoptosis**

**Definition**: Apoptosis is a programmed and regulated form of cell death that occurs in a controlled manner, without causing inflammation.

**Mechanisms**:

a. **Intrinsic Pathway**: Triggered by internal signals such as DNA damage or oxidative stress, involving the mitochondria and activation of caspases.

b. **Extrinsic Pathway**: Initiated by external signals through death receptors on the cell surface, leading to caspase activation and cell death.

**Features**:

a. **Cell Shrinkage**: Cells undergo shrinkage and condensation.

b. **Nuclear Fragmentation**: The nucleus fragments into small bodies.

c. **Formation of Apoptotic Bodies**: Cells break into membrane-bound apoptotic bodies that are phagocytosed by neighboring cells or macrophages.

**Clinical Relevance**:

a. **Homeostasis**: Apoptosis is crucial for maintaining cellular homeostasis and tissue remodeling.

b. **Disease**: Dysregulation of apoptosis can lead to diseases such as cancer (anti-apoptotic) and neurodegenerative disorders (pro-apoptotic).

## 2. Necrosis

**Definition**: Necrosis is an uncontrolled and pathological form of cell death characterized by the loss of cell membrane integrity and subsequent inflammation.

**Mechanisms**:

a. **Cell Swelling**: Cells swell due to impaired ion pumps and accumulation of intracellular water.

b. **Membrane Rupture**: The cell membrane ruptures, leading to the release of cellular contents into the extracellular space.

c. **Inflammation**: The released contents trigger an inflammatory response in the surrounding tissue.

**Features**:

a. **Cellular Swelling**: Initial swelling followed by rupture.

b. **Cellular Disintegration**: Breakdown of cellular components.

c. **Inflammatory Response**: Recruitment of immune cells and release of inflammatory mediators.

**Clinical Relevance**:

a. **Pathology**: Necrosis is associated with conditions such as myocardial infarction, stroke, and gangrene.

b. **Diagnosis**: Identifying necrotic tissue can aid in diagnosing and managing acute injuries and infections.

## 3. Autophagy

**Definition**: Autophagy is a cellular process that involves the degradation of damaged or redundant organelles and proteins through lysosomal pathways.

**Mechanisms**:

a. **Autophagosome Formation**: Damaged organelles or proteins are encapsulated in a double-membraned vesicle.

b. **Fusion with Lysosomes**: The autophagosome fuses with lysosomes, where the contents are degraded by lysosomal enzymes.

c. **Recycling**: Degraded products are recycled to support cellular metabolism.

**Features**:

a. **Cellular Maintenance**: Helps maintain cellular homeostasis and remove damaged components.

b. **Adaptive Response**: Can be a protective response to stress, but excessive or insufficient autophagy can contribute to diseases.

**Clinical Relevance**:

a. **Disease**: Dysregulation of autophagy is linked to diseases such as cancer, neurodegenerative disorders, and infections.

## ACIDOSIS & ALKALOSIS

Acidosis and alkalosis are disturbances in the acid-base balance of the body that can significantly impact cellular function and overall physiological homeostasis. They involve changes in the pH of the blood and tissues, leading to various cellular adaptations and injuries. Here's a detailed examination of acidosis and alkalosis:

**Acidosis**

**Definition**: Acidosis refers to a condition where there is an excess of hydrogen ions ($H^+$) in the body, resulting in a decrease in blood pH below the normal range (7.35–7.45).

**Types of Acidosis:**

1. **Metabolic Acidosis**:
   a. **Definition**: A decrease in blood pH due to a primary decrease in bicarbonate ($HCO_3^-$) concentration.
   b. **Causes**:
      i. **Increased Acid Production**: Conditions like diabetic ketoacidosis or lactic acidosis increase acid levels.
      ii. **Decreased Acid Excretion**: Renal failure impairs the kidney's ability to excrete acids.
      iii. **Loss of Bicarbonate**: Diarrhea or certain renal disorders can lead to a loss of bicarbonate.
   c. **Compensatory Mechanism**: Respiratory compensation through hyperventilation to reduce $CO_2$ levels and partially counteract the acidosis.
2. **Respiratory Acidosis**:
   a. **Definition**: A decrease in blood pH due to an increase in $CO_2$ levels.
   b. **Causes**:
      i. **Impaired Gas Exchange**: Conditions like chronic obstructive pulmonary disease (COPD) or asthma can impair $CO_2$ exhalation.
      ii. **Respiratory Depression**: Central nervous system disorders or drug overdose can reduce respiratory drive.
   c. **Compensatory Mechanism**: Renal compensation through increased reabsorption of bicarbonate and increased acid excretion.

**Effects on Cells and Tissues**:
1. **Decreased Enzyme Activity**: Low pH can alter enzyme activity, affecting metabolic processes.
2. **Altered Membrane Potential**: Changes in pH can affect ion channel activity and membrane potential.

3. **Cellular Injury**: Severe acidosis can lead to cell dysfunction, impaired oxygen delivery, and potential cell death.

**Clinical Implications**:

1. **Diagnosis**: Measured using arterial blood gas (ABG) analysis. Metabolic acidosis is indicated by low bicarbonate levels, while respiratory acidosis is indicated by high $CO_2$ levels.

2. **Treatment**: Addressing the underlying cause (e.g., administering bicarbonate for metabolic acidosis or improving ventilation for respiratory acidosis).

**Alkalosis**

**Definition**: Alkalosis refers to a condition where there is a deficiency of hydrogen ions, leading to an increase in blood pH above the normal range.

**Types of Alkalosis**:

1. **Metabolic Alkalosis**:

    a. **Definition**: An increase in blood pH due to a primary increase in bicarbonate concentration.

    b. **Causes**:

        i. **Excessive Bicarbonate**: Overuse of antacids or bicarbonate-containing solutions.

        ii. **Loss of Acid**: Vomiting or gastric suction can lead to loss of hydrogen ions.

        iii. **Diuretic Use**: Certain diuretics can cause loss of potassium and hydrogen ions.

    c. **Compensatory Mechanism**: Respiratory compensation through hypoventilation to increase $CO_2$ levels and partially counteract the alkalosis.

2. **Respiratory Alkalosis**:

    a. **Definition**: An increase in blood pH due to a decrease in $CO_2$ levels.

b. **Causes**:

    i. **Hyperventilation**: Conditions like anxiety, pain, or hypoxia can cause excessive breathing and reduced $CO_2$ levels.

    ii. **High Altitude**: Reduced atmospheric $CO_2$ can contribute to respiratory alkalosis.

c. **Compensatory Mechanism**: Renal compensation through decreased reabsorption of bicarbonate and reduced acid excretion.

**Effects on Cells and Tissues**:

1. **Increased Enzyme Activity**: High pH can enhance enzyme activity, potentially disrupting normal metabolic processes.

2. **Altered Membrane Potential**: Changes in pH can affect ion channel activity and neuronal excitability.

3. **Cellular Dysfunction**: Severe alkalosis can lead to neuromuscular symptoms like muscle cramps, tetany, and potentially seizures.

**Clinical Implications**:

1. **Diagnosis**: Measured using arterial blood gas (ABG) analysis. Metabolic alkalosis is indicated by high bicarbonate levels, while respiratory alkalosis is indicated by low $CO_2$ levels.

2. **Treatment**: Addressing the underlying cause (e.g., reducing hyperventilation for respiratory alkalosis or managing electrolyte imbalances for metabolic alkalosis).

## ELECTROLYTE IMBALANCE

Electrolyte imbalance refers to disturbances in the levels of electrolytes in the body, which are essential for maintaining various physiological functions, including fluid balance, nerve conduction, and muscle contraction. These imbalances can lead to significant cellular and systemic effects. Here's a detailed examination of electrolyte imbalance, including its causes, effects, and management:

**Key Electrolytes**

1. Sodium ($Na^+$)

2. Potassium ($K^+$)

3. Calcium ($Ca^{2+}$)

4. Magnesium ($Mg^{2+}$)

5. Chloride ($Cl^-$)

6. Bicarbonate ($HCO_3^-$)

**Types of Electrolyte Imbalances**

**1. Sodium Imbalance**

**Hyponatremia (Low Sodium Levels):**

a. **Definition**: Serum sodium levels below 135 mEq/L.

b. **Causes**:

   i. **Excessive Fluid Intake**: Overhydration or administration of hypotonic fluids.

   ii. **Sodium Loss**: Conditions like diarrhea, vomiting, or excessive sweating.

   iii. **Syndrome of Inappropriate Antidiuretic Hormone (SIADH)**: Excessive secretion of ADH leading to water retention.

c. **Effects**:

   i. **Cell Swelling**: Low sodium levels lead to water influx into cells, causing cellular swelling and potential lysis.

   ii. **Neurological Symptoms**: Confusion, seizures, or coma due to brain cell swelling.

d. **Management**: Correction involves fluid restriction, careful sodium replacement, and addressing underlying causes.

**Hypernatremia (High Sodium Levels):**

a. **Definition**: Serum sodium levels above 145 mEq/L.

b. **Causes**:

   i. **Dehydration**: Inadequate fluid intake or excessive fluid loss.

ii. **Hyperaldosteronism**: Excessive aldosterone leading to sodium retention.

c. **Effects**:

   i. **Cell Shrinkage**: High sodium levels cause water to leave cells, leading to cellular dehydration.

   ii. **Neurological Symptoms**: Irritability, lethargy, or seizures due to brain cell dehydration.

d. **Management**: Involves controlled fluid replacement and managing the underlying cause.

## 2. Potassium Imbalance

**Hypokalemia (Low Potassium Levels)**:

a. **Definition**: Serum potassium levels below 3.5 mEq/L.

b. **Causes**:

   i. **Increased Loss**: Diuretics, vomiting, or diarrhea.

   ii. **Shift into Cells**: Conditions like alkalosis or insulin administration.

c. **Effects**:

   i. **Muscle Weakness**: Due to impaired muscle contraction.

   ii. **Cardiac Arrhythmias**: Potassium is crucial for normal cardiac rhythm, and its deficiency can lead to arrhythmias.

d. **Management**: Potassium replacement through oral or intravenous means and addressing the underlying cause.

**Hyperkalemia (High Potassium Levels)**:

a. **Definition**: Serum potassium levels above 5.0 mEq/L.

b. **Causes**:

   i. **Renal Failure**: Impaired excretion of potassium.

   ii. **Cellular Release**: Conditions like rhabdomyolysis or hemolysis.

c. **Effects**:

   i. **Cardiac Arrhythmias**: High potassium levels can cause life-threatening arrhythmias.

ii.    **Muscle Weakness**: Due to impaired neuromuscular function.

d. **Management**: Includes medications to shift potassium into cells, increase excretion, and treat the underlying condition.

## 3. Calcium Imbalance

**Hypocalcemia (Low Calcium Levels):**

a. **Definition**: Serum calcium levels below 8.5 mg/dL.

b. **Causes**:

i.    **Hypoparathyroidism**: Reduced parathyroid hormone levels.

ii.    **Vitamin D Deficiency**: Inadequate calcium absorption.

iii.    **Renal Failure**: Impaired calcium metabolism.

c. **Effects**:

i.    **Neuromuscular Symptoms**: Muscle cramps, tetany, or seizures.

ii.    **Cardiac Arrhythmias**: Impaired cardiac function.

d. **Management**: Calcium supplementation and addressing the underlying cause.

**Hypercalcemia (High Calcium Levels):**

a. **Definition**: Serum calcium levels above 10.5 mg/dL.

b. **Causes**:

i.    **Hyperparathyroidism**: Excessive parathyroid hormone.

ii.    **Malignancy**: Certain cancers can increase calcium release from bones.

iii.    **Vitamin D Excess**: Overuse of vitamin D supplements.

c. **Effects**:

i.    **Neurological Symptoms**: Confusion, lethargy, or coma.

ii.    **Renal Stones**: Increased calcium can lead to kidney stones.

d. **Management**: Hydration, medications to reduce calcium levels, and treatment of the underlying cause.

## 4. Magnesium Imbalance

**Hypomagnesemia (Low Magnesium Levels):**

a. **Definition**: Serum magnesium levels below 1.8 mg/dL.

b. **Causes**:

    i. **Gastrointestinal Losses**: Vomiting, diarrhea.

    ii. **Renal Losses**: Certain diuretics or renal disorders.

c. **Effects**:

    i. **Neuromuscular Symptoms**: Tremors, muscle cramps, or seizures.

    ii. **Cardiac Arrhythmias**: Similar to other electrolyte disturbances.

d. **Management**: Magnesium supplementation and addressing underlying causes.

**Hypermagnesemia (High Magnesium Levels)**:

a. **Definition**: Serum magnesium levels above 2.5 mg/dL.

b. **Causes**:

    i. **Renal Failure**: Impaired excretion.

    ii. **Excessive Supplementation**: Overuse of magnesium-containing medications.

c. **Effects**:

    i. **Neuromuscular Symptoms**: Muscle weakness, lethargy.

    ii. **Cardiac Issues**: Bradycardia, hypotension.

d. **Management**: Discontinuation of magnesium sources, hydration, and treatment of the underlying condition.

## 5. Chloride Imbalance

**Hypochloremia (Low Chloride Levels)**:

a. **Definition**: Serum chloride levels below 98 mEq/L.

b. **Causes**:

    i. **Losses**: Vomiting, diarrhea, or use of diuretics.

    ii. **Metabolic Alkalosis**: Often associated with chloride loss.

c. **Effects**:

    i. **Metabolic Alkalosis**: Associated with low chloride levels.

    ii. **Neurological Symptoms**: Can include confusion or irritability.

d. **Management**: Addressing the underlying cause and chloride replacement.

**Hyperchloremia (High Chloride Levels):**

a. **Definition**: Serum chloride levels above 106 mEq/L.

b. **Causes**:

    i. **Dehydration**: Excessive fluid loss or poor fluid intake.

    ii. **Metabolic Acidosis**: Often associated with high chloride levels.

c. **Effects**:

    i. **Metabolic Acidosis**: Often accompanies high chloride levels.

    ii. **Fluid Imbalance**: Can affect overall fluid balance and distribution.

d. **Management**: Correcting fluid imbalances and addressing underlying causes.

**Multiple Choice Questions (MCQs)**

1. What is the primary cause of cell injury due to physical agents?

    a) Chemical toxins

    b) Trauma

    c) Bacterial infection

    d) Nutritional imbalance

2. Which of the following is NOT a mechanism of cell injury?

    a) ATP depletion

    b) Oxidative stress

    c) Membrane damage

    d) Cellular proliferation

3. What is the primary effect of increased intracellular calcium levels in cell injury?

    a) Reduced ATP production

    b) Activation of damaging enzymes

c) Decreased protein synthesis

d) Enhanced cellular proliferation

4. Which of the following characterizes reversible cell injury?

    a) Necrosis

    b) Apoptosis

    c) Cellular swelling

    d) Cellular fragmentation

5. What type of cell death is characterized by inflammation?

    a) Apoptosis

    b) Necrosis

    c) Autophagy

    d) Senescence

6. Which adaptation involves an increase in cell size due to increased workload?

    a) Hyperplasia

    b) Hypertrophy

    c) Atrophy

    d) Metaplasia

7. What is the main cause of atrophy?

    a) Increased workload

    b) Reduced workload

    c) Increased cell division

    d) Replacement of one cell type with another

8. Which adaptation involves an increase in cell number due to increased cell division?

    a) Hypertrophy

    b) Hyperplasia

    c) Atrophy

    d) Dysplasia

9. Which type of adaptation involves the replacement of one cell type with another?

- a) Hyperplasia
- b) Hypertrophy
- c) Metaplasia
- d) Atrophy

10. What is the primary cause of dystrophic calcification?

- a) Elevated serum calcium levels
- b) Tissue damage or necrosis
- c) Increased parathyroid hormone
- d) Excessive vitamin D

11. What is the main mechanism leading to cell swelling?

- a) Increased ATP production
- b) Impaired sodium-potassium pump function
- c) Enhanced protein synthesis
- d) Increased cellular proliferation

12. What is a common cause of hypernatremia?

- a) Overhydration
- b) Dehydration
- c) Excessive diuretic use
- d) Renal failure

13. What is a characteristic feature of necrosis?

- a) Cell shrinkage
- b) Formation of apoptotic bodies
- c) Cell swelling and rupture
- d) Controlled cell death without inflammation

14. Which condition is primarily associated with elevated serum potassium levels?

- a) Hypokalemia

b) Hyperkalemia

c) Hyponatremia

d) Hypernatremia

15. What is a common cause of metabolic acidosis?

a) Excessive bicarbonate

b) Increased acid production

c) Hyperventilation

d) Decreased acid excretion

16. What is the primary cause of respiratory alkalosis?

a) Increased $CO_2$ levels

b) Decreased $CO_2$ levels

c) Increased bicarbonate levels

d) Decreased bicarbonate levels

17. What is the primary mechanism of dystrophic calcification?

a) Elevated serum calcium levels

b) Calcification of healthy tissues

c) Deposition of calcium in damaged tissues

d) Decreased parathyroid hormone levels

18. What type of cellular adaptation is seen in chronic irritation or inflammation?

a) Atrophy

b) Hyperplasia

c) Hypertrophy

d) Metaplasia

19. What is a common consequence of severe hypokalemia?

a) Muscle weakness

b) Hyperactivity

c) Increased appetite

d) Weight gain

20. What enzyme is often elevated in cases of liver cell damage?

    a) Lactate dehydrogenase (LDH)

    b) Creatine kinase (CK)

    c) Alanine aminotransferase (ALT)

    d) Alkaline phosphatase (ALP)

**Short Answer Type Questions (Subjective)**

1. Define cell injury and list its primary causes.

2. Explain the mechanism of ATP depletion in cell injury.

3. What is oxidative stress, and how does it contribute to cell injury?

4. Describe the process of apoptosis and its significance.

5. What are the main characteristics of necrosis?

6. Explain the difference between hypertrophy and hyperplasia.

7. What causes metaplasia, and why does it occur?

8. Describe the mechanisms leading to cell swelling.

9. What is the role of calcium in cell injury?

10. Explain the difference between dystrophic and metastatic calcification.

11. What are the main causes of hyponatremia?

12. Describe the effects of hyperkalemia on the body.

13. What is metabolic acidosis, and what are its primary causes?

14. How does respiratory alkalosis develop?

15. Explain the significance of enzyme leakage in diagnosing cell injury.

16. Describe the consequences of intracellular accumulation of lipids.

17. What are the main mechanisms of cell adaptation?

18. How does hyperplasia differ from dysplasia?

19. Explain the role of homeostasis in cellular function.

20. Describe the impact of electrolyte imbalances on cellular function.

**Long Answer Type Questions (Subjective)**

1. Discuss the mechanisms of cell injury and how they lead to cell death.

2. Explain the different types of cell adaptation and provide examples of each.

3. Describe the process of necrosis and how it differs from apoptosis.

4. Discuss the causes, mechanisms, and consequences of intracellular accumulation.

5. Explain the role of homeostasis in maintaining cellular function and how its disruption leads to disease.

6. Describe the causes and mechanisms of calcification and its effects on tissues.

7. Explain the different types of acid-base imbalances and their impact on the body.

8. Discuss the mechanisms and effects of electrolyte imbalances, with a focus on sodium and potassium.

9. Describe the role of enzyme leakage in diagnosing and understanding cell injury.

10. Explain the significance of oxidative stress in cellular injury and the mechanisms by which it damages cells.

**Answer Key for MCQs**

1. b) Trauma

2. d) Cellular proliferation

3. b) Activation of damaging enzymes

4. c) Cellular swelling

5. b) Necrosis

6. b) Hypertrophy

7. b) Reduced workload

8. b) Hyperplasia

9. c) Metaplasia

10. b) Tissue damage or necrosis

11. b) Impaired sodium-potassium pump function

12.b) Dehydration

13.c) Cell swelling and rupture

14.b) Hyperkalemia

15.b) Increased acid production

16.b) Decreased $CO_2$ levels

17.c) Deposition of calcium in damaged tissues

18.d) Metaplasia

19.a) Muscle weakness

20.c) Alanine aminotransferase (ALT)

# CHAPTER – 2

## BASIC MECHANISM INVOLVED IN THE PROCESS OF INFLAMMATION AND REPAIR

**Introduction:**

The process of inflammation and repair is crucial for maintaining tissue homeostasis and responding to injury or infection. Here's a detailed overview of the basic mechanisms involved:

**1. Inflammation**

Inflammation is a complex biological response to harmful stimuli, such as pathogens, damaged cells, or irritants. Its primary goals are to eliminate the initial cause of cell injury, clear out dead cells, and repair tissue.

**Phases of Inflammation:**

**a. Acute Inflammation**

1. **Onset:** Rapid onset (minutes to hours).
2. **Duration:** Short-lived (minutes to days).
3. **Key Features:** Edema (swelling), redness, heat, pain, and loss of function.
4. **Mechanisms:**
   i. **Vascular Response:**
      a. **Vasodilation:** Blood vessels widen to increase blood flow to the affected area, which helps deliver immune cells and nutrients.

b. **Increased Permeability:** Blood vessel walls become more permeable, allowing proteins and cells to pass into the tissue.

ii. **Cellular Response:**

a. **Leukocyte Recruitment:** White blood cells, especially neutrophils, migrate from the bloodstream to the site of injury. This process is guided by chemotactic signals.

b. **Phagocytosis:** Immune cells engulf and destroy pathogens and debris.

iii. **Chemical Mediators:** Various chemicals (e.g., histamine, prostaglandins, cytokines) are released to orchestrate the inflammatory response.

## b. Chronic Inflammation

1. **Onset:** Gradual onset.
2. **Duration:** Prolonged (weeks to years).
3. **Key Features:** Persistent inflammation with tissue destruction and healing occurring simultaneously.
4. **Mechanisms:**

    i. **Persistent Inflammation:** Continuous presence of irritants or pathogens leads to prolonged activation of the immune system.

    ii. **Cellular Infiltrate:** Involves a mix of macrophages, lymphocytes, and plasma cells.

    iii. **Fibrosis:** Chronic inflammation can lead to excessive connective tissue formation, resulting in scar tissue.

## 2. Repair

Repair is the process by which tissue architecture and function are restored following injury. This process can occur via regeneration or fibrosis.

**Repair Mechanisms:**

**a. Regeneration**

1. **Definition:** Replacement of lost tissue with the same type of cells, restoring normal function.

2. **Process:**

   i.   **Cell Proliferation:** Cells divide to replace damaged or lost cells.

   ii.  **Tissue Regeneration:** Tissue architecture is restored to its normal state.

**b. Fibrosis (Scar Formation)**

1. **Definition:** Replacement of damaged tissue with fibrous connective tissue (scar tissue) when regeneration is not possible.

2. **Process:**

   i.   **Angiogenesis:** Formation of new blood vessels to supply the growing tissue.

   ii.  **Fibroblast Proliferation:** Fibroblasts produce collagen and extracellular matrix components to form the scar.

   iii. **Scar Maturation:** The initial granulation tissue matures into a fibrous scar with reduced cellularity and increased collagen deposition.

**Key Factors Influencing Repair:**

1. **Type and Extent of Injury:** The severity and type of injury affect the repair process and outcomes.

2. **Tissue Type:** Different tissues have varying capacities for regeneration (e.g., skin vs. cardiac muscle).

3. **Systemic Factors:** Age, nutritional status, and overall health can impact the repair process.

**Overall Integration**

The inflammatory response and repair process are tightly regulated to ensure proper healing and restoration of tissue function. Dysregulation in these processes can lead to chronic inflammation, impaired healing, and disease development. Understanding these mechanisms provides insights into various pathologies and guides therapeutic strategies for managing inflammation and promoting effective tissue repair.

## CLINICAL SIGNS OF INFLAMMATION

The classical signs of inflammation, first described by Aulus Cornelius Celsus in the 1st century AD, are:

1. **Redness (Rubor)**: This occurs due to the dilation of small blood vessels within the damaged area.
2. **Heat (Calor)**: An increase in temperature is seen in the inflamed area, which is also a result of increased blood flow.
3. **Swelling (Tumor)**: This is caused by the accumulation of fluid outside the blood vessels.
4. **Pain (Dolor)**: This can be due to the release of chemicals that stimulate nerve endings or the increased pressure on nerve endings from the swelling.
5. **Loss of Function (Functio Laesa)**: This can be a result of pain or severe swelling, which inhibits the normal function of the tissue.

**Basic Mechanism of Inflammation and Repair**

**1. Recognition of Injury or Infection:**

a. **Pathogen Recognition:**

i. **Receptors:** Pathogen Recognition Receptors (PRRs), such as Toll-like receptors (TLRs) and NOD-like receptors (NLRs).

ii.  **Function:** Detect pathogen-associated molecular patterns (PAMPs) and damage-associated molecular patterns (DAMPs) to initiate an inflammatory response.

b.  **Endothelial Cell Activation:**

i.  **Stimuli:** Inflammatory cytokines (e.g., TNF-α, IL-1).

ii.  **Effect:** Upregulation of adhesion molecules (e.g., selectins, integrins), leading to increased leukocyte adhesion and migration.

**2. Vascular Changes:**

a.  **Vasodilation:**

i.  **Mediators:** Histamine, prostaglandins.

ii.  **Effect:** Increases blood flow to the affected area, causing redness (rubor) and heat (calor).

b.  **Increased Vascular Permeability:**

i.  **Mediators:** Histamine, bradykinin, leukotrienes.

ii.  **Effect:** Endothelial cell contraction or damage, allowing fluid, proteins, and cells to leak into the tissue, causing swelling (tumor).

**3. Leukocyte Recruitment and Activation:**

a.  **Chemotaxis:**

i.  **Chemotactic Factors:** C5a, LTB4, IL-8.

ii.  **Function:** Directs leukocytes to the site of injury or infection.

b.  **Leukocyte Adhesion and Migration:**

i.  **Selectins:** Mediate rolling of leukocytes on the endothelium.

ii.  **Integrins:** Facilitate firm adhesion of leukocytes to the endothelium.

iii.  **PECAM-1 (CD31):** Assists in transmigration of leukocytes through the endothelium.

c.  **Phagocytosis:**

i.  **Phagocytes:** Neutrophils, macrophages.

ii. **Process:** Engulfment and destruction of pathogens and debris, enhanced by opsonization.

## 4. Removal of the Injurious Agent:

a. **Degranulation:**

   i. **Cells:** Mast cells, neutrophils.

   ii. **Mediators:** Release of histamine, enzymes, and other inflammatory mediators.

b. **Production of Reactive Oxygen Species (ROS):**

   i. **Source:** Neutrophils and macrophages.

   ii. **Function:** Kill pathogens but can also contribute to tissue damage if excessive.

c. **Release of Enzymes:**

   i. **Examples:** Proteases, lipases.

   ii. **Function:** Break down extracellular matrix components and pathogens.

## 5. Resolution of Inflammation:

a. **Anti-inflammatory Mediators:**

   i. **Cytokines:** IL-10, TGF-$\beta$.

   ii. **Lipoxins, Resolvins:** Produced to counteract inflammation and promote healing.

b. **Apoptosis of Neutrophils:**

   i. **Process:** Programmed cell death followed by clearance by macrophages.

c. **Phagocytosis of Apoptotic Cells:**

   i. **Macrophages:** Engulf and clear apoptotic cells and debris.

## 6. Tissue Repair:

a. **Regeneration:**

   i. **Process:** Replacement of damaged cells with the same cell type, restoring normal function.

b. **Fibrosis:**

   i. **Formation:** Deposition of collagen and extracellular matrix components by fibroblasts.

   ii. **Mediators:** TGF-β, fibroblast growth factor (FGF).

c. **Angiogenesis:**

   i. **Growth Factors:** VEGF, FGF.

   ii. **Function:** Formation of new blood vessels to supply nutrients and oxygen.

d. **Remodeling:**

   i. **Process:** Matrix metalloproteinases (MMPs) remodel the ECM to restore normal tissue architecture.

**Clinical Signs of Inflammation**

The clinical signs of inflammation are direct manifestations of the underlying inflammatory processes and can vary depending on the location and extent of the inflammation. They are typically summarized as:

1. **Redness (Rubor):**

   a. **Cause:** Increased blood flow to the affected area due to vasodilation.

   b. **Mechanism:** Prostaglandins and histamine induce vasodilation, leading to an influx of blood.

2. **Heat (Calor):**

   a. **Cause:** Increased blood flow (hyperemia) to the inflamed area.

   b. **Mechanism:** Similar to redness, vasodilation results in increased blood flow, raising the local temperature.

3. **Swelling (Tumor):**

   a. **Cause:** Accumulation of fluid (edema) and cells in the interstitial tissue.

   b. **Mechanism:** Increased vascular permeability allows fluid, proteins, and cells to leak into the tissue.

4. **Pain (Dolor):**
   a. **Cause:** Release of pain-inducing mediators and increased pressure from swelling.
   b. **Mechanism:** Prostaglandins and bradykinin sensitize nerve endings, and the pressure from swelling stimulates pain receptors.
5. **Loss of Function (Functio laesa):**
   a. **Cause:** Pain, swelling, and tissue damage affect normal function.
   b. **Mechanism:** Pain and swelling limit movement or function of the affected area, and tissue damage can impair organ function.

**Molecular Mediators of Inflammation and Repair**

Molecular mediators play crucial roles in the regulation and progression of inflammation and tissue repair. They include cytokines, chemokines, eicosanoids, and growth factors, each contributing to different aspects of the inflammatory response and repair processes.

**1. Cytokines**

a. **Tumor Necrosis Factor-alpha (TNF-α):**
   i. **Source:** Macrophages, T-cells, and other cells.
   ii. **Function:** Promotes inflammation by inducing fever, activating endothelial cells, and stimulating the production of other cytokines.

b. **Interleukin-1 (IL-1):**
   i. **Source:** Macrophages, endothelial cells.
   ii. **Function:** Similar to TNF-α, it promotes inflammation and fever, and enhances the expression of adhesion molecules on endothelial cells.

c. **Interleukin-6 (IL-6):**
   i. **Source:** Macrophages, T-cells.
   ii. **Function:** Stimulates the acute phase response, leading to increased production of acute-phase proteins by the liver.

d. **Interleukin-10 (IL-10):**

  i. **Source:** Macrophages, T-cells.

  ii. **Function:** Anti-inflammatory cytokine that inhibits the production of pro-inflammatory cytokines and promotes resolution of inflammation.

e. **Transforming Growth Factor-beta (TGF-β):**

  i. **Source:** Macrophages, fibroblasts.

  ii. **Function:** Regulates the immune response and promotes fibrosis and tissue repair.

## 2. Chemokines

a. **Interleukin-8 (IL-8):**

  i. **Source:** Macrophages, endothelial cells.

  ii. **Function:** Attracts neutrophils to the site of inflammation through chemotaxis.

b. **Monocyte Chemoattractant Protein-1 (MCP-1 or CCL2):**

  i. **Source:** Macrophages, endothelial cells.

  ii. **Function:** Recruits monocytes to sites of inflammation.

## 3. Eicosanoids

a. **Prostaglandins:**

  i. **Source:** Produced from arachidonic acid by cyclooxygenase enzymes (COX-1 and COX-2).

  ii. **Function:** Mediate pain, fever, and vasodilation; some also contribute to the resolution of inflammation.

b. **Leukotrienes:**

  i. **Source:** Produced from arachidonic acid by lipoxygenase enzymes.

  ii. **Function:** Promote leukocyte adhesion, increase vascular permeability, and contribute to bronchoconstriction in asthma.

c. **Thromboxanes:**

   i.   **Source:** Platelets.

   ii.  **Function:** Promote platelet aggregation and vasoconstriction.

## 4. Growth Factors

a. **Vascular Endothelial Growth Factor (VEGF):**

   i.   **Source:** Macrophages, fibroblasts.

   ii.  **Function:** Stimulates angiogenesis (formation of new blood vessels) to support tissue repair.

b. **Fibroblast Growth Factor (FGF):**

   i.   **Source:** Fibroblasts, endothelial cells.

   ii.  **Function:** Promotes fibroblast proliferation and tissue repair.

c. **Platelet-Derived Growth Factor (PDGF):**

   i.   **Source:** Platelets, macrophages.

   ii.  **Function:** Stimulates fibroblast proliferation and collagen production, contributing to tissue repair and fibrosis.

## Clinical Signs of Inflammation and Their Molecular Mediators

1. **Redness (Rubor):**

   a. **Mediators:** Prostaglandins (e.g., PGE2), nitric oxide (NO).

   b. **Mechanism:** Prostaglandins and NO cause vasodilation, increasing blood flow to the affected area.

2. **Heat (Calor):**

   a. **Mediators:** Prostaglandins, histamine.

   b. **Mechanism:** Increased blood flow and metabolic activity result in elevated local temperature.

3. **Swelling (Tumor):**

   a. **Mediators:** Histamine, bradykinin, leukotrienes.

   b. **Mechanism:** Increased vascular permeability allows fluid, proteins, and cells to leak into the tissue.

4. **Pain (Dolor):**

   a. **Mediators:** Prostaglandins, bradykinin.

   b. **Mechanism:** Prostaglandins and bradykinin sensitize pain receptors, contributing to the sensation of pain.

5. **Loss of Function (Functio laesa):**

   a. **Mediators:** Overall impact of pain, swelling, and tissue damage.

   b. **Mechanism:** Pain and swelling reduce mobility and function, while tissue damage impairs normal function.

## DIFFERENT TYPES OF INFLAMMATION

Inflammation can be classified based on its duration, underlying cause, and the type of immune response involved. The main types of inflammation are acute and chronic inflammation, each with distinct characteristics and mechanisms.

### Acute Inflammation

**Acute inflammation** is the body's immediate and early response to injury or infection, characterized by rapid onset and short duration. It aims to eliminate the cause of injury, clear damaged tissues, and initiate tissue repair. Here's a detailed look at acute inflammation and its mechanisms.

### Key Features of Acute Inflammation

1. **Onset and Duration:**

   a. **Onset:** Rapid, occurring within minutes to hours.

   b. **Duration:** Short-term, usually resolving within a few days.

2. **Clinical Signs:**

   a. **Redness (Rubor):** Due to increased blood flow (hyperemia).

   b. **Heat (Calor):** Also due to increased blood flow.

   c. **Swelling (Tumor):** Due to increased vascular permeability and edema.

   d. **Pain (Dolor):** Resulting from the release of pain-inducing mediators and pressure from swelling.

e. **Loss of Function (Functio laesa):** Due to pain and tissue damage.

**Basic Mechanisms Involved in Acute Inflammation**

1. **Recognition of Injury or Infection:**
   a. **Pathogen Recognition Receptors (PRRs):**
      i. **Examples:** Toll-like receptors (TLRs), NOD-like receptors (NLRs).
      ii. **Function:** Recognize pathogen-associated molecular patterns (PAMPs) and damage-associated molecular patterns (DAMPs), initiating the inflammatory response.
   b. **Endothelial Cell Activation:**
      i. **Stimuli:** Cytokines like TNF-α and IL-1.
      ii. **Effect:** Upregulation of adhesion molecules (e.g., selectins, integrins) on endothelial cells, facilitating leukocyte adhesion.

2. **Vascular Changes:**
   a. **Vasodilation:**
      i. **Mediators:** Histamine, prostaglandins.
      ii. **Effect:** Increases blood flow to the affected area, causing redness and heat.
   b. **Increased Vascular Permeability:**
      i. **Mediators:** Histamine, bradykinin, leukotrienes.
      ii. **Effect:** Endothelial cells contract or become damaged, allowing fluid, proteins, and leukocytes to leak into the tissue, causing swelling (edema).

3. **Leukocyte Recruitment and Activation:**
   a. **Chemotaxis:**
      i. **Chemotactic Factors:** C5a, LTB4, IL-8.
      ii. **Function:** Directs leukocytes to the site of injury or infection.
   b. **Leukocyte Adhesion:**
      i. **Selectins:** Mediate rolling of leukocytes on the endothelium.

ii. **Integrins:** Facilitate firm adhesion to the endothelium.

iii. **PECAM-1 (CD31):** Assists in transmigration of leukocytes through the endothelium.

c. **Phagocytosis:**

i. **Phagocytes:** Neutrophils, macrophages.

ii. **Process:** Engulfment and destruction of pathogens and debris. Enhanced by opsonization (coating of pathogens with opsonins like C3b and antibodies).

4. **Removal of the Injurious Agent:**

a. **Degranulation:**

i. **Cells:** Mast cells, neutrophils.

ii. **Mediators:** Release of histamine, enzymes, and other inflammatory mediators.

b. **Production of Reactive Oxygen Species (ROS):**

i. **Source:** Neutrophils and macrophages.

ii. **Function:** Kill pathogens but can also contribute to tissue damage if excessive.

c. **Release of Enzymes:**

i. **Examples:** Proteases, lipases.

ii. **Function:** Break down extracellular matrix components and pathogens.

5. **Resolution of Inflammation:**

a. **Anti-Inflammatory Mediators:**

i. **Cytokines:** IL-10, TGF-β.

ii. **Lipoxins, Resolvins:** Produced to counteract the inflammatory response and promote healing.

b. **Apoptosis of Neutrophils:**

i. **Process:** Programmed cell death of neutrophils followed by clearance by macrophages.

c. **Phagocytosis of Apoptotic Cells:**

    i. **Macrophages:** Engulf and clear apoptotic cells and debris, preventing secondary inflammation.

**Types of Acute Inflammation:**

1. **Serous Inflammation:**

    a. **Characteristics:** Fluid accumulation with low protein content.

    b. **Examples:** Blister formation, serous effusions.

2. **Fibrinous Inflammation:**

    a. **Characteristics:** Fibrin deposition in the extracellular space.

    b. **Examples:** Pericarditis, fibrinous pleuritis.

3. **Purulent (Suppurative) Inflammation:**

    a. **Characteristics:** Accumulation of pus (neutrophils, dead cells, and fluid).

    b. **Examples:** Abscesses, bacterial infections.

4. **Hemorrhagic Inflammation:**

    a. **Characteristics:** Presence of blood in the inflammatory exudate.

    b. **Examples:** Severe infections, trauma.

## Chronic Inflammation

**Chronic inflammation** is a prolonged inflammatory response that can last for months or years. It often results from the failure to eliminate the cause of acute inflammation or from a continuous exposure to an injurious agent. Chronic inflammation is characterized by the presence of macrophages, lymphocytes, and plasma cells, and it leads to tissue destruction and repair.

**Key Features of Chronic Inflammation**

1. **Onset and Duration:**

    a. **Onset:** Gradual, can follow acute inflammation or occur insidiously.

    b. **Duration:** Long-term, lasting months to years.

2. **Clinical Signs:**

a. **Persistent Symptoms:** May include fatigue, weight loss, and low-grade fever.

b. **Localized Effects:** Dependent on the affected organ or tissue, such as chronic cough in chronic bronchitis or abdominal pain in inflammatory bowel disease.

**Basic Mechanisms Involved in Chronic Inflammation**

1. **Ongoing Injury or Insult:**

   a. **Persistent Pathogen or Antigen:** Continued presence of microorganisms (e.g., tuberculosis) or foreign bodies (e.g., splinters).

   b. **Autoimmune Reactions:** The immune system attacks normal tissues (e.g., rheumatoid arthritis).

2. **Cellular Infiltration:**

   a. **Macrophages:**

      i. **Role:** Dominant in chronic inflammation, they phagocytize pathogens, dead cells, and debris.

      ii. **Activation:** Macrophages can be classically activated (M1) to produce pro-inflammatory cytokines or alternatively activated (M2) to promote tissue repair and fibrosis.

   b. **Lymphocytes:**

      i. **Types:** T-cells (CD4+, CD8+), B-cells.

      ii. **Function:** Produce cytokines, provide help to macrophages, and mediate adaptive immune responses.

   c. **Plasma Cells:**

      i. **Origin:** Differentiated B-cells.

      ii. **Function:** Produce antibodies against persistent antigens.

3. **Tissue Destruction and Repair:**

   a. **Continued Damage:** Persistent inflammation leads to ongoing tissue destruction.

b. **Fibrosis:** Excessive deposition of collagen and extracellular matrix components by fibroblasts. This results in scar formation and loss of normal tissue architecture.

    i. **Mediators:** Transforming growth factor-beta (TGF-β), fibroblast growth factor (FGF).

4. **Granuloma Formation:**

a. **Definition:** A specialized form of chronic inflammation where macrophages aggregate to form granulomas, often surrounded by a fibrous capsule.

b. **Types:**

    i. **Caseating Granulomas:** Characterized by central necrosis, seen in tuberculosis.

    ii. **Non-caseating Granulomas:** Without central necrosis, seen in sarcoidosis.

c. **Purpose:** To isolate and contain the persistent antigen or pathogen.

5. **Mediators of Chronic Inflammation:**

a. **Cytokines:**

    i. **Examples:** Interferon-gamma (IFN-γ), Tumor necrosis factor-alpha (TNF-α), Interleukin-6 (IL-6).

    ii. **Function:** Promote and sustain inflammation by activating macrophages and lymphocytes.

b. **Chemokines:**

    i. **Examples:** CCL2 (MCP-1), CXCL9.

    ii. **Function:** Recruit leukocytes to the site of inflammation.

c. **Growth Factors:**

    i. **Examples:** Vascular endothelial growth factor (VEGF), TGF-β.

    ii. **Function:** Promote angiogenesis and fibrosis.

6. **Resolution and Repair:**

a. **Impaired Resolution:** In chronic inflammation, the mechanisms that normally resolve inflammation are often overwhelmed or impaired.

b. **Healing:** May involve fibrosis and scar formation if regeneration is not possible. Chronic inflammation can lead to functional impairment and structural changes in affected tissues.

**Types of Chronic Inflammation**

1. **Chronic Active Inflammation:**

   a. **Characteristics:** Ongoing inflammation with active tissue destruction and repair.

   b. **Examples:** Chronic infections, autoimmune diseases.

2. **Chronic Granulomatous Inflammation:**

   a. **Characteristics:** Formation of granulomas.

   b. **Examples:** Tuberculosis, sarcoidosis, Crohn's disease.

3. **Chronic Fibrosing Inflammation:**

   a. **Characteristics:** Excessive fibrosis and scarring.

   b. **Examples:** Pulmonary fibrosis, liver cirrhosis.

## MECHANISM OF INFLAMMATION

## ALTERATION IN VASCULAR PERMEABILITY AND BLOOD FLOW:

**Vascular Changes in Inflammation:**

1. **Vasodilation:**

   a. **Initial Vasoconstriction:** Brief and transient, typically lasting only a few seconds.

   b. **Subsequent Vasodilation:** Mediated by histamine, nitric oxide, and other vasoactive mediators, leading to increased blood flow (hyperemia) and the classic signs of redness (rubor) and heat (calor).

2. **Increased Vascular Permeability:**

a. **Immediate Transient Response:** Occurs within minutes and is mediated by histamine and bradykinin, causing endothelial cells to contract and form gaps.

b. **Delayed Prolonged Response:** Mediated by cytokines such as TNF-α and IL-1, leading to retraction of endothelial cells over hours to days.

c. **Direct Endothelial Injury:** Can cause sustained leakage due to endothelial cell necrosis or detachment, often seen in severe burns or infections.

3. **Stasis and Margination:**

a. **Stasis:** Blood flow slows down due to increased vascular permeability, resulting in more concentrated blood cells.

b. **Margination:** Leukocytes move toward and adhere to the endothelial lining of the blood vessels.

4. **Leukocyte Extravasation:**

a. **Rolling:** Selectins on endothelial cells and leukocytes facilitate a rolling interaction.

b. **Adhesion:** Integrins on leukocytes bind to intercellular adhesion molecules (ICAMs) on endothelial cells.

c. **Transmigration (Diapedesis):** Leukocytes pass through the endothelial layer and basement membrane into the tissue.

**Basic Mechanism Involved in the Process of Inflammation and Repair**

**1. Recognition of the Injurious Agent:**

a. **Pathogen Recognition Receptors (PRRs):**

   i. PRRs such as Toll-like receptors (TLRs) on macrophages and dendritic cells recognize PAMPs (pathogen-associated molecular patterns) and DAMPs (damage-associated molecular patterns).

**2. Recruitment of Leukocytes:**

a. **Chemotaxis:**

i. Chemokines and other chemotactic factors direct the migration of leukocytes to the site of injury.

ii. C5a, leukotriene B4, and bacterial products are common chemotactic agents.

b. **Leukocyte Adhesion and Migration:**

i. **Selectins:** Mediate weak, rolling interactions.

ii. **Integrins:** Mediate firm adhesion to the endothelium.

iii. **PECAM-1 (Platelet Endothelial Cell Adhesion Molecule-1):** Facilitates transmigration of leukocytes.

## 3. Removal of the Injurious Agent:

a. **Phagocytosis:**

i. Neutrophils and macrophages engulf pathogens and debris.

ii. Phagocytosis is enhanced by opsonins such as antibodies and complement proteins (e.g., C3b).

b. **Degranulation and Release of Mediators:**

i. Mast cells and basophils release histamine and other granules containing inflammatory mediators.

ii. Activated macrophages and neutrophils release reactive oxygen species (ROS) and enzymes to kill pathogens.

## 4. Resolution of Inflammation:

a. **Anti-Inflammatory Cytokines:**

i. IL-10 and TGF-$\beta$ play crucial roles in dampening the inflammatory response.

ii. Lipoxins, resolvins, and protectins also contribute to the resolution phase.

b. **Apoptosis and Clearance of Neutrophils:**

i. Neutrophils undergo apoptosis and are phagocytosed by macrophages.

## 5. Tissue Repair:

a. **Regeneration:**

    i. If the injury is mild and the tissue has a high proliferative capacity (e.g., epithelial cells), regeneration occurs.

b. **Fibrosis (Scar Formation):**

    i. When regeneration is not possible, fibroblasts proliferate and deposit extracellular matrix (ECM) components, leading to scar formation.

c. **Angiogenesis:**

    i. New blood vessels form to supply nutrients and oxygen to the healing tissue.

    ii. Mediated by growth factors such as VEGF (vascular endothelial growth factor).

d. **Remodeling:**

    i. ECM is remodeled by matrix metalloproteinases (MMPs) to restore normal tissue architecture.

## Molecular Mediators of Inflammation and Repair:

1. **Vasoactive Amines:**

a. **Histamine:** Released by mast cells and basophils, causing vasodilation and increased vascular permeability.

b. **Serotonin:** Released by platelets, also contributing to vasodilation and increased permeability.

2. **Eicosanoids:**

a. **Prostaglandins:** Mediate vasodilation, fever, and pain.

b. **Leukotrienes:** Increase vascular permeability and leukocyte chemotaxis.

3. **Cytokines:**

a. **TNF-α and IL-1:** Promote leukocyte recruitment and activation, as well as endothelial activation.

4. **Complement System:**
   a. **C3a and C5a:** Anaphylatoxins that increase vascular permeability and attract leukocytes.
5. **Growth Factors:**
   a. **EGF (Epidermal Growth Factor), FGF (Fibroblast Growth Factor), VEGF:** Stimulate cell proliferation, differentiation, and angiogenesis.

## MIGRATION OF WBC'S

The migration of white blood cells (WBCs), also known as leukocytes, from the bloodstream to the site of tissue injury or infection is a critical step in the inflammatory response. This process involves several well-coordinated steps, including margination, rolling, adhesion, and transmigration. Here is a detailed overview:

**Steps of Leukocyte Migration**

1. **Margination:**
   a. **Blood Flow Dynamics:** In normal conditions, leukocytes travel in the center of the bloodstream. During inflammation, blood flow slows down (due to vasodilation), and leukocytes move closer to the vessel wall (marginate).
2. **Rolling:**
   a. **Selectins:** Endothelial cells express selectins (E-selectin and P-selectin) on their surface in response to inflammatory mediators like histamine and thrombin.
   b. **Leukocyte Interaction:** Selectins on the endothelial cells bind to carbohydrate ligands (e.g., sialyl Lewis X) on the leukocytes, causing the leukocytes to "roll" along the inner surface of the blood vessel.
3. **Adhesion:**

a. **Integrins:** Leukocytes express integrins (e.g., LFA-1, Mac-1) on their surface in a low-affinity state.

b. **Activation of Integrins:** Chemokines presented on the endothelial surface activate these integrins, increasing their affinity for adhesion molecules.

c. **Adhesion Molecules:** Endothelial cells express intercellular adhesion molecules (ICAM-1, VCAM-1). Activated integrins on leukocytes bind firmly to these adhesion molecules, causing the leukocytes to adhere strongly to the endothelium.

4. **Transmigration (Diapedesis):**

a. **Transendothelial Migration:** After adhesion, leukocytes extend pseudopodia and migrate between endothelial cells through the basement membrane. This process involves the interaction of PECAM-1 (CD31) on both leukocytes and endothelial cells.

b. **Basement Membrane Degradation:** Leukocytes secrete proteolytic enzymes (e.g., collagenases) to degrade the basement membrane, allowing them to pass through the vessel wall.

5. **Chemotaxis:**

a. **Migration to the Site of Injury:** Once in the tissue, leukocytes follow a gradient of chemotactic factors (e.g., bacterial products, complement components like C5a, chemokines like IL-8) that guide them to the site of infection or injury.

**Molecular Mediators Involved in Leukocyte Migration**

1. **Selectins:**

a. **E-Selectin:** Induced on endothelial cells by IL-1 and TNF.

b. **P-Selectin:** Stored in Weibel-Palade bodies of endothelial cells and released in response to histamine and thrombin.

c. **L-Selectin:** Found on leukocytes and plays a role in their initial tethering and rolling.

2. **Integrins:**

   a. **LFA-1 (CD11a/CD18):** Binds to ICAM-1.

   b. **Mac-1 (CD11b/CD18):** Binds to ICAM-1 and ICAM-2.

   c. **VLA-4 (CD49d/CD29):** Binds to VCAM-1.

3. **Adhesion Molecules:**

   a. **ICAM-1 (Intercellular Adhesion Molecule-1):** Expressed on endothelial cells and binds to LFA-1 and Mac-1.

   b. **VCAM-1 (Vascular Cell Adhesion Molecule-1):** Expressed on endothelial cells and binds to VLA-4.

4. **Chemokines:**

   a. **IL-8 (CXCL8):** Attracts neutrophils and promotes their adhesion.

   b. **MCP-1 (CCL2):** Attracts monocytes.

   c. **RANTES (CCL5):** Attracts T cells and monocytes.

**Regulation and Resolution**

1. **Anti-Inflammatory Signals:** To prevent excessive tissue damage, the migration of leukocytes is tightly regulated. Anti-inflammatory cytokines (e.g., IL-10, TGF-β) and specialized pro-resolving mediators (e.g., lipoxins, resolvins) help resolve the inflammation by inhibiting further leukocyte recruitment and promoting the clearance of apoptotic cells.

2. **Apoptosis of Neutrophils:** Neutrophils undergo apoptosis after fulfilling their role, and macrophages clear them to prevent prolonged inflammation and tissue damage.

## MEDIATORS OF INFLAMMATION

Inflammation is regulated by a variety of chemical mediators, which are produced by both plasma proteins and cells. These mediators play critical roles in the initiation, amplification, and resolution of the inflammatory response.

**1. Vasoactive Amines**

   a. **Histamine:**

i. **Source:** Mast cells, basophils, platelets.

ii. **Function:** Causes vasodilation and increases vascular permeability by inducing endothelial cell contraction.

b. **Serotonin:**

i. **Source:** Platelets.

ii. **Function:** Acts similarly to histamine in increasing vascular permeability and promoting vasodilation.

## 2. Plasma Proteins

a. **Complement System:**

i. **Components:** C3a, C5a (anaphylatoxins), C3b, C5b-9 (membrane attack complex).

ii. **Function:** Enhance phagocytosis (opsonization), increase vascular permeability, and attract leukocytes (chemotaxis).

b. **Kinins:**

i. **Example:** Bradykinin.

ii. **Function:** Causes vasodilation, increases vascular permeability, and induces pain.

c. **Coagulation and Fibrinolysis Systems:**

i. **Components:** Thrombin, fibrin degradation products.

ii. **Function:** Thrombin promotes inflammation by activating protease-activated receptors (PARs) on cells, leading to increased vascular permeability and leukocyte adhesion.

## 3. Eicosanoids

a. **Prostaglandins:**

i. **Source:** Arachidonic acid via cyclooxygenase (COX) pathway.

ii. **Examples:** PGE2, PGD2.

iii. **Function:** Cause vasodilation, increase vascular permeability, and induce fever and pain.

b. **Leukotrienes:**

    i.   **Source:** Arachidonic acid via lipoxygenase (LOX) pathway.

    ii.   **Examples:** LTB4, LTC4, LTD4, LTE4.

    iii.   **Function:** LTB4 is chemotactic for leukocytes; LTC4, LTD4, and LTE4 increase vascular permeability and cause bronchoconstriction.

c. **Lipoxins:**

    i.   **Source:** Arachidonic acid via alternative pathways.

    ii.   **Function:** Inhibit leukocyte recruitment and promote the resolution of inflammation.

## 4. Cytokines and Chemokines

a. **Pro-inflammatory Cytokines:**

    i.   **Examples:** Tumor necrosis factor (TNF-α), Interleukin-1 (IL-1), IL-6.

    ii.   **Function:** Induce endothelial activation, promote leukocyte recruitment, and stimulate the acute-phase response.

b. **Anti-inflammatory Cytokines:**

    i.   **Examples:** Interleukin-10 (IL-10), Transforming growth factor-beta (TGF-β).

    ii.   **Function:** Inhibit the inflammatory response and promote healing.

c. **Chemokines:**

    i.   **Examples:** IL-8 (CXCL8), MCP-1 (CCL2).

    ii.   **Function:** Direct the migration of leukocytes to the site of inflammation.

## 5. Reactive Oxygen Species (ROS)

- **Source:** Produced by activated leukocytes (neutrophils and macrophages).

- **Function:** Destroy pathogens and contribute to tissue damage if produced in excess.

## 6. Nitric Oxide (NO)

a. **Source:** Endothelial cells, macrophages, neurons.

b. **Function:** Causes vasodilation, reduces platelet aggregation and adhesion, and has antimicrobial properties.

## 7. Neuropeptides

a. **Examples:** Substance P, neurokinin A.

b. **Function:** Transmit pain signals, regulate vascular tone, and modulate immune responses.

**Basic Mechanism Involved in the Process of Inflammation and Repair**

## 1. Recognition of the Injurious Agent

a. **Pathogen Recognition Receptors (PRRs):**

    i. **Examples:** Toll-like receptors (TLRs), NOD-like receptors (NLRs).

    ii. **Function:** Recognize PAMPs and DAMPs to initiate the inflammatory response.

## 2. Recruitment of Leukocytes

a. **Chemotaxis:**

    i. **Chemotactic Factors:** C5a, LTB4, IL-8.

    ii. **Function:** Attract leukocytes to the site of injury.

b. **Leukocyte Adhesion and Migration:**

    i. **Selectins:** Mediate leukocyte rolling on the endothelium.

    ii. **Integrins:** Facilitate firm adhesion of leukocytes to endothelial cells.

    iii. **PECAM-1:** Assists in transmigration of leukocytes across the endothelium.

## 3. Removal of the Injurious Agent

a. **Phagocytosis:**

    i. **Phagocytes:** Neutrophils, macrophages.

    ii. **Process:** Engulfment and digestion of pathogens and debris.

b. **Degranulation:**

   i. **Cells:** Mast cells, basophils.

   ii. **Function:** Release granules containing histamine and other inflammatory mediators.

## 4. Resolution of Inflammation

a. **Anti-inflammatory Signals:**

   i. **Mediators:** IL-10, TGF-$\beta$, lipoxins, resolvins.

   ii. **Function:** Suppress pro-inflammatory pathways and promote healing.

b. **Apoptosis and Clearance of Neutrophils:**

   i. **Process:** Neutrophils undergo programmed cell death and are phagocytosed by macrophages.

## 5. Tissue Repair

a. **Regeneration:**

   i. **Tissue:** Replacement of damaged cells with the same cell type.

b. **Fibrosis:**

   i. **Formation:** Deposition of collagen and ECM components by fibroblasts.

   ii. **Result:** Scar tissue formation if regeneration is not possible.

c. **Angiogenesis:**

   i. **Growth Factors:** VEGF, FGF.

   ii. **Function:** Formation of new blood vessels to supply nutrients and oxygen to the healing tissue.

d. **Remodeling:**

   i. **Process:** Matrix metalloproteinases (MMPs) remodel the ECM to restore normal tissue architecture.

**BASIC PRINCIPLES OF WOUND HEALING IN THE SKIN**

Wound healing in the skin is a complex and dynamic process that involves multiple overlapping phases: hemostasis, inflammation, proliferation, and remodeling. Each phase is characterized by specific cellular and molecular events aimed at restoring the integrity and function of the injured skin.

**Phases of Wound Healing**

Wound healing in the skin is a well-coordinated process that can be divided into four overlapping phases: hemostasis, inflammation, proliferation, and remodeling. Each phase is characterized by specific cellular and molecular activities essential for effective tissue repair.

**1. Hemostasis Phase**

**Immediate Response:**

a. **Vasoconstriction:** Blood vessels constrict immediately after injury to minimize blood loss.

b. **Platelet Activation:** Platelets adhere to the exposed extracellular matrix and aggregate to form a primary plug.

c. **Clot Formation:** The coagulation cascade is activated, leading to the conversion of fibrinogen to fibrin, which stabilizes the platelet plug, forming a stable clot that seals the wound and provides a provisional matrix for incoming cells.

**Key Players:**

a. **Platelets:** Release clotting factors and growth factors (e.g., PDGF, TGF-β) that initiate and regulate healing.

**2. Inflammation Phase**

**Vascular and Cellular Responses:**

a. **Vasodilation and Increased Permeability:** Histamine, bradykinin, and other inflammatory mediators cause vasodilation and increase vascular permeability, leading to the influx of plasma and immune cells into the wound site, resulting in edema.

b. **Leukocyte Recruitment:** Neutrophils arrive first to clear debris and pathogens through phagocytosis, followed by macrophages, which continue phagocytosis and secrete cytokines and growth factors.

**Key Molecular Mediators:**

a. **Cytokines:** TNF-α, IL-1, IL-6.

b. **Chemokines:** IL-8 (CXCL8) that attract neutrophils.

**Key Players:**

a. **Neutrophils:** Clear pathogens and debris.

b. **Macrophages:** Release cytokines and growth factors, regulate the transition to the proliferative phase.

## 3. Proliferation Phase

**Tissue Formation:**

a. **Re-epithelialization:** Keratinocytes at the wound edges proliferate and migrate across the wound bed to cover the wound. EGF and KGF are crucial for this process.

b. **Angiogenesis:** New blood vessels form from existing ones to supply nutrients and oxygen to the healing tissue, driven by VEGF.

c. **Fibroplasia and Collagen Deposition:** Fibroblasts proliferate and synthesize extracellular matrix components, primarily collagen, which provides structural support.

d. **Formation of Granulation Tissue:** Granulation tissue, composed of new blood vessels, fibroblasts, and extracellular matrix, fills the wound bed and provides a scaffold for further tissue regeneration.

**Key Molecular Mediators:**

a. **Growth Factors:** PDGF, TGF-β, VEGF.

b. **Cytokines:** IL-6, TNF-α.

**Key Players:**

a. **Keratinocytes:** Proliferate and migrate to re-epithelialize the wound.

b. **Fibroblasts:** Synthesize and deposit collagen and other extracellular matrix components.

c. **Endothelial Cells:** Form new blood vessels through angiogenesis.

## 4. Remodeling Phase

**Tissue Strengthening and Remodeling:**

a. **Collagen Maturation and Remodeling:** Initially deposited collagen type III is gradually replaced by collagen type I, which is stronger and more organized. This process involves matrix metalloproteinases (MMPs) and their inhibitors (TIMPs).

b. **Wound Contraction:** Myofibroblasts, which express contractile proteins, pull the edges of the wound together, reducing its size.

c. **Scar Formation:** As remodeling progresses, the vascularity of the granulation tissue decreases, leading to the formation of a less cellular and less vascular scar. The scar tissue continues to mature and gain tensile strength over time.

**Key Molecular Mediators:**

a. **MMPs:** Degrade extracellular matrix components.

b. **TIMPs:** Inhibit MMP activity to regulate remodeling.

**Key Players:**

a. **Myofibroblasts:** Mediate wound contraction.

b. **Fibroblasts:** Continue to synthesize and remodel collagen.

**Cellular and Molecular Mediators**

The wound healing process involves a variety of cells and molecular mediators that coordinate to restore tissue integrity and function. These mediators play specific roles in each phase of wound healing: hemostasis, inflammation, proliferation, and remodeling.

**Hemostasis Phase**

**Cellular Mediators:**

a. **Platelets:** These are the first responders to vascular injury. They aggregate at the site of injury to form a primary plug and release granules containing clotting factors and growth factors.

**Molecular Mediators:**

a. **Clotting Factors:** Proteins in the blood that are essential for coagulation. They include fibrinogen, which is converted to fibrin to form a stable clot.

b. **Growth Factors:**

   i. **Platelet-Derived Growth Factor (PDGF):** Released by platelets to recruit neutrophils, macrophages, and fibroblasts to the wound site.

   ii. **Transforming Growth Factor-Beta (TGF-β):** Released by platelets and other cells to promote fibrosis and regulate inflammation.

**Inflammation Phase**

**Cellular Mediators:**

a. **Neutrophils:** The first leukocytes to arrive at the wound site, they clear debris and pathogens through phagocytosis.

b. **Macrophages:** These cells arrive later and continue phagocytosis. They release cytokines and growth factors to regulate the healing process and transition to the proliferative phase.

c. **Mast Cells:** Release histamine and other mediators that increase vascular permeability.

**Molecular Mediators:**

a. **Cytokines:**

   i. **Tumor Necrosis Factor-Alpha (TNF-α):** Produced by macrophages, it promotes inflammation and the recruitment of additional immune cells.

ii. **Interleukin-1 (IL-1):** Produced by macrophages and other cells, it induces fever, promotes inflammation, and recruits leukocytes.

iii. **Interleukin-6 (IL-6):** Promotes the acute phase response and recruits leukocytes.

b. **Chemokines:**

i. **Interleukin-8 (IL-8 or CXCL8):** Attracts neutrophils to the wound site.

c. **Histamine:** Released by mast cells, it increases vascular permeability, allowing immune cells to enter the wound site.

d. **Bradykinin:** Increases vascular permeability and stimulates pain receptors.

**Proliferation Phase**

**Cellular Mediators:**

a. **Keratinocytes:** Proliferate and migrate to cover the wound (re-epithelialization).

b. **Fibroblasts:** Proliferate and synthesize extracellular matrix components, particularly collagen.

c. **Endothelial Cells:** Form new blood vessels through angiogenesis.

d. **Myofibroblasts:** Differentiated fibroblasts that express contractile proteins to pull the wound edges together.

**Molecular Mediators:**

a. **Growth Factors:**

i. **Vascular Endothelial Growth Factor (VEGF):** Stimulates angiogenesis.

ii. **Epidermal Growth Factor (EGF):** Promotes keratinocyte proliferation and migration.

iii. **Keratinocyte Growth Factor (KGF):** Stimulates keratinocyte proliferation.

iv. **Fibroblast Growth Factor (FGF):** Promotes fibroblast proliferation and angiogenesis.

b. **Cytokines:**

i. **Transforming Growth Factor-Beta (TGF-β):** Promotes fibroblast activity and collagen synthesis.

ii. **Interleukin-6 (IL-6):** Continued role in recruiting leukocytes and supporting fibroblast activity.

c. **Matrix Metalloproteinases (MMPs):** Enzymes that degrade the extracellular matrix, allowing for cell migration and remodeling.

**Remodeling Phase**

**Cellular Mediators:**

a. **Myofibroblasts:** Mediate wound contraction by expressing contractile proteins.

b. **Fibroblasts:** Continue to produce and remodel collagen and other extracellular matrix components.

**Molecular Mediators:**

a. **Matrix Metalloproteinases (MMPs):** Degrade extracellular matrix components to allow for remodeling.

b. **Tissue Inhibitors of Metalloproteinases (TIMPs):** Regulate the activity of MMPs to prevent excessive degradation.

c. **Collagen:** Type III collagen is initially deposited and later replaced by the stronger type I collagen.

d. **Cytokines and Growth Factors:**

i. **TGF-β:** Continues to regulate collagen synthesis and fibroblast activity.

ii. **PDGF:** Supports the remodeling process by stimulating fibroblast activity.

**Key Growth Factors and Cytokines**

Growth factors and cytokines are crucial for regulating the various phases of wound healing. They influence cell migration, proliferation, differentiation, and tissue remodeling. Here's a detailed look at the key growth factors and cytokines involved in the wound healing process:

**1. Hemostasis and Inflammation Phases**

**Cytokines:**

   a. **Tumor Necrosis Factor-Alpha (TNF-α):**

      i.  **Source:** Macrophages, T cells, and other immune cells.

      ii.  **Function:** Promotes inflammation, fever, and the activation of endothelial cells. It also stimulates the production of other cytokines and growth factors.

   b. **Interleukin-1 (IL-1):**

      i.  **Source:** Macrophages, fibroblasts, and endothelial cells.

      ii.  **Function:** Induces fever, promotes inflammation, and enhances the recruitment of leukocytes. It also plays a role in the activation of other immune responses.

   c. **Interleukin-6 (IL-6):**

      i.  **Source:** Macrophages, fibroblasts, and endothelial cells.

      ii.  **Function:** Promotes the acute phase response, recruits leukocytes, and stimulates fibroblast proliferation.

**Growth Factors:**

   a. **Platelet-Derived Growth Factor (PDGF):**

      i.  **Source:** Platelets, macrophages, and endothelial cells.

      ii.  **Function:** Attracts neutrophils, macrophages, and fibroblasts to the wound site. Stimulates fibroblast proliferation and collagen synthesis.

   b. **Transforming Growth Factor-Beta (TGF-β):**

      i.  **Source:** Platelets, macrophages, and fibroblasts.

ii. **Function:** Regulates inflammation, promotes fibroblast activity, collagen deposition, and tissue remodeling.

## 2. Proliferation Phase

**Growth Factors:**

a. **Vascular Endothelial Growth Factor (VEGF):**
   i. **Source:** Macrophages, fibroblasts, and endothelial cells.
   ii. **Function:** Stimulates angiogenesis by promoting the proliferation and migration of endothelial cells to form new blood vessels.

b. **Epidermal Growth Factor (EGF):**
   i. **Source:** Platelets, macrophages, and fibroblasts.
   ii. **Function:** Promotes keratinocyte proliferation and migration, essential for re-epithelialization.

c. **Keratinocyte Growth Factor (KGF):**
   i. **Source:** Fibroblasts and other mesenchymal cells.
   ii. **Function:** Stimulates keratinocyte proliferation and migration, supporting the restoration of the epithelial layer.

d. **Fibroblast Growth Factor (FGF):**
   i. **Source:** Platelets, macrophages, and fibroblasts.
   ii. **Function:** Promotes fibroblast proliferation, angiogenesis, and extracellular matrix production.

**Cytokines:**

a. **Interleukin-8 (IL-8):**
   i. **Source:** Macrophages, fibroblasts, and endothelial cells.
   ii. **Function:** Attracts neutrophils to the wound site, facilitating inflammation and debris clearance.

b. **Transforming Growth Factor-Beta (TGF-β):**
   i. **Continued Role:** Regulates fibroblast proliferation, collagen production, and modulates the inflammatory response.

**3. Remodeling Phase**

**Growth Factors:**

a. **Matrix Metalloproteinases (MMPs):**
   i. **Source:** Fibroblasts, macrophages, and endothelial cells.
   ii. **Function:** Enzymes that degrade extracellular matrix components, allowing for tissue remodeling and repair.

b. **Tissue Inhibitors of Metalloproteinases (TIMPs):**
   i. **Source:** Fibroblasts and other cells.
   ii. **Function:** Regulate MMP activity to prevent excessive degradation of the extracellular matrix and control remodeling.

**Cytokines:**

a. **Interleukin-10 (IL-10):**
   i. **Source:** Macrophages and other immune cells.
   ii. **Function:** Anti-inflammatory cytokine that helps resolve inflammation and promote tissue repair.

**PATHOPHYSIOLOGY OF ATHEROSCLEROSIS**

Atherosclerosis is a chronic inflammatory disease of the arterial walls characterized by the formation of atherosclerotic plaques. These plaques consist of lipids, inflammatory cells, smooth muscle cells, and connective tissue. The disease progresses through several stages and involves complex interactions between various cellular and molecular mechanisms.

**Stages of Atherosclerosis:**

1. **Endothelial Dysfunction:**
   a. **Initiation:** The earliest step in atherosclerosis involves damage to the endothelial lining of arteries due to factors such as hypertension, smoking, diabetes, and high cholesterol levels.

b. **Mechanism:** Endothelial cells lose their ability to produce nitric oxide (NO), a vasodilator and anti-inflammatory molecule, leading to increased vascular permeability and leukocyte adhesion.

2. **Lipoprotein Entry and Modification:**

   a. **LDL Accumulation:** Low-density lipoprotein (LDL) particles penetrate the damaged endothelium and accumulate in the intima (inner layer) of the arterial wall.

   b. **Oxidation:** LDL particles undergo oxidation to form oxidized LDL (oxLDL), which is highly atherogenic and promotes inflammation.

3. **Leukocyte Recruitment and Foam Cell Formation:**

   a. **Leukocyte Adhesion:** Endothelial cells express adhesion molecules (e.g., VCAM-1, ICAM-1) that facilitate the attachment of monocytes and T-cells to the endothelium.

   b. **Migration:** Monocytes migrate into the intima and differentiate into macrophages.

   c. **Foam Cells:** Macrophages engulf oxLDL via scavenger receptors, transforming into foam cells. These foam cells are a hallmark of early atherosclerotic lesions known as fatty streaks.

4. **Plaque Progression:**

   a. **Smooth Muscle Cell Migration and Proliferation:** Smooth muscle cells (SMCs) migrate from the media (middle layer) to the intima and proliferate in response to growth factors such as platelet-derived growth factor (PDGF).

   b. **Extracellular Matrix (ECM) Production:** SMCs produce ECM components, including collagen and elastin, contributing to plaque stability.

   c. **Necrotic Core Formation:** As foam cells die, they release their lipid content, forming a necrotic core surrounded by fibrous tissue.

5. **Plaque Complications:**
   a. **Fibrous Cap Formation:** A fibrous cap forms over the plaque, composed of SMCs and ECM. The stability of this cap determines the risk of plaque rupture.
   b. **Calcification:** Calcium deposits accumulate within the plaque, contributing to its hardening.
   c. **Plaque Rupture and Thrombosis:** If the fibrous cap ruptures, it exposes the necrotic core to the bloodstream, triggering platelet aggregation and thrombus (blood clot) formation. This can lead to partial or complete occlusion of the artery, resulting in ischemic events such as myocardial infarction (heart attack) or stroke.

**Basic Mechanism Involved in the Process of Inflammation and Repair**

**1. Recognition of the Injurious Agent:**
   a. **Pathogen Recognition Receptors (PRRs):**
      i. **Examples:** Toll-like receptors (TLRs), NOD-like receptors (NLRs).
      ii. **Function:** Recognize PAMPs (pathogen-associated molecular patterns) and DAMPs (damage-associated molecular patterns) to initiate the inflammatory response.

**2. Recruitment of Leukocytes:**
   a. **Chemotaxis:**
      i. **Chemotactic Factors:** C5a, LTB4, IL-8.
      ii. **Function:** Attract leukocytes to the site of injury.
   b. **Leukocyte Adhesion and Migration:**
      i. **Selectins:** Mediate leukocyte rolling on the endothelium.
      ii. **Integrins:** Facilitate firm adhesion of leukocytes to endothelial cells.

iii. **PECAM-1:** Assists in transmigration of leukocytes across the endothelium.

## 3. Removal of the Injurious Agent:

a. **Phagocytosis:**

   i. **Phagocytes:** Neutrophils, macrophages.

   ii. **Process:** Engulfment and digestion of pathogens and debris.

b. **Degranulation:**

   i. **Cells:** Mast cells, basophils.

   ii. **Function:** Release granules containing histamine and other inflammatory mediators.

## 4. Resolution of Inflammation:

a. **Anti-inflammatory Signals:**

   i. **Mediators:** IL-10, TGF-$\beta$, lipoxins, resolvins.

   ii. **Function:** Suppress pro-inflammatory pathways and promote healing.

b. **Apoptosis and Clearance of Neutrophils:**

   i. **Process:** Neutrophils undergo programmed cell death and are phagocytosed by macrophages.

## 5. Tissue Repair:

a. **Regeneration:**

   i. **Tissue:** Replacement of damaged cells with the same cell type.

b. **Fibrosis:**

   i. **Formation:** Deposition of collagen and ECM components by fibroblasts.

   ii. **Result:** Scar tissue formation if regeneration is not possible.

c. **Angiogenesis:**

   i. **Growth Factors:** VEGF, FGF.

   ii. **Function:** Formation of new blood vessels to supply nutrients and oxygen to the healing tissue.

d. **Remodeling:**

    i. **Process:** Matrix metalloproteinases (MMPs) remodel the ECM to restore normal tissue architecture.

## Mediators of Inflammation

Inflammation is regulated by a variety of chemical mediators, which are produced by both plasma proteins and cells. These mediators play critical roles in the initiation, amplification, and resolution of the inflammatory response.

### 1. Vasoactive Amines

a. **Histamine:**

    i. **Source:** Mast cells, basophils, platelets.

    ii. **Function:** Causes vasodilation and increases vascular permeability by inducing endothelial cell contraction.

b. **Serotonin:**

    i. **Source:** Platelets.

    ii. **Function:** Acts similarly to histamine in increasing vascular permeability and promoting vasodilation.

### 2. Plasma Proteins

a. **Complement System:**

    i. **Components:** C3a, C5a (anaphylatoxins), C3b, C5b-9 (membrane attack complex).

    ii. **Function:** Enhance phagocytosis (opsonization), increase vascular permeability, and attract leukocytes (chemotaxis).

b. **Kinins:**

    i. **Example:** Bradykinin.

    ii. **Function:** Causes vasodilation, increases vascular permeability, and induces pain.

c. **Coagulation and Fibrinolysis Systems:**

    i. **Components:** Thrombin, fibrin degradation products.

ii. **Function:** Thrombin promotes inflammation by activating protease-activated receptors (PARs) on cells, leading to increased vascular permeability and leukocyte adhesion.

## 3. Eicosanoids

a. **Prostaglandins:**

   i. **Source:** Arachidonic acid via cyclooxygenase (COX) pathway.

   ii. **Examples:** PGE2, PGD2.

   iii. **Function:** Cause vasodilation, increase vascular permeability, and induce fever and pain.

b. **Leukotrienes:**

   i. **Source:** Arachidonic acid via lipoxygenase (LOX) pathway.

   ii. **Examples:** LTB4, LTC4, LTD4, LTE4.

   iii. **Function:** LTB4 is chemotactic for leukocytes; LTC4, LTD4, and LTE4 increase vascular permeability and cause bronchoconstriction.

c. **Lipoxins:**

   i. **Source:** Arachidonic acid via alternative pathways.

   ii. **Function:** Inhibit leukocyte recruitment and promote the resolution of inflammation.

## 4. Cytokines and Chemokines

a. **Pro-inflammatory Cytokines:**

   i. **Examples:** Tumor necrosis factor (TNF-α), Interleukin-1 (IL-1), IL-6.

   ii. **Function:** Induce endothelial activation, promote leukocyte recruitment, and stimulate the acute-phase response.

b. **Anti-inflammatory Cytokines:**

   i. **Examples:** Interleukin-10 (IL-10), Transforming growth factor-beta (TGF-β).

   ii. **Function:** Inhibit the inflammatory response and promote healing.

c. **Chemokines:**
  - i. **Examples:** IL-8 (CXCL8), MCP-1 (CCL2).
  - ii. **Function:** Direct the migration of leukocytes to the site of inflammation.

## 5. Reactive Oxygen Species (ROS)

a. **Source:** Produced by activated leukocytes (neutrophils and macrophages).

b. **Function:** Destroy pathogens and contribute to tissue damage if produced in excess.

## 6. Nitric Oxide (NO)

a. **Source:** Endothelial cells, macrophages, neurons.

b. **Function:** Causes vasodilation, reduces platelet aggregation and adhesion, and has antimicrobial properties.

## 7. Neuropeptides

a. **Examples:** Substance P, neurokinin A.

b. **Function:** Transmit pain signals, regulate vascular tone, and modulate immune responses.

**Multiple-Choice Questions (Objective)**

1. What is the primary goal of inflammation?
   - a) To increase blood pressure
   - b) To eliminate the initial cause of cell injury
   - c) To decrease body temperature
   - d) To reduce white blood cell count

2. Which of the following is NOT a key feature of acute inflammation?
   - a) Rapid onset
   - b) Short duration
   - c) Tissue destruction and healing simultaneously
   - d) Edema

3. What causes vasodilation during the acute inflammatory response?

   a) Decreased blood flow

   b) Vasoconstriction

   c) Increased blood flow

   d) Decreased vascular permeability

4. What type of leukocyte is primarily recruited during acute inflammation?

   a) Eosinophils

   b) Basophils

   c) Neutrophils

   d) Lymphocytes

5. Which of the following is a characteristic of chronic inflammation?

   a) Rapid onset

   b) Short-lived

   c) Persistent inflammation

   d) Immediate resolution

6. What is the definition of fibrosis in the context of tissue repair?

   a) Replacement of damaged tissue with the same type of cells

   b) Formation of new blood vessels

   c) Replacement of damaged tissue with fibrous connective tissue

   d) Cell division to replace lost cells

7. What factor influences the capacity of a tissue to regenerate?

   a) Age of the individual

   b) Nutritional status

   c) Type and extent of injury

   d) All of the above

8. Which chemical mediator is primarily responsible for increasing vascular permeability?

   a) Histamine

   b) Serotonin

     c) Interleukin-1

     d) Tumor necrosis factor-alpha

9. Which cells release histamine during an inflammatory response?

     a) Neutrophils

     b) Macrophages

     c) Mast cells

     d) Fibroblasts

10. What is the main function of cytokines such as TNF-α and IL-1 in inflammation?

     a) Promote anti-inflammatory effects

     b) Induce endothelial activation

     c) Decrease leukocyte recruitment

     d) Inhibit the acute-phase response

11. What triggers the recruitment of leukocytes to the site of injury?

     a) Blood clotting

     b) Chemotactic factors

     c) Platelet aggregation

     d) Reduced blood flow

12. Which phase of wound healing involves re-epithelialization?

     a) Hemostasis

     b) Inflammation

     c) Proliferation

     d) Remodeling

13. Which mediator is involved in the formation of new blood vessels during wound healing?

     a) TGF-β

     b) VEGF

     c) PDGF

     d) EGF

14. What role do macrophages play in the inflammatory response?

   a) Release histamine

   b) Produce cytokines and growth factors

   c) Form blood clots

   d) Increase vascular permeability

15. Which of the following is a symptom of acute inflammation?

   a) Increased heart rate

   b) Redness

   c) Muscle cramps

   d) Joint stiffness

16. What is the primary cause of endothelial dysfunction in atherosclerosis?

   a) Hypertension

   b) High cholesterol levels

   c) Smoking

   d) All of the above

17. Which cells transform into foam cells in the development of atherosclerosis?

   a) Lymphocytes

   b) Neutrophils

   c) Macrophages

   d) Platelets

18. What is the primary function of matrix metalloproteinases (MMPs) in wound healing?

   a) Promote fibrosis

   b) Degrade extracellular matrix components

   c) Increase vascular permeability

   d) Stimulate collagen production

19. Which cytokine is primarily anti-inflammatory and promotes healing?

   a) TNF-$\alpha$

   b) IL-1

c) IL-6

d) IL-10

20.What is the function of selectins in the inflammatory response?

a) Mediate leukocyte rolling

b) Facilitate leukocyte firm adhesion

c) Assist in transmigration of leukocytes

d) Enhance phagocytosis

**Short Answer Type Questions (Subjective)**

1. What are the primary goals of inflammation?

2. Describe the key features of acute inflammation.

3. Explain the process of leukocyte recruitment during acute inflammation.

4. What are the main differences between acute and chronic inflammation?

5. How does the body achieve vasodilation during an inflammatory response?

6. What is fibrosis and how does it occur?

7. Describe the role of macrophages in the inflammatory response.

8. What are the clinical signs of inflammation and their underlying mechanisms?

9. Explain the process of phagocytosis during inflammation.

10.How does histamine contribute to the inflammatory response?

11.Describe the different phases of wound healing.

12.What factors influence tissue repair and regeneration?

13.Explain the role of cytokines in the inflammatory response.

14.What is the significance of VEGF in wound healing?

15.How does endothelial dysfunction contribute to the development of atherosclerosis?

16.Describe the formation and role of foam cells in atherosclerosis.

17.Explain the function of matrix metalloproteinases (MMPs) in tissue remodeling.

18. What is the role of chemokines in leukocyte migration?

19. How do anti-inflammatory cytokines contribute to the resolution of inflammation?

20. Describe the process of angiogenesis during wound healing.

## Long Answer Type Questions (Subjective)

1. Discuss the basic mechanisms involved in the process of inflammation, including recognition, recruitment, and removal of the injurious agent.

2. Describe the differences between acute and chronic inflammation, including their mechanisms, key features, and clinical significance.

3. Explain the phases of wound healing in the skin, detailing the cellular and molecular mediators involved in each phase.

4. Discuss the pathophysiology of atherosclerosis, including the stages of plaque formation and the role of inflammation.

5. Explain the role of chemical mediators in the regulation of inflammation, including vasoactive amines, cytokines, and eicosanoids.

6. Describe the clinical signs of inflammation and the molecular mechanisms underlying these signs.

7. Discuss the process of leukocyte migration during inflammation, including the roles of selectins, integrins, and chemokines.

8. Explain the role of macrophages in both the initiation and resolution of inflammation.

9. Discuss the factors that influence tissue repair and regeneration, including the type and extent of injury and systemic factors.

10. Describe the molecular mediators of inflammation and repair, focusing on their sources, functions, and interactions.

## Answer Key for MCQ Questions

1. b) To eliminate the initial cause of cell injure

2.  c) Tissue destruction and healing simultaneously

3.  c) Increased blood flow

4.  c) Neutrophils

5.  c) Persistent inflammation

6.  c) Replacement of damaged tissue with fibrous connective tissue

7.  d) All of the above

8.  a) Histamine

9.  c) Mast cells

10. b) Induce endothelial activation

11. b) Chemotactic factors

12. c) Proliferation

13. b) VEGF

14. b) Produce cytokines and growth factors

15. b) Redness

16. d) All of the above

17. c) Macrophages

18. b) Degrade extracellular matrix components

19. d) IL-10

20. a) Mediate leukocyte rolling

# CHAPTER – 3

## CARDIOVASCULAR AND RESPIRATORY SYSTEM

Cardiovascular System:

**Anatomy**

1. **Heart**: A muscular organ located in the thoracic cavity, consisting of four chambers:
    a. **Right Atrium**: Receives deoxygenated blood from the body via the superior and inferior vena cavae.
    b. **Right Ventricle**: Pumps deoxygenated blood to the lungs via the pulmonary arteries.
    c. **Left Atrium**: Receives oxygenated blood from the lungs via the pulmonary veins.
    d. **Left Ventricle**: Pumps oxygenated blood to the rest of the body via the aorta.
2. **Blood Vessels**:
    a. **Arteries**: Carry blood away from the heart (e.g., aorta, pulmonary arteries).
    b. **Veins**: Return blood to the heart (e.g., superior and inferior vena cavae, pulmonary veins).
    c. **Capillaries**: Microscopic vessels where gas and nutrient exchange occurs.
3. **Blood**: Composed of plasma, red blood cells, white blood cells, and platelets.

**Physiology**

1. **Circulatory Routes**:
   a. **Systemic Circulation**: Delivers oxygen-rich blood from the left side of the heart to the body and returns deoxygenated blood to the right side of the heart.
   b. **Pulmonary Circulation**: Carries deoxygenated blood from the right side of the heart to the lungs for oxygenation and returns oxygenated blood to the left side of the heart.
2. **Cardiac Cycle**:
   a. **Systole**: Contraction phase of the heart where blood is pumped out of the ventricles.
   b. **Diastole**: Relaxation phase where the heart chambers fill with blood.
3. **Regulation**:
   a. **Autonomic Nervous System**: Regulates heart rate and force of contraction via sympathetic (increases) and parasympathetic (decreases) input.
   b. **Hormonal Control**: Includes hormones like adrenaline and aldosterone that affect heart function and blood pressure.

**Respiratory System:**

**Anatomy**

1. **Upper Respiratory Tract**:
   a. **Nose/Nasal Cavity**: Filters, warms, and moistens air.
   b. **Pharynx**: Passageway for air and food.
   c. **Larynx**: Voice box containing vocal cords.
2. **Lower Respiratory Tract**:
   a. **Trachea**: Main airway leading to the bronchi.

b. **Bronchi**: Two main branches from the trachea that lead to each lung.

c. **Bronchioles**: Smaller branches of the bronchi.

d. **Alveoli**: Tiny air sacs in the lungs where gas exchange occurs.

3. **Lungs**: Paired organs in the thoracic cavity responsible for gas exchange. Each lung has lobes (three in the right lung, two in the left).

**Physiology**

1. **Ventilation**:
   a. **Inspiration**: The process of inhaling air into the lungs, driven by the contraction of the diaphragm and intercostal muscles.
   b. **Expiration**: The process of exhaling air out of the lungs, typically a passive process driven by the relaxation of these muscles.

2. **Gas Exchange**:
   a. **External Respiration**: Exchange of gases (oxygen and carbon dioxide) between the alveoli and the blood in the pulmonary capillaries.
   b. **Internal Respiration**: Exchange of gases between the blood in systemic capillaries and the body's tissues.

3. **Regulation**:
   a. **Medullary Respiratory Centers**: Located in the brainstem, these centers regulate the rate and depth of breathing based on $CO_2$ levels and pH in the blood.
   b. **Chemoreceptors**: Located in the carotid arteries and aorta, they detect changes in blood pH, $CO_2$, and $O_2$ levels and adjust respiratory rate accordingly.

**Interrelation between Cardiovascular and Respiratory Systems**

1. **Gas Exchange**: The cardiovascular and respiratory systems work together to deliver oxygen to tissues and remove carbon dioxide from the body.

2. **Circulatory Support**: The heart pumps oxygenated blood from the lungs to the body and deoxygenated blood back to the lungs for gas exchange.

3. **Regulatory Feedback**: Both systems have feedback mechanisms that help maintain homeostasis, such as adjusting heart rate and breathing rate in response to changes in blood gas levels.

## HYPERTENSION:

Hypertension, commonly known as high blood pressure, is a chronic medical condition in which the blood pressure in the arteries is persistently elevated. It is a significant risk factor for cardiovascular and respiratory diseases.

### Introduction:

**Hypertension** is defined as having a systolic blood pressure (SBP) of 130 mmHg or higher, or a diastolic blood pressure (DBP) of 80 mmHg or higher. It is a major cause of morbidity and mortality worldwide and is often referred to as the "silent killer" because it frequently has no warning signs or symptoms.

### Pathophysiology:

### 1. Blood Pressure Regulation:

   a. Blood pressure is determined by cardiac output (CO) and peripheral vascular resistance (PVR).

   b. Factors influencing these include the autonomic nervous system, the renin-angiotensin-aldosterone system (RAAS), and the balance of sodium and water.

### 2. Mechanisms Leading to Hypertension:

   a. **Genetic Factors:** Family history and genetic predisposition.

b. **Environmental Factors:** High salt intake, obesity, physical inactivity, and excessive alcohol consumption.

c. **Renal Dysfunction:** Impaired excretion of sodium, leading to increased blood volume and pressure.

d. **Endothelial Dysfunction:** Reduced production of vasodilators like nitric oxide.

e. **Sympathetic Nervous System Overactivity:** Increased heart rate and vasoconstriction.

f. **RAAS Activation:** Increased levels of angiotensin II, causing vasoconstriction and aldosterone secretion, leading to sodium and water retention.

## Epidemiology:

### 1. Prevalence:

a. Hypertension affects approximately 1.3 billion people worldwide.

b. It is more common in older adults, with prevalence increasing with age.

c. Higher prevalence in certain populations, such as African Americans.

### 2. Risk Factors:

a. **Non-Modifiable:** Age, family history, race/ethnicity, gender.

b. **Modifiable:** Diet (high salt intake), obesity, sedentary lifestyle, alcohol and tobacco use, stress, and other comorbid conditions like diabetes.

## Symptoms and Complications:

### Symptoms:

a. Often asymptomatic, especially in the early stages.

b. When present, symptoms may include headaches, dizziness, shortness of breath, chest pain, and visual disturbances.

### Complications:

a. **Cardiovascular System:**

    i. Heart disease (left ventricular hypertrophy, coronary artery disease, heart failure).

ii.   Stroke (ischemic and hemorrhagic).

b. **Respiratory System:**

i.   Pulmonary hypertension (leading to right heart failure).

ii.   Increased risk of obstructive sleep apnea.

c. **Renal System:**

i.   Chronic kidney disease.

ii.   Nephrosclerosis.

d. **Vascular System:**

i.   Atherosclerosis.

ii.   Peripheral artery disease.

e. **Eyes:**

i.   Hypertensive retinopathy.

**Diagnosis:**

**1. Blood Pressure Measurement:**

a. Multiple readings on different occasions.

b. Use of proper techniques and equipment (sphygmomanometer).

c. Ambulatory blood pressure monitoring (ABPM) or home blood pressure monitoring (HBPM) for accurate assessment.

**2. Laboratory Tests:**

a. Blood tests (electrolytes, renal function, lipid profile).

b. Urinalysis (to check for proteinuria).

c. Electrocardiogram (ECG) and echocardiography (to assess cardiac effects).

**3. Additional Assessments:**

a. Evaluation of secondary causes (e.g., endocrine disorders, renal artery stenosis).

b. Assessment of target organ damage (e.g., retinal examination, urine albumin-to-creatinine ratio).

**Treatment:**

**1. Lifestyle Modifications:**

a. **Diet:** DASH (Dietary Approaches to Stop Hypertension) diet, reducing salt intake, increasing potassium intake, limiting alcohol consumption.

b. **Physical Activity:** Regular aerobic exercise.

c. **Weight Management:** Achieving and maintaining a healthy weight.

d. **Smoking Cessation:** Eliminating tobacco use.

e. **Stress Management:** Techniques like relaxation therapy and mindfulness.

**2. Pharmacologic Therapy:**

a. **First-Line Medications:**

i. **Diuretics:** Thiazide diuretics (e.g., hydrochlorothiazide).

ii. **ACE Inhibitors:** (e.g., enalapril, lisinopril).

iii. **ARBs:** Angiotensin II receptor blockers (e.g., losartan, valsartan).

iv. **Calcium Channel Blockers:** (e.g., amlodipine, diltiazem).

v. **Beta-Blockers:** (e.g., metoprolol, atenolol) - not first-line for primary hypertension but useful in certain populations.

b. **Second-Line Medications:**

i. **Aldosterone Antagonists:** (e.g., spironolactone).

ii. **Direct Renin Inhibitors:** (e.g., aliskiren).

iii. **Alpha-Blockers:** (e.g., prazosin).

iv. **Central Alpha Agonists:** (e.g., clonidine).

**3. Treatment Goals:**

a. Generally, target BP < 130/80 mmHg.

b. Individualized targets based on age, comorbidities, and risk factors.

**Complications:**

**1. Medication Side Effects:**

a. Diuretics: Electrolyte imbalances (e.g., hypokalemia), hyperuricemia.

b. ACE Inhibitors/ARBs: Cough, hyperkalemia, renal impairment.

c. Calcium Channel Blockers: Edema, bradycardia.

d. Beta-Blockers: Fatigue, bradycardia, worsening asthma.

## 2. Non-Adherence:

a. Due to side effects, cost, complexity of regimens, lack of symptoms.

## Prevention:

## 1. Primary Prevention:

a. Public health strategies to reduce risk factors (e.g., reducing salt intake in processed foods).

b. Promoting healthy lifestyle choices from a young age.

c. Screening and early detection in high-risk populations.

## 2. Secondary Prevention:

a. Regular monitoring and follow-up for individuals diagnosed with hypertension.

b. Patient education on the importance of adherence to lifestyle modifications and medications.

## 3. Tertiary Prevention:

a. Managing and preventing complications through comprehensive care (e.g., regular cardiovascular assessments, controlling comorbid conditions like diabetes).

## CONGESTIVE HEART FAILURE

Congestive heart failure (CHF) is a chronic progressive condition where the heart is unable to pump sufficient blood to meet the body's needs. This leads to a buildup of fluid in the lungs and other tissues.

**Introduction:**

**Congestive Heart Failure (CHF),** also known simply as heart failure, is a syndrome characterized by the heart's inability to provide adequate blood flow to the body, leading to a range of symptoms and systemic effects. It can result from various underlying cardiovascular conditions.

**Pathophysiology:**

**1. Heart's Pumping Ability:**

a. CHF can result from systolic dysfunction (reduced contractility) or diastolic dysfunction (impaired filling).

**2. Mechanisms Leading to CHF:**

a. **Systolic Dysfunction:** Decreased ejection fraction due to weakened heart muscle, often caused by conditions like myocardial infarction (heart attack) or dilated cardiomyopathy.

b. **Diastolic Dysfunction:** Normal ejection fraction but impaired ventricular filling due to stiff or thickened heart muscle, often seen in hypertensive heart disease and hypertrophic cardiomyopathy.

c. **Increased Afterload:** Conditions like hypertension and aortic stenosis increase resistance against which the heart must pump.

d. **Increased Preload:** Conditions like valvular regurgitation increase the volume of blood returning to the heart, causing volume overload.

**3. Compensatory Mechanisms:**

a. **Neurohormonal Activation:** Activation of the sympathetic nervous system and the renin-angiotensin-aldosterone system (RAAS) increases heart rate and blood pressure but can lead to further heart damage over time.

b. **Ventricular Remodeling:** Structural changes in the heart, such as dilation and hypertrophy, occur in response to chronic pressure and volume overload.

**Epidemiology:**

**1. Prevalence:**

a. CHF affects over 6 million adults in the United States.

b. It is more common in older adults, with prevalence increasing with age.

**2. Risk Factors:**

a. **Non-Modifiable:** Age, family history, gender (higher incidence in men), and race (higher incidence in African Americans).

b. **Modifiable:** Hypertension, coronary artery disease, diabetes, obesity, smoking, and sedentary lifestyle.

**Symptoms and Complications;**

**Symptoms:**

a. **Left-Sided Heart Failure:** Pulmonary congestion and edema, leading to symptoms such as shortness of breath (dyspnea), orthopnea (difficulty breathing while lying flat), paroxysmal nocturnal dyspnea (PND), and cough.

b. **Right-Sided Heart Failure:** Systemic congestion, leading to symptoms such as peripheral edema, ascites (abdominal swelling), hepatomegaly (enlarged liver), and jugular venous distension (JVD).

**Complications:**

a. **Cardiovascular System:**
   i. Arrhythmias (e.g., atrial fibrillation).
   ii. Myocardial infarction.
   iii. Sudden cardiac death.

b. **Respiratory System:**
   i. Pulmonary edema.
   ii. Pleural effusion.
   iii. Increased risk of respiratory infections.

c. **Renal System:**
   i. Worsening renal function (cardiorenal syndrome).

d. **Others:**
   i. Cachexia (severe weight loss and muscle wasting).
   ii. Depression and anxiety due to chronic illness.

**Diagnosis:**

**1. Clinical Evaluation:**

a. Detailed medical history and physical examination.

b. Assessment of symptoms and functional status (e.g., New York Heart Association (NYHA) classification).

**2. Diagnostic Tests:**

a. **Echocardiography:** Key test for evaluating heart structure and function, including ejection fraction.

b. **Electrocardiogram (ECG):** To assess heart rhythm and identify ischemic changes.

c. **Chest X-ray:** To detect pulmonary congestion and cardiomegaly.

d. **Blood Tests:**

   i. B-type natriuretic peptide (BNP) or N-terminal proBNP (NT-proBNP): Elevated levels indicate heart failure.

   ii. Complete blood count, kidney function tests, electrolytes, and thyroid function tests.

e. **Other Imaging:**

   i. Cardiac MRI or CT scan for detailed structural and functional assessment.

   ii. Coronary angiography if ischemic heart disease is suspected.

**Treatment:**

**1. Lifestyle Modifications:**

a. **Diet:** Low-sodium diet to reduce fluid retention.

b. **Exercise:** Regular physical activity as tolerated to improve cardiovascular fitness.

c. **Weight Management:** Maintaining a healthy weight to reduce cardiac workload.

d. **Smoking Cessation:** Eliminating tobacco use.

e. **Alcohol Restriction:** Limiting alcohol intake.

**2. Pharmacologic Therapy:**

a. **First-Line Medications:**

i. **ACE Inhibitors/ARBs:** Reduce afterload and improve survival (e.g., enalapril, losartan).

ii. **Beta-Blockers:** Reduce heart rate, improve ejection fraction, and reduce mortality (e.g., metoprolol, carvedilol).

iii. **Diuretics:** Manage fluid overload and reduce symptoms (e.g., furosemide, spironolactone).

iv. **Aldosterone Antagonists:** Reduce morbidity and mortality in severe heart failure (e.g., spironolactone, eplerenone).

b. **Other Medications:**

i. **Vasodilators:** Improve symptoms and reduce afterload (e.g., hydralazine, isosorbide dinitrate).

ii. **Digoxin:** Improves symptoms and reduces hospitalization in select patients.

3. **Advanced Therapies:**

a. **Device Therapy:**

i. **Implantable Cardioverter-Defibrillator (ICD):** Prevents sudden cardiac death in patients with reduced ejection fraction.

ii. **Cardiac Resynchronization Therapy (CRT):** Improves symptoms and survival in patients with heart failure and ventricular dyssynchrony.

b. **Surgical Interventions:**

i. **Coronary Artery Bypass Grafting (CABG):** For patients with ischemic heart disease.

ii. **Heart Valve Surgery:** For patients with significant valvular disease.

iii. **Left Ventricular Assist Device (LVAD):** Mechanical pump for patients with end-stage heart failure.

iv. **Heart Transplant:** For select patients with refractory heart failure.

**Complications:**

**1. Medication Side Effects:**

   a. Diuretics: Electrolyte imbalances (e.g., hypokalemia, hyponatremia).

   b. ACE Inhibitors/ARBs: Hyperkalemia, renal impairment, cough (with ACE inhibitors).

   c. Beta-Blockers: Bradycardia, fatigue.

   d. Digoxin: Digoxin toxicity (nausea, visual disturbances, arrhythmias).

**2. Disease Progression:**

   a. Worsening heart failure despite optimal treatment.

   b. Frequent hospitalizations and reduced quality of life.

**Prevention:**

**1. Primary Prevention:**

   a. Addressing modifiable risk factors early (e.g., hypertension, diabetes, obesity).

   b. Promoting healthy lifestyle choices from a young age.

   c. Screening and early detection in high-risk populations.

**2. Secondary Prevention:**

   a. Regular monitoring and follow-up for individuals with known cardiovascular disease.

   b. Aggressive management of comorbid conditions (e.g., diabetes, hypertension).

   c. Patient education on the importance of adherence to lifestyle modifications and medications.

**3. Tertiary Prevention:**

   a. Comprehensive care to manage and prevent complications.

   b. Regular cardiovascular assessments.

   c. Multidisciplinary approach involving cardiologists, primary care physicians, dietitians, and exercise physiologists.

# ISCHEMIC HEART DISEASE (ANGINA, MYOCARDIAL INFARCTION, ATHEROSCLEROSIS AND ARTERIOSCLEROSIS)

Ischemic heart disease (IHD), also known as coronary artery disease (CAD), is a condition characterized by reduced blood flow to the heart muscle due to narrowing or blockage of the coronary arteries. This leads to various clinical manifestations, including angina pectoris and myocardial infarction (heart attack).

**Introduction:**

**Ischemic Heart Disease (IHD)** encompasses conditions resulting from reduced coronary blood flow and oxygen supply to the heart muscle, primarily due to atherosclerosis of the coronary arteries. The most common forms of IHD are angina pectoris and myocardial infarction.

**Pathophysiology:**

**1. Atherosclerosis:**

    a. **Development:** Begins with endothelial injury due to factors like hypertension, smoking, and high LDL cholesterol.

    b. **Progression:** Formation of fatty streaks, development of fibrous plaques, and eventual plaque rupture or erosion leading to thrombosis.

**2. Arteriosclerosis:**

    a. General term for the thickening and hardening of arterial walls, often associated with aging and hypertension.

    b. Includes atherosclerosis as a specific type.

**3. Angina Pectoris:**

    a. **Stable Angina:** Predictable chest pain triggered by physical exertion or stress due to fixed atherosclerotic plaques.

    b. **Unstable Angina:** Unpredictable chest pain, occurring at rest or with minimal exertion, indicating plaque instability and risk of myocardial infarction.

**4. Myocardial Infarction (MI):**

a. **Mechanism:** Complete or near-complete occlusion of a coronary artery by a thrombus following plaque rupture, leading to ischemia and necrosis of heart muscle.

**Epidemiology:**

**1. Prevalence:**

a. Leading cause of death globally, affecting millions annually.

b. Higher prevalence in older adults, with men typically affected earlier than women.

**2. Risk Factors:**

a. **Non-Modifiable:** Age, male gender, family history, and genetic predisposition.

b. **Modifiable:** Hypertension, hyperlipidemia, diabetes, smoking, obesity, physical inactivity, and unhealthy diet.

**Symptoms and Complications;**

**Symptoms:**

a. **Angina Pectoris:** Chest pain or discomfort, often described as pressure, squeezing, or burning. It may radiate to the shoulders, arms, neck, jaw, or back.

b. **Myocardial Infarction:** Severe, prolonged chest pain not relieved by rest or nitroglycerin, associated with symptoms like shortness of breath, nausea, sweating, and lightheadedness.

**Complications:**

a. **Cardiovascular System:**

   i. Heart failure.

   ii. Arrhythmias (e.g., ventricular fibrillation, atrial fibrillation).

   iii. Cardiogenic shock.

   iv. Sudden cardiac death.

b. **Other Systems:**

   i. Left ventricular aneurysm.

    ii.    Mitral regurgitation due to papillary muscle dysfunction or rupture.

    iii.    Pericarditis (inflammation of the pericardium).

**Diagnosis:**

**1. Clinical Evaluation:**

    a.  Detailed medical history and physical examination.

    b.  Assessment of risk factors and symptomatology.

**2. Diagnostic Tests:**

    a.  **Electrocardiogram (ECG):** To detect ischemic changes, ST-segment abnormalities, and arrhythmias.

    b.  **Cardiac Biomarkers:** Elevated troponin levels indicate myocardial damage.

    c.  **Echocardiography:** To assess cardiac structure and function.

    d.  **Stress Testing:** Exercise or pharmacologic stress tests to evaluate myocardial perfusion and ischemic response.

    e.  **Coronary Angiography:** Gold standard for visualizing coronary artery stenosis and blockages.

    f.  **Non-invasive Imaging:**

        i.    Coronary computed tomography angiography (CTA).

        ii.    Cardiac magnetic resonance imaging (MRI).

**Treatment:**

**1. Lifestyle Modifications:**

    a.  **Diet:** Heart-healthy diet rich in fruits, vegetables, whole grains, and lean proteins. Reduce intake of saturated fats, trans fats, and sodium.

    b.  **Exercise:** Regular physical activity, such as brisk walking or aerobic exercises.

    c.  **Weight Management:** Achieving and maintaining a healthy weight.

    d.  **Smoking Cessation:** Complete elimination of tobacco use.

    e.  **Alcohol Moderation:** Limiting alcohol intake.

**2. Pharmacologic Therapy:**

    a. **Antiplatelet Agents:** Aspirin, clopidogrel to prevent thrombosis.

    b. **Statins:** To lower LDL cholesterol and stabilize plaques.

    c. **Beta-Blockers:** To reduce myocardial oxygen demand and improve survival post-MI.

    d. **ACE Inhibitors/ARBs:** To reduce blood pressure and myocardial workload.

    e. **Nitrates:** To relieve angina by dilating coronary arteries.

    f. **Calcium Channel Blockers:** To reduce angina and lower blood pressure.

    g. **Ranolazine:** For refractory angina.

**3. Revascularization Procedures:**

    a. **Percutaneous Coronary Intervention (PCI):** Balloon angioplasty with stent placement to open blocked arteries.

    b. **Coronary Artery Bypass Grafting (CABG):** Surgical bypass of occluded coronary arteries using grafts.

**Complications:**

**1. Medication Side Effects:**

    a. Antiplatelets: Increased risk of bleeding.

    b. Statins: Muscle pain, liver dysfunction.

    c. Beta-Blockers: Bradycardia, fatigue.

    d. ACE Inhibitors/ARBs: Cough (ACE inhibitors), hyperkalemia, renal impairment.

**2. Procedure-Related Complications:**

    a. PCI: Restenosis, stent thrombosis.

    b. CABG: Graft occlusion, wound infections.

**3. Disease Progression:**

    a. Recurrent angina or myocardial infarction.

    b. Worsening heart failure.

**Prevention:**

**1. Primary Prevention:**

   a. Addressing modifiable risk factors early (e.g., controlling hypertension, hyperlipidemia, diabetes).

   b. Promoting healthy lifestyle choices from a young age.

   c. Screening and early detection in high-risk populations.

**2. Secondary Prevention:**

   a. Regular monitoring and follow-up for individuals with known cardiovascular disease.

   b. Aggressive management of comorbid conditions (e.g., diabetes, hypertension).

   c. Patient education on the importance of adherence to lifestyle modifications and medications.

**3. Tertiary Prevention:**

   a. Comprehensive care to manage and prevent complications.

   b. Regular cardiovascular assessments.

   c. Multidisciplinary approach involving cardiologists, primary care physicians, dietitians, and exercise physiologists.

**Specific Conditions under Ischemic Heart Disease:**

**1. Angina Pectoris:**

   a. **Stable Angina:** Managed with lifestyle changes, medications, and possibly revascularization.

   b. **Unstable Angina:** Requires urgent medical evaluation and treatment to prevent myocardial infarction.

**2. Myocardial Infarction (MI):**

   a. **Acute Management:** Immediate reperfusion therapy (PCI or thrombolysis), antiplatelet agents, anticoagulants, and supportive care.

   b. **Post-MI Care:** Long-term medications (beta-blockers, ACE inhibitors, statins), lifestyle modifications, and cardiac rehabilitation.

**3. Atherosclerosis and Arteriosclerosis:**

  a. **Management:** Focus on reducing risk factors (e.g., hyperlipidemia, hypertension), lifestyle changes, and medications (statins, antihypertensives).

**RESPIRATORY SYSTEM**

**ASTHMA**

Asthma is a chronic inflammatory disorder of the airways characterized by recurrent episodes of wheezing, breathlessness, chest tightness, and coughing. These episodes are often associated with variable airflow obstruction that is often reversible either spontaneously or with treatment.

**Introduction:**

**Asthma** is a chronic respiratory condition involving inflammation and narrowing of the airways, leading to difficulty in breathing. It affects people of all ages and is influenced by a combination of genetic and environmental factors.

**Pathophysiology**

**1. Airway Inflammation:**

  a. Chronic inflammation leads to swelling of the airway walls, increased mucus production, and hyperresponsiveness to various stimuli.

**2. Bronchoconstriction:**

  a. Contraction of smooth muscles around the airways, narrowing them and causing airflow limitation.

**3. Airway Remodeling:**

  a. Persistent inflammation may lead to structural changes in the airways, such as thickening of the airway walls, increased smooth muscle mass, and fibrosis, which may contribute to irreversible airflow obstruction.

**4. Triggers:**

a. Common triggers include allergens (pollen, dust mites, pet dander), respiratory infections, exercise, cold air, smoke, pollution, and certain medications (e.g., NSAIDs, beta-blockers).

**Epidemiology:**

**1. Prevalence:**

a. Asthma affects approximately 300 million people worldwide.

b. It is one of the most common chronic diseases in children, but it can develop at any age.

**2. Risk Factors:**

a. **Genetic:** Family history of asthma or other allergic conditions.

b. **Environmental:** Exposure to allergens, tobacco smoke, air pollution, occupational irritants.

c. **Other Factors:** Respiratory infections during early childhood, low birth weight, and obesity.

**Symptoms and Complications:**

**Symptoms:**

a. Wheezing (a high-pitched whistling sound during breathing).

b. Shortness of breath.

c. Chest tightness.

d. Coughing, especially at night or early morning.

e. Symptoms may vary in frequency and severity and can be episodic.

**Complications:**

a. **Acute Exacerbations:** Severe episodes of asthma that require urgent medical attention, often triggered by infections, allergens, or irritants.

b. **Chronic Symptoms:** Persistent symptoms that affect daily activities and quality of life.

c. **Respiratory Failure:** Severe asthma attacks that do not respond to standard treatments can lead to life-threatening respiratory failure.

d. **Lung Infections:** Increased risk of infections such as pneumonia.

e. **Airway Remodeling:** Long-term changes in the airway structure that can lead to persistent airflow limitation.

**Diagnosis:**

**1. Clinical Evaluation:**

a. Detailed medical history, including family history and exposure to potential triggers.

b. Physical examination focusing on respiratory system.

**2. Diagnostic Tests:**

a. **Spirometry:** Measures airflow obstruction and reversibility with bronchodilator therapy.

b. **Peak Expiratory Flow (PEF):** Monitoring peak flow rates to detect variability in airway obstruction.

c. **Bronchoprovocation Testing:** Assess airway hyperresponsiveness using methacholine or exercise challenge.

d. **Allergy Testing:** Skin prick tests or specific IgE blood tests to identify potential allergens.

e. **Chest X-ray:** To rule out other conditions mimicking asthma.

**Treatment:**

**1. Pharmacologic Therapy:**

a. **Quick-Relief Medications:**

  i. **Short-Acting Beta-Agonists (SABAs):** For rapid relief of acute symptoms (e.g., albuterol).

b. **Long-Term Control Medications:**

  i. **Inhaled Corticosteroids (ICS):** First-line therapy for persistent asthma to reduce inflammation (e.g., fluticasone, budesonide).

  ii. **Long-Acting Beta-Agonists (LABAs):** Used in combination with ICS for better control (e.g., salmeterol, formoterol).

  iii. **Leukotriene Modifiers:** Reduce inflammation and bronchoconstriction (e.g., montelukast).

iv. **Long-Acting Muscarinic Antagonists (LAMAs):** For maintenance treatment (e.g., tiotropium).

v. **Biologic Therapies:** For severe asthma not controlled with standard therapies (e.g., omalizumab, mepolizumab).

## 2. Non-Pharmacologic Therapy:

a. **Trigger Avoidance:** Identifying and minimizing exposure to known triggers (e.g., allergens, smoke, pollution).

b. **Allergy Management:** Immunotherapy for allergic asthma.

c. **Asthma Action Plan:** Personalized plan developed with a healthcare provider to manage symptoms and exacerbations.

d. **Patient Education:** Teaching proper inhaler technique, self-monitoring, and recognizing early signs of exacerbations.

## 3. Emergency Management:

a. **Acute Exacerbations:** Use of SABAs, systemic corticosteroids, and possibly oxygen therapy or hospitalization for severe cases.

## Complications:

## 1. Medication Side Effects:

a. **Inhaled Corticosteroids:** Oral thrush, hoarseness, and potential for long-term effects like osteoporosis.

b. **Beta-Agonists:** Tremors, palpitations, and potential for tolerance with overuse.

c. **Leukotriene Modifiers:** Headache, gastrointestinal disturbances.

d. **Biologics:** Risk of allergic reactions and injection site reactions.

## 2. Disease Progression:

a. **Frequent Exacerbations:** Can lead to increased airway remodeling and chronic symptoms.

b. **Chronic Symptoms:** Persistent cough, wheezing, and breathlessness impacting quality of life.

**Prevention:**

**1. Primary Prevention:**

    a. **Avoidance of Risk Factors:** Reducing exposure to tobacco smoke, air pollution, and occupational irritants.

    b. **Healthy Lifestyle:** Promoting regular exercise, a balanced diet, and maintaining a healthy weight.

**2. Secondary Prevention:**

    a. **Early Diagnosis and Treatment:** Prompt identification and management of asthma to prevent progression and complications.

    b. **Regular Monitoring:** Ongoing assessment of asthma control and adjustment of therapy as needed.

**3. Tertiary Prevention:**

    a. **Comprehensive Management:** Implementing an asthma action plan, ensuring adherence to medications, and regular follow-up with healthcare providers.

    b. **Education and Support:** Providing resources and support for patients and caregivers to effectively manage asthma.

## CHRONIC OBSTRUCTIVE AIRWAYS DISEASES

Chronic obstructive pulmonary disease (COPD) is a progressive lung disease characterized by persistent respiratory symptoms and airflow limitation due to airway and/or alveolar abnormalities, usually caused by significant exposure to noxious particles or gases. COPD includes emphysema and chronic bronchitis.

**Introduction:**

**Chronic Obstructive Pulmonary Disease (COPD)** is a group of chronic inflammatory lung diseases that cause obstructed airflow from the lungs. It is primarily associated with long-term exposure to irritating gases or particulate matter, most often from cigarette smoke. The main conditions that comprise COPD are emphysema and chronic bronchitis.

**Pathophysiology:**

**1. Chronic Bronchitis:**

a. Characterized by chronic inflammation of the bronchi, leading to increased mucus production, airway narrowing, and cough.

b. Defined clinically by a productive cough lasting for at least three months in two consecutive years.

**2. Emphysema:**

a. Characterized by the destruction of alveolar walls, leading to reduced surface area for gas exchange and loss of lung elasticity.

b. Results in airflow limitation and air trapping.

**3. Airflow Limitation:**

a. Persistent and progressive, caused by small airway disease (e.g., inflammation, fibrosis, and increased resistance) and parenchymal destruction (loss of alveolar attachments).

**4. Inflammation:**

a. Involves the recruitment of inflammatory cells (neutrophils, macrophages, and lymphocytes) and the release of inflammatory mediators.

b. Oxidative stress and protease-antiprotease imbalance contribute to tissue damage and remodeling.

**Epidemiology:**

**1. Prevalence:**

a. COPD affects approximately 65 million people globally and is a leading cause of morbidity and mortality.

b. Higher prevalence in older adults, with smoking being the most significant risk factor.

**2. Risk Factors:**

a. **Primary:** Smoking (both active and passive), occupational exposures to dust and chemicals, and indoor and outdoor air pollution.

b. **Genetic:** Alpha-1 antitrypsin deficiency, which predisposes individuals to early-onset emphysema.

c. **Other Factors:** Respiratory infections in childhood, low socioeconomic status, and age.

**Symptoms and Complications:**

**Symptoms:**

a. Chronic cough with sputum production.

b. Dyspnea (shortness of breath), initially on exertion and eventually at rest.

c. Wheezing and chest tightness.

d. Frequent respiratory infections.

**Complications:**

a. **Exacerbations:** Acute worsening of symptoms, often triggered by infections or environmental factors.

b. **Respiratory Failure:** Severe cases may result in inadequate oxygenation and/or carbon dioxide removal.

c. **Pulmonary Hypertension:** Increased pressure in the pulmonary arteries due to chronic hypoxia.

d. **Cor Pulmonale:** Right-sided heart failure secondary to chronic lung disease.

e. **Osteoporosis:** Due to systemic inflammation and corticosteroid use.

f. **Weight Loss and Muscle Wasting:** Due to increased work of breathing and systemic inflammation.

**Diagnosis:**

**1. Clinical Evaluation:**

a. Detailed medical history, including smoking history and exposure to environmental or occupational irritants.

b. Physical examination focusing on respiratory system (e.g., wheezing, prolonged expiration, use of accessory muscles).

**2. Diagnostic Tests:**

a. **Spirometry:** Key diagnostic test showing persistent airflow limitation with a reduced FEV1/FVC ratio (<70% post-bronchodilator).

b. **Chest X-ray:** To rule out other conditions and assess for signs of hyperinflation, bullae, or other structural changes.

c. **CT Scan:** High-resolution CT can provide detailed images of emphysematous changes and airway disease.

d. **Arterial Blood Gas (ABG):** To assess oxygenation and ventilation status, especially in severe cases.

e. **Alpha-1 Antitrypsin Level:** To screen for genetic deficiency in younger patients or those with a family history.

**Treatment:**

**1. Lifestyle Modifications:**

a. **Smoking Cessation:** Most crucial step to slow disease progression and improve survival.

b. **Avoidance of Irritants:** Reducing exposure to air pollutants and occupational hazards.

c. **Vaccinations:** Annual influenza vaccination and pneumococcal vaccination to reduce the risk of respiratory infections.

**2. Pharmacologic Therapy:**

a. **Bronchodilators:**

   i. **Short-Acting Beta-Agonists (SABAs):** For quick relief of symptoms (e.g., albuterol).

   ii. **Long-Acting Beta-Agonists (LABAs):** For maintenance therapy (e.g., salmeterol, formoterol).

   iii. **Anticholinergics:**

      - **Short-Acting (SAMA):** Ipratropium.

      - **Long-Acting (LAMA):** Tiotropium, aclidinium.

b. **Inhaled Corticosteroids (ICS):** Often used in combination with LABAs for patients with frequent exacerbations (e.g., fluticasone/salmeterol).

c. **Phosphodiesterase-4 Inhibitors:** Roflumilast for severe COPD with chronic bronchitis and a history of exacerbations.

d. **Mucolytics:** To reduce sputum viscosity in chronic bronchitis.

3. **Non-Pharmacologic Therapy:**

a. **Pulmonary Rehabilitation:** Multidisciplinary program including exercise training, education, and support.

b. **Oxygen Therapy:** For patients with chronic hypoxemia (PaO2 ≤55 mmHg or SaO2 ≤88%).

c. **Surgical Interventions:**

   i. **Lung Volume Reduction Surgery (LVRS):** For selected patients with severe emphysema.

   ii. **Bullectomy:** Removal of large bullae that compress functioning lung tissue.

   iii. **Lung Transplantation:** For end-stage COPD in select patients.

**Complications:**

**1. Medication Side Effects:**

a. **Bronchodilators:** Tachycardia, tremors, dry mouth.

b. **Inhaled Corticosteroids:** Oral thrush, dysphonia, increased risk of pneumonia.

c. **Phosphodiesterase-4 Inhibitors:** Nausea, weight loss, psychiatric symptoms.

**2. Disease Progression:**

a. **Frequent Exacerbations:** Leading to accelerated decline in lung function.

b. **Chronic Respiratory Failure:** Persistent hypoxemia and hypercapnia.

c. **Systemic Effects:** Weight loss, muscle wasting, osteoporosis.

**Prevention:**

**1. Primary Prevention:**

    a. **Smoking Prevention and Cessation:** Public health campaigns, smoking cessation programs, and policies to reduce tobacco use.

    b. **Reducing Exposure to Pollutants:** Implementing regulations to reduce air pollution and occupational exposures.

    c. **Vaccinations:** Preventing respiratory infections through influenza and pneumococcal vaccines.

**2. Secondary Prevention:**

    a. **Early Detection:** Screening for COPD in high-risk individuals (e.g., smokers, those with a history of occupational exposure).

    b. **Management of Comorbidities:** Controlling conditions like hypertension, diabetes, and cardiovascular diseases.

**3. Tertiary Prevention:**

    a. **Optimizing Treatment:** Regular follow-up and adjustment of therapy to control symptoms and prevent exacerbations.

    b. **Pulmonary Rehabilitation:** Improving functional status and quality of life through comprehensive rehabilitation programs.

    c. **Patient Education:** Teaching self-management skills, proper inhaler technique, and recognizing early signs of exacerbations.

## RENAL SYSTEM

### ACUTE AND CHRONIC RENAL FAILURE

Renal failure, also known as kidney failure, refers to a condition where the kidneys lose their ability to filter waste products from the blood effectively. It can be acute (sudden onset) or chronic (gradual onset and long-term).

**Introduction:**

**Acute Renal Failure (ARF),** also known as acute kidney injury (AKI), is a sudden loss of kidney function that develops within hours to days. It often results from conditions that reduce blood flow to the kidneys, damage the kidneys, or obstruct urine flow from the kidneys.

**Chronic Renal Failure (CRF)**, also known as chronic kidney disease (CKD), is a gradual loss of kidney function over months to years. It is often the result of long-term conditions such as hypertension and diabetes.

**Pathophysiology:**

**Acute Renal Failure (ARF):**

    a. **Prerenal Causes:** Decreased blood flow to the kidneys (e.g., due to dehydration, heart failure, shock).

    b. **Intrarenal Causes:** Direct damage to the kidneys (e.g., acute tubular necrosis, glomerulonephritis, nephrotoxins).

    c. **Postrenal Causes:** Obstruction of urine outflow (e.g., kidney stones, tumors, enlarged prostate).

**Chronic Renal Failure (CRF):**

    a. **Diabetic Nephropathy:** High blood sugar levels damage the glomeruli over time.

    b. **Hypertensive Nephropathy:** High blood pressure causes chronic damage to blood vessels in the kidneys.

    c. **Glomerulonephritis:** Chronic inflammation and scarring of the glomeruli.

    d. **Polycystic Kidney Disease:** Genetic disorder causing cysts to form in the kidneys.

    e. **Other Causes:** Chronic obstruction, recurrent infections, autoimmune diseases.

**Epidemiology:**

**Acute Renal Failure:**

    a. Affects about 1-2% of hospitalized patients, with higher rates in critical care settings.

b. More common in older adults, those with chronic diseases, and those undergoing major surgery.

**Chronic Renal Failure:**

a. Affects about 10% of the global population.

b. More common in older adults, with increasing prevalence due to aging populations and rising rates of diabetes and hypertension.

**Symptoms and Complications**

**Acute Renal Failure:**

a. **Symptoms:** Sudden decrease in urine output, fluid retention, swelling, fatigue, confusion, nausea, chest pain, shortness of breath.

b. **Complications:** Metabolic acidosis, electrolyte imbalances (e.g., hyperkalemia), fluid overload, uremia, acute respiratory distress syndrome (ARDS), infections.

**Chronic Renal Failure:**

a. **Symptoms:** Gradual development of fatigue, weakness, nausea, vomiting, loss of appetite, itching, fluid retention, shortness of breath, hypertension.

b. **Complications:** Anemia, bone disease, cardiovascular disease, fluid and electrolyte imbalances, hyperkalemia, metabolic acidosis, peripheral neuropathy.

**Diagnosis:**

**Acute Renal Failure:**

a. **History and Physical Examination:** Assessing risk factors and symptoms.

b. **Laboratory Tests:** Serum creatinine, blood urea nitrogen (BUN), electrolytes, complete blood count (CBC).

c. **Urinalysis:** To check for protein, blood, and other abnormalities.

d. **Imaging:** Ultrasound, CT scan, MRI to evaluate kidney size, structure, and obstructions.

e. **Kidney Biopsy:** In certain cases to determine the underlying cause.

**Chronic Renal Failure:**

a. **History and Physical Examination:** Assessing long-term health conditions and symptoms.

b. **Laboratory Tests:** Serum creatinine, BUN, estimated glomerular filtration rate (eGFR), electrolytes, hemoglobin, parathyroid hormone (PTH).

c. **Urinalysis:** Proteinuria, hematuria, urine albumin-to-creatinine ratio.

d. **Imaging:** Ultrasound to assess kidney size and detect structural abnormalities.

e. **Kidney Biopsy:** In select cases to determine the underlying cause and guide treatment.

**Treatment:**

**Acute Renal Failure:**

a. **Address Underlying Cause:** Restore blood flow, treat infections, remove obstructions.

b. **Supportive Care:** Fluid and electrolyte management, avoiding nephrotoxic drugs, dialysis if necessary.

c. **Medications:** Diuretics (for fluid overload), vasopressors (for shock), antibiotics (for infections).

**Chronic Renal Failure:**

a. **Lifestyle Modifications:** Dietary changes (low protein, low sodium, low potassium), smoking cessation, weight management, regular exercise.

b. **Medications:** Antihypertensives (ACE inhibitors, ARBs), blood glucose control (for diabetes), erythropoiesis-stimulating agents (for anemia), phosphate binders, vitamin D supplements.

c. **Dialysis:** Hemodialysis or peritoneal dialysis for end-stage renal disease (ESRD).

d. **Kidney Transplant:** For eligible patients with ESRD.

**Complications:**

**Acute Renal Failure:**

a. **Electrolyte Imbalances:** Hyperkalemia, hyponatremia.

b. **Metabolic Acidosis:** Accumulation of acid in the blood.

c. **Fluid Overload:** Leading to edema and congestive heart failure.

d. **Infections:** Increased risk due to weakened immune system and invasive procedures.

**Chronic Renal Failure:**

a. **Cardiovascular Disease:** Leading cause of death in CKD patients.

b. **Bone Disease:** Renal osteodystrophy due to impaired calcium and phosphate metabolism.

c. **Anemia:** Due to decreased erythropoietin production.

d. **Malnutrition:** Due to dietary restrictions and reduced appetite.

e. **Peripheral Neuropathy:** Due to accumulation of uremic toxins.

**Prevention:**

**Acute Renal Failure:**

a. **Hydration:** Adequate fluid intake to maintain blood flow to the kidneys.

b. **Avoid Nephrotoxins:** Minimize use of medications and substances that can damage the kidneys.

c. **Manage Underlying Conditions:** Control blood pressure, treat infections promptly, monitor kidney function in at-risk patients.

**Chronic Renal Failure:**

a. **Control Risk Factors:** Effective management of diabetes and hypertension, regular monitoring of kidney function.

b. **Healthy Lifestyle:** Balanced diet, regular exercise, avoiding smoking and excessive alcohol intake.

c. **Regular Screening:** For high-risk individuals (e.g., those with diabetes, hypertension, family history of kidney disease).

d. **Early Intervention:** Prompt treatment of acute kidney injury to prevent progression to chronic kidney disease.

**Multiple-Choice Questions (Objective)**

1. What chamber of the heart receives deoxygenated blood from the body?
   a) Left Atrium
   b) Left Ventricle
   c) Right Atrium
   d) Right Ventricle

2. Which blood vessels carry oxygenated blood from the lungs to the heart?
   a) Pulmonary arteries
   b) Pulmonary veins
   c) Aorta
   d) Superior vena cava

3. What is the primary function of capillaries?
   a) Pump blood
   b) Exchange gases and nutrients
   c) Transport blood to the lungs
   d) Return blood to the heart

4. During which phase of the cardiac cycle do the ventricles contract?
   a) Diastole
   b) Systole
   c) Relaxation
   d) Refilling

5. What regulates the rate and depth of breathing based on $CO_2$ levels in the blood?
   a) Pulmonary arteries
   b) Chemoreceptors
   c) Medullary respiratory centers

d) Diaphragm

6. Which part of the respiratory system is the main airway leading to the bronchi?

   a) Trachea

   b) Pharynx

   c) Larynx

   d) Alveoli

7. What is the condition characterized by high blood pressure in the arteries?

   a) Hypotension

   b) Hypertension

   c) Arrhythmia

   d) Bradycardia

8. Which hormone increases heart rate and force of contraction?

   a) Insulin

   b) Adrenaline

   c) Estrogen

   d) Thyroxine

9. What is the medical term for heart failure due to the heart's inability to pump sufficient blood?

   a) Myocardial infarction

   b) Congestive heart failure

   c) Atherosclerosis

   d) Angina pectoris

10. What is the leading cause of myocardial infarction?

    a) Hyperlipidemia

    b) Atherosclerosis

    c) Diabetes

    d) Smoking

11. Which condition involves chronic inflammation and narrowing of the airways?

    a) Asthma

    b) COPD

    c) Bronchitis

    d) Emphysema

12. Which diagnostic test measures airflow obstruction and reversibility in asthma?

    a) ECG

    b) Spirometry

    c) Chest X-ray

    d) Blood gas analysis

13. What is a common symptom of chronic obstructive pulmonary disease (COPD)?

    a) Chest pain

    b) Shortness of breath

    c) High fever

    d) Swelling of the legs

14. Which medication is commonly used for quick relief of asthma symptoms?

    a) Beta-blockers

    b) Statins

    c) Short-acting beta-agonists (SABAs)

    d) ACE inhibitors

15. What is the primary cause of chronic renal failure?

    a) Acute infections

    b) Genetic mutations

    c) Long-term hypertension and diabetes

    d) Trauma

16. What type of dialysis involves the filtration of blood through an external machine?

    a) Peritoneal dialysis

    b) Hemodialysis

    c) Continuous ambulatory peritoneal dialysis

    d) None of the above

17. Which hormone helps regulate blood pressure and fluid balance by causing the kidneys to retain sodium and water?

    a) Aldosterone

    b) Insulin

    c) Cortisol

    d) Glucagon

18. What condition is characterized by the destruction of alveolar walls and loss of lung elasticity?

    a) Chronic bronchitis

    b) Asthma

    c) Emphysema

    d) Pulmonary fibrosis

19. What diagnostic tool is used to visualize coronary artery stenosis and blockages?

    a) Spirometry

    b) Electrocardiogram (ECG)

    c) Coronary angiography

    d) Chest X-ray

20. Which type of cell is primarily responsible for transporting oxygen in the blood?

    a) White blood cells

    b) Platelets

    c) Red blood cells

d) Plasma cells

**Short Answer Type Questions (Subjective)**

1. Describe the main functions of the heart in the cardiovascular system.
2. Explain the process of gas exchange in the alveoli.
3. What factors influence blood pressure regulation?
4. How does hypertension affect the cardiovascular system?
5. Describe the pathophysiology of congestive heart failure.
6. What are the main symptoms and complications of chronic obstructive pulmonary disease (COPD)?
7. How is asthma diagnosed and managed?
8. Explain the differences between acute and chronic renal failure.
9. What is the role of the autonomic nervous system in regulating heart function?
10. How do the lungs and cardiovascular system work together to maintain oxygenation?
11. What are the primary causes of myocardial infarction?
12. Describe the diagnostic tests used to assess chronic kidney disease (CKD).
13. How does diabetes contribute to the development of chronic kidney disease?
14. What lifestyle modifications can help manage hypertension?
15. Explain the role of bronchodilators in the treatment of asthma.
16. Describe the complications associated with untreated hypertension.
17. How does smoking contribute to the development of COPD?
18. What are the common treatments for acute renal failure?
19. Explain the concept of airway remodeling in asthma.
20. Describe the preventive measures for cardiovascular diseases.

**Long Answer Type Questions (Subjective)**

1. Discuss the structure and functions of the heart, including its chambers, valves, and blood vessels.
2. Explain the pathophysiology, symptoms, and treatment options for hypertension.
3. Describe the mechanisms of congestive heart failure and its impact on the body.
4. Explain the pathophysiology, diagnosis, and management of chronic obstructive pulmonary disease (COPD).
5. Discuss the interrelation between the cardiovascular and respiratory systems in maintaining homeostasis.
6. Describe the pathophysiology, symptoms, and treatment of myocardial infarction.
7. Explain the differences between asthma and COPD, including their causes, symptoms, and treatments.
8. Discuss the pathophysiology, diagnosis, and management of chronic kidney disease (CKD).
9. Explain the role of lifestyle modifications and pharmacologic therapy in the management of cardiovascular diseases.
10. Discuss the impact of chronic diseases like hypertension and diabetes on kidney function and the development of chronic renal failure.

**Answer Key for MCQ Questions**

1. c) Right Atrium
2. b) Pulmonary veins
3. b) Exchange gases and nutrients
4. b) Systole
5. c) Medullary respiratory centers

6. a) Trachea

7. b) Hypertension

8. b) Adrenaline

9. b) Congestive heart failure

10.b) Atherosclerosis

11.a) Asthma

12.b) Spirometry

13.b) Shortness of breath

14.c) Short-acting beta-agonists (SABAs)

15.c) Long-term hypertension and diabetes

16.b) Hemodialysis

17.a) Aldosterone

18.c) Emphysema

19.c) Coronary angiography

20.c) Red blood cells

## CHAPTER – 4

## HAEMATOLOGICAL DISEASE AND ENDOCRINE SYSTEM

Hematological diseases affect the blood, bone marrow, and lymphatic systems. They can impact the production, function, and quality of blood cells and can be broadly classified into several categories:

1. **Anemias**: Conditions characterized by a deficiency in the number or quality of red blood cells (RBCs) or hemoglobin, leading to reduced oxygen delivery to tissues. Examples include:

   a. **Iron Deficiency Anemia**: Caused by a lack of iron, which is crucial for hemoglobin production.

   b. **Vitamin B12 and Folate Deficiency Anemia**: Resulting from insufficient vitamin B12 or folate, essential for RBC production.

   c. **Aplastic Anemia**: A condition where the bone marrow fails to produce adequate amounts of blood cells.

2. **Leukemias**: Cancers of the blood and bone marrow characterized by the overproduction of abnormal white blood cells (WBCs). Types include:

   a. **Acute Lymphoblastic Leukemia (ALL)**: A rapid-growing leukemia affecting lymphoblasts.

   b. **Acute Myeloid Leukemia (AML)**: Affects myeloid cells and progresses quickly.

   c. **Chronic Lymphocytic Leukemia (CLL)**: A slow-growing leukemia affecting B lymphocytes.

   d. **Chronic Myeloid Leukemia (CML)**: Affects myeloid cells and is characterized by the presence of the Philadelphia chromosome.

3. **Lymphomas**: Cancers that originate in the lymphatic system. Major types are:

a. **Hodgkin Lymphoma**: Characterized by the presence of Reed-Sternberg cells.

b. **Non-Hodgkin Lymphoma**: A diverse group of blood cancers that includes various subtypes, such as diffuse large B-cell lymphoma (DLBCL) and follicular lymphoma.

4. **Myeloma**: Cancer of plasma cells in the bone marrow, leading to the production of abnormal antibodies. **Multiple Myeloma** is the most common form, characterized by bone pain, anemia, and kidney dysfunction.

5. **Bleeding Disorders**: Conditions that impair blood clotting, leading to excessive bleeding or bruising. Examples include:

   a. **Hemophilia**: A genetic disorder resulting in insufficient clotting factors.

   b. **Von Willebrand Disease**: A bleeding disorder caused by a deficiency or dysfunction of von Willebrand factor.

6. **Polycythemia**: Conditions characterized by an overproduction of red blood cells. **Polycythemia Vera** is a primary form associated with JAK2 mutation.

**Endocrine System:**

The endocrine system is responsible for producing and regulating hormones that control various physiological processes. Key components include:

1. **Hypothalamus**: Regulates the pituitary gland and controls the release of hormones that influence growth, metabolism, and stress responses.

2. **Pituitary Gland**: Known as the "master gland," it secretes hormones that regulate other endocrine glands. It has two main lobes:

   a. **Anterior Pituitary**: Produces hormones like growth hormone (GH), adrenocorticotropic hormone (ACTH), thyroid-stimulating hormone (TSH), luteinizing hormone (LH), and follicle-stimulating hormone (FSH).

b. **Posterior Pituitary**: Releases hormones such as oxytocin and antidiuretic hormone (ADH) produced by the hypothalamus.

3. **Thyroid Gland**: Produces thyroid hormones (thyroxine T4 and triiodothyronine T3) that regulate metabolism, energy levels, and growth.

4. **Parathyroid Glands**: Secrete parathyroid hormone (PTH), which regulates calcium and phosphate levels in the blood and bones.

5. **Adrenal Glands**: Located on top of the kidneys, they produce hormones such as cortisol (involved in stress response), aldosterone (regulates blood pressure), and adrenal androgens.

6. **Pancreas**: Functions as both an endocrine and exocrine gland. The endocrine component produces insulin and glucagon, which regulate blood sugar levels.

7. **Gonads**:

    a. **Ovaries**: Produce estrogen and progesterone, which regulate reproductive functions and secondary sexual characteristics.

    b. **Testes**: Produce testosterone, which regulates sperm production and secondary sexual characteristics.

8. **Pineal Gland**: Produces melatonin, which regulates sleep-wake cycles.

**Interactions Between Hematological Diseases and the Endocrine System**

1. **Endocrine Disorders and Blood Cell Production**: Conditions like hypothyroidism or hyperthyroidism can affect red and white blood cell production. For example, hypothyroidism can lead to anemia, while hyperthyroidism might cause increased red cell turnover.

2. **Adrenal Disorders**: Diseases such as Addison's disease (adrenal insufficiency) or Cushing's syndrome (excess cortisol) can impact various blood parameters, including blood pressure and glucose levels.

3. **Diabetes and Hematological Health**: Chronic diabetes can lead to various hematological complications, including an increased risk of infections due to impaired immune function.

## HEMATOLOGICAL DISEASES

### A. Iron deficiency:

### Introduction

**Iron deficiency** is one of the most common nutritional deficiencies worldwide, impacting various aspects of hematological and endocrine health. Iron is crucial for producing hemoglobin, which transports oxygen in the blood. Iron deficiency can lead to anemia and various systemic issues, impacting overall health and quality of life.

### Pathophysiology

Iron deficiency impairs hemoglobin production due to insufficient iron availability. Hemoglobin is essential for oxygen transport in the blood, and low iron levels reduce its synthesis, leading to decreased oxygen delivery to tissues. The pathophysiology of iron deficiency anemia (IDA) involves:

1. **Reduced Hemoglobin Production**: Low iron levels limit the synthesis of hemoglobin, leading to smaller and fewer red blood cells (RBCs).
2. **Impaired Oxygen Transport**: Anemia reduces the blood's oxygen-carrying capacity, affecting cellular metabolism and function.
3. **Increased Erythropoiesis**: The body tries to compensate by increasing red blood cell production, which may not be effective without adequate iron.

### Epidemiology

Iron deficiency is prevalent globally and can affect any age group. The incidence varies by region and demographic factors:

1. **Infants and Children**: Rapid growth and increased iron requirements make them vulnerable. Iron deficiency is common in developing countries due to poor diet and inadequate breastfeeding.
2. **Pregnant Women**: Increased iron needs due to fetal development and blood volume expansion.

3. **Women of Reproductive Age**: Menstrual blood loss can contribute to iron deficiency.

4. **Elderly**: Chronic diseases, poor dietary intake, and gastrointestinal bleeding can lead to iron deficiency.

5. **Athletes**: Increased iron loss through sweat and high demand can result in deficiency.

**Symptoms and Complications**

**Symptoms of Iron Deficiency**:

1. **Fatigue and Weakness**: Due to reduced oxygen delivery to tissues.

2. **Paleness**: Due to low hemoglobin levels.

3. **Shortness of Breath and Dizziness**: Especially during physical activity.

4. **Cold Hands and Feet**: Due to poor circulation.

5. **Brittle Nails and Hair Loss**: Reflecting poor cellular function.

6. **Pica**: Craving for non-nutritive substances like ice, dirt, or starch.

**Complications**:

1. **Severe Anemia**: Can lead to cardiovascular complications, including heart failure.

2. **Pregnancy Complications**: Increased risk of preterm birth, low birth weight, and postpartum depression.

3. **Impaired Cognitive and Developmental Function**: In children, iron deficiency can affect cognitive development and academic performance.

**Diagnosis**

**Diagnostic Tests**:

1. **Complete Blood Count (CBC)**: To evaluate red blood cell count, hemoglobin levels, and hematocrit.

2. **Serum Ferritin**: Measures the amount of stored iron in the body. Low levels indicate iron deficiency.

3. **Serum Iron**: Measures the amount of circulating iron. Low levels can indicate deficiency.

4. **Total Iron-Binding Capacity (TIBC)**: Elevated in iron deficiency; measures the blood's ability to bind iron.

5. **Transferrin Saturation**: Low percentage indicates iron deficiency.

**Additional Tests**:

1. **Peripheral Blood Smear**: To observe red blood cell morphology (e.g., microcytic, hypochromic cells).

2. **Bone Marrow Aspiration**: In some cases, to evaluate iron stores if the diagnosis is unclear.

**Treatment**

**Iron Supplementation**:

1. **Oral Iron Supplements**: Ferrous sulfate, ferrous gluconate, or ferrous fumarate are commonly used. Usually prescribed at a dose of 100-200 mg of elemental iron per day.

2. **Intravenous Iron**: For patients who cannot tolerate oral iron or have severe deficiency. Examples include iron sucrose, ferric gluconate, and iron dextran.

**Dietary Changes**:

1. **Iron-Rich Foods**: Incorporate sources like red meat, poultry, fish, lentils, beans, and fortified cereals.

2. **Vitamin C**: Enhances iron absorption. Include citrus fruits, tomatoes, and peppers in the diet.

**Addressing Underlying Causes**:

1. **Gastrointestinal Disorders**: Treat conditions like peptic ulcers or celiac disease that may contribute to iron deficiency.

2. **Menstrual Issues**: Address heavy menstrual bleeding with appropriate treatments.

**Prevention**

**General Recommendations**:

1. **Balanced Diet**: Ensure adequate intake of iron-rich foods, particularly in high-risk populations.
2. **Iron Supplementation**: For at-risk groups such as pregnant women, infants, and individuals with chronic conditions.
3. **Regular Screening**: For populations at risk (e.g., pregnant women, children, and the elderly) to detect iron deficiency early.
4. **Education and Awareness**: Promote dietary diversity and awareness of iron-rich foods and proper supplement use.

**Specific Interventions**:

1. **Pregnant Women**: Routine iron supplementation during pregnancy.
2. **Infants and Children**: Supplementation and dietary guidance to prevent deficiency.

Effective management of iron deficiency involves a combination of appropriate treatment, addressing underlying causes, and preventive measures to ensure optimal health outcomes.

## B. Megaloblastic anemia (Vit B$_{12}$ and folic acid):

**Introduction**

**Megaloblastic anemia** is a type of anemia characterized by the presence of abnormally large and immature red blood cells (megaloblasts) in the bone marrow and peripheral blood. It is primarily caused by deficiencies in vitamin B12 (cobalamin) or folic acid (vitamin B9), both of which are essential for proper DNA synthesis and red blood cell maturation.

**Pathophysiology**

1. **Vitamin B12 Deficiency**:
   a. **Impaired DNA Synthesis**: Vitamin B12 is essential for DNA synthesis and cell division. Its deficiency leads to impaired DNA replication, resulting in the production of large, immature red blood cells.

b. **Neurological Effects**: Vitamin B12 is also crucial for maintaining myelin sheaths in nerves. Deficiency can lead to neurological symptoms due to demyelination.

2. **Folic Acid Deficiency**:

   a. **Impaired Cell Division**: Folic acid is vital for DNA synthesis and cell division. Deficiency leads to the production of large, dysfunctional red blood cells.

   b. **Effect on Rapidly Dividing Cells**: Folic acid deficiency affects rapidly dividing cells, including those in the bone marrow, leading to megaloblastic anemia.

**Epidemiology**

1. **Vitamin B12 Deficiency**:

   a. More common in older adults due to decreased absorption in the gastrointestinal tract.

   b. Higher prevalence in individuals with gastrointestinal disorders (e.g., Crohn's disease, pernicious anemia) or those undergoing gastric surgery.

   c. Vegetarians and vegans are at higher risk due to the absence of vitamin B12 in plant-based diets.

2. **Folic Acid Deficiency**:

   a. Common in pregnant women due to increased demand.

   b. Higher incidence in individuals with poor dietary intake, alcoholism, or malabsorption issues (e.g., celiac disease).

   c. Certain medications (e.g., methotrexate, antiepileptics) can interfere with folic acid metabolism.

**Symptoms and Complications**

**Symptoms**:

1. **General Anemia Symptoms**: Fatigue, weakness, pallor, and shortness of breath.

2. **Vitamin B12 Deficiency Symptoms**:

    a. **Neurological Symptoms**: Numbness or tingling in extremities, difficulty walking, and memory loss.

    b. **Glossitis**: Inflammation of the tongue.

    c. **Mood Changes**: Depression or irritability.

3. **Folic Acid Deficiency Symptoms**:

    a. **Glossitis and Mouth Ulcers**: Inflammation and sores in the mouth.

    b. **Diarrhea**: Gastrointestinal discomfort.

    c. **Pregnancy Complications**: Neural tube defects in the fetus if deficiency occurs during pregnancy.

**Complications**:

1. **Neurological Damage**: Irreversible neurological damage if vitamin B12 deficiency is not treated promptly.

2. **Pregnancy Complications**: Increased risk of birth defects, including neural tube defects in the baby.

3. **Impaired Immune Function**: Both deficiencies can impact immune system function, leading to increased susceptibility to infections.

**Diagnosis**

**Diagnostic Tests**:

1. **Complete Blood Count (CBC)**: Shows macrocytic anemia with high mean corpuscular volume (MCV).

2. **Peripheral Blood Smear**: Reveals megaloblasts and hypersegmented neutrophils.

3. **Serum Vitamin B12 Levels**: Low levels indicate deficiency.

4. **Serum Folate Levels**: Low levels indicate deficiency.

5. **Methylmalonic Acid (MMA)**: Elevated in vitamin B12 deficiency.

6. **Homocysteine Levels**: Elevated in both vitamin B12 and folic acid deficiencies, but more specific to vitamin B12 deficiency.

**Additional Tests**:

1. **Intrinsic Factor Antibodies**: To diagnose pernicious anemia (a common cause of vitamin B12 deficiency).
2. **Bone Marrow Biopsy**: In some cases, to assess for megaloblasts and rule out other causes of anemia.

**Treatment**

**Vitamin B12 Deficiency**:

1. **Oral Supplements**: Typically prescribed at 1,000-2,000 µg daily if absorption is adequate.
2. **Intramuscular Injections**: 1,000 µg of vitamin B12 administered intramuscularly weekly or monthly, depending on the severity and cause of the deficiency.

**Folic Acid Deficiency**:

1. **Oral Supplements**: Typically prescribed at 1 mg daily.
2. **Dietary Changes**: Increase intake of folate-rich foods such as leafy greens, legumes, and fortified cereals.

**Addressing Underlying Causes**:

1. **Vitamin B12 Malabsorption**: Treat underlying conditions like pernicious anemia or gastrointestinal issues.
2. **Folic Acid Absorption Issues**: Address any underlying causes, such as malabsorption syndromes or drug interactions.

**Complications**

1. **Neurological Damage**: Especially in vitamin B12 deficiency, if treatment is delayed.
2. **Persistent Anemia**: If the underlying cause is not addressed, anemia may persist or recur.
3. **Pregnancy Complications**: Inadequate folic acid intake during pregnancy can lead to serious fetal developmental issues.

**Prevention**

**General Recommendations**:

1. **Balanced Diet**: Ensure adequate intake of vitamin B12 and folic acid through a varied diet.
2. **Supplements**: For individuals at risk, such as the elderly, pregnant women, and those with malabsorption issues.

**Specific Interventions**:

1. **Pregnant Women**: Routine supplementation of folic acid to prevent neural tube defects.
2. **Vegetarians and Vegans**: Regular vitamin B12 supplementation or fortified foods.
3. **Elderly Individuals**: Regular screening and supplementation if needed.

**C. Sickle cell anemia:**

**Introduction**

**Sickle cell anemia** is a genetic disorder characterized by the production of abnormal hemoglobin, known as hemoglobin S (HbS). This condition leads to the deformation of red blood cells (RBCs) into a sickle shape, which can cause blockages in blood vessels and result in various complications.

**Pathophysiology**

1. **Genetic Mutation**:
   a. **Hemoglobin S Production**: Sickle cell anemia is caused by a mutation in the HBB gene on chromosome 11, leading to the production of hemoglobin S instead of normal hemoglobin A.
   b. **Inheritance Pattern**: It follows an autosomal recessive pattern. Individuals with two copies of the mutated gene (homozygous) have sickle cell anemia, while those with one copy (heterozygous) are carriers (sickle cell trait).

2. **Red Blood Cell Deformation**:

   a. **Sickle Shape**: Hemoglobin S causes RBCs to assume a rigid, crescent or sickle shape, particularly under low oxygen conditions.

   b. **Cell Rigidity and Aggregation**: Sickle-shaped cells are less flexible and more prone to clumping together, leading to blockages in small blood vessels.

3. **Vaso-Occlusive Crises**:

   a. **Blockage of Blood Flow**: The sickle cells can obstruct blood flow, leading to tissue ischemia and pain. This can cause acute vaso-occlusive crises.

   b. **Chronic Organ Damage**: Repeated blockages and ischemia can lead to chronic damage in organs such as the spleen, liver, kidneys, and bones.

4. **Hemolysis**:

   a. **Destruction of RBCs**: Sickle cells have a shorter lifespan (10-20 days compared to the normal 120 days), leading to chronic hemolytic anemia.

   b. **Increased Bilirubin**: Hemolysis releases hemoglobin into the bloodstream, which is converted to bilirubin, potentially causing jaundice.

**Epidemiology**

1. **Prevalence**:

   a. **Global**: Sickle cell anemia is most common in sub-Saharan Africa, the Middle East, and parts of India and the Mediterranean.

   b. **United States**: It affects about 1 in 365 African-American births and 1 in 16,300 Hispanic-American births.

2. **Carrier Frequency**:

a. **High Incidence in Endemic Regions**: In regions where malaria is prevalent, the sickle cell trait provides a selective advantage, resulting in higher carrier rates.

**Symptoms and Complications**

**Symptoms**:

1. **Pain Crises**: Acute pain episodes due to vaso-occlusive crises.
2. **Anemia Symptoms**: Fatigue, pallor, and shortness of breath.
3. **Frequent Infections**: Due to spleen damage and impaired immune function.
4. **Delayed Growth**: In children, due to chronic anemia and pain.
5. **Jaundice**: Resulting from hemolysis and increased bilirubin levels.

**Complications**:

1. **Acute Chest Syndrome**: A life-threatening condition involving chest pain, fever, and difficulty breathing, often triggered by infection or vaso-occlusive crisis.
2. **Stroke**: Due to blockages in cerebral vessels, leading to neurological deficits.
3. **Organ Damage**: Chronic damage to the spleen, liver, kidneys, and bones.
4. **Leg Ulcers**: Chronic skin ulcers, particularly on the lower legs.
5. **Priapism**: Painful, prolonged erections in males due to blocked blood flow.

**Diagnosis**

**Diagnostic Tests**:

1. **Hemoglobin Electrophoresis**: Identifies hemoglobin S, confirming the diagnosis of sickle cell anemia.
2. **Complete Blood Count (CBC)**: Shows anemia and an increased number of reticulocytes (immature RBCs).
3. **Peripheral Blood Smear**: Reveals sickle-shaped cells and possible Howell-Jolly bodies (indicative of splenic dysfunction).

4. **Prenatal Testing**: For identifying sickle cell anemia in newborns or during pregnancy, through chorionic villus sampling or amniocentesis.

**Additional Tests**:

1. **Genetic Testing**: To confirm the presence of mutations in the HBB gene and identify carriers.
2. **Imaging Studies**: Such as ultrasound to assess organ damage or to monitor complications like stroke.

**Treatment**

**Supportive Care**:

1. **Pain Management**: Analgesics, including opioids and non-steroidal anti-inflammatory drugs (NSAIDs), to manage pain crises.
2. **Hydration**: Maintaining adequate fluid intake to reduce blood viscosity and prevent sickling.

**Medications**:

1. **Hydroxyurea**: Increases fetal hemoglobin (HbF) levels, which can reduce the frequency of pain crises and other complications.
2. **Folic Acid Supplements**: To support red blood cell production and mitigate anemia.
3. **Antibiotics**: To prevent infections, particularly in patients with spleen damage.

**Blood Transfusions**:

1. **Regular Transfusions**: To manage severe anemia or prevent stroke in high-risk individuals.
2. **Exchange Transfusions**: To reduce the proportion of sickle cells in the bloodstream during acute complications.

**Curative Treatments**:

1. **Bone Marrow Transplantation**: The only potential cure for sickle cell anemia, used in selected patients. Involves replacing defective bone marrow with healthy donor marrow.

**Emerging Therapies**:

1. **Gene Therapy**: Research is ongoing into gene editing technologies, such as CRISPR/Cas9, to correct the sickle cell mutation.

**Complications**

1. **Chronic Pain**: Persistent pain due to repeated vaso-occlusive crises.
2. **Organ Failure**: Progressive damage to organs, including the spleen, liver, kidneys, and heart.
3. **Increased Risk of Infections**: Due to compromised spleen function and weakened immune system.
4. **Developmental Delays**: In children, including delays in physical and cognitive development.

**Prevention**

**Primary Prevention**:

1. **Genetic Counseling**: For couples at risk, particularly in regions where sickle cell disease is common, to understand the risk and make informed reproductive choices.

**Secondary Prevention**:

1. **Newborn Screening**: Early detection and management to improve outcomes.
2. **Regular Monitoring and Care**: Routine check-ups to manage symptoms and prevent complications.

**Tertiary Prevention**:

1. **Education and Support**: Providing patients and families with information about managing the disease and accessing support services.

Sickle cell anemia management focuses on alleviating symptoms, preventing complications, and improving the quality of life for affected individuals. Advances in research continue to offer hope for more effective treatments and potential cures.

**D. Thalassemia:**

**Introduction**

**Thalassemia** is a group of inherited blood disorders characterized by the reduced production of hemoglobin, the protein in red blood cells responsible for oxygen transport. This leads to anemia and other related complications. The condition results from mutations in the genes responsible for hemoglobin production, affecting either the alpha or beta globin chains.

**Pathophysiology**

1. **Genetic Mutations**:
   a. **Alpha Thalassemia**: Caused by mutations in the genes responsible for alpha globin chain production (HBA1 and HBA2). There are four alpha globin genes, and the severity of the disease depends on the number of affected genes.
   b. **Beta Thalassemia**: Caused by mutations in the HBB gene, which codes for the beta globin chain. There are two beta globin genes, and the severity depends on the nature of the mutations.
2. **Impaired Hemoglobin Production**:
   a. **Alpha Thalassemia**: Results in reduced alpha globin chain production, leading to excess beta globin chains that form unstable hemoglobin.
   b. **Beta Thalassemia**: Results in reduced beta globin chain production, leading to excess alpha globin chains that aggregate, forming unstable hemoglobin.
3. **Ineffective Erythropoiesis**:
   a. **Bone Marrow Expansion**: Due to ineffective erythropoiesis, the body tries to produce more red blood cells, leading to expansion of the bone marrow and potentially causing bone deformities.

b. **Hemolysis**: Abnormal red blood cells are destroyed prematurely, leading to chronic anemia.

4. **Compensatory Mechanisms**:

    a. **Extramedullary Hematopoiesis**: To compensate for ineffective erythropoiesis, blood cell production may occur in the spleen and liver, leading to organ enlargement.

## Epidemiology

1. **Global Prevalence**:

    a. **Alpha Thalassemia**: Common in Southeast Asia, sub-Saharan Africa, and the Mediterranean region.

    b. **Beta Thalassemia**: Common in the Mediterranean Basin, the Middle East, Central Asia, and parts of Africa and South Asia.

2. **Carrier Rates**:

    a. **Alpha Thalassemia**: Higher in regions with high malaria prevalence, as carriers may have some protection against malaria.

    b. **Beta Thalassemia**: Higher in regions where thalassemia has been historically prevalent.

## Symptoms and Complications

**Symptoms:**

1. **General Symptoms**: Fatigue, weakness, and pallor due to anemia.

2. **Alpha Thalassemia**:

    a. **Mild Cases**: Often asymptomatic or with mild anemia.

    b. **Severe Cases (Hemoglobin H Disease)**: Symptoms can include jaundice, splenomegaly, and bone deformities.

3. **Beta Thalassemia**:

    a. **Beta Thalassemia Minor (Trait)**: Mild anemia and often asymptomatic.

b. **Beta Thalassemia Major (Cooley's Anemia)**: Severe anemia, growth retardation, bone deformities, splenomegaly, and liver enlargement.

**Complications**:

1. **Iron Overload**: Due to frequent blood transfusions, which can lead to damage of organs such as the heart, liver, and endocrine glands.
2. **Bone Deformities**: Thinning of bones and expansion of bone marrow can lead to skeletal abnormalities.
3. **Endocrine Disorders**: Such as diabetes mellitus and hypoparathyroidism due to iron deposition in endocrine organs.
4. **Infections**: Increased risk of infections due to splenectomy or compromised spleen function.

**Diagnosis**

**Diagnostic Tests**:

1. **Complete Blood Count (CBC)**: Shows anemia and abnormal red blood cell indices.
2. **Hemoglobin Electrophoresis**: Identifies abnormal hemoglobin patterns; useful for diagnosing beta thalassemia.
3. **Genetic Testing**: Detects mutations in the alpha or beta globin genes for precise diagnosis.
4. **Peripheral Blood Smear**: Reveals microcytic, hypochromic red blood cells and target cells.
5. **Iron Studies**: To assess iron levels and differentiate thalassemia from iron deficiency anemia.

**Additional Tests**:

1. **Bone Marrow Biopsy**: May be performed in severe cases to evaluate erythropoiesis.
2. **Prenatal Testing**: Includes chorionic villus sampling (CVS) or amniocentesis for early diagnosis in at-risk pregnancies.

**Treatment**

**Supportive Care**:

1. **Blood Transfusions**: Regular transfusions to manage anemia, particularly in beta thalassemia major.

2. **Iron Chelation Therapy**: To prevent iron overload from repeated transfusions. Agents include deferoxamine, deferasirox, and deferiprone.

**Specific Treatments**:

1. **Alpha Thalassemia**: Management varies depending on severity; severe cases may require regular blood transfusions.

2. **Beta Thalassemia**:

   a. **Hydroxyurea**: Increases fetal hemoglobin (HbF) levels, which can reduce symptoms.

   b. **Bone Marrow Transplantation**: The only potential cure, suitable for some patients with a suitable donor.

**Emerging Therapies**:

1. **Gene Therapy**: Research into correcting the genetic mutations responsible for thalassemia.

2. **Gene Editing**: Techniques like CRISPR/Cas9 are being explored to directly correct mutations.

**Complications**

1. **Iron Overload**: Leading to heart disease, liver cirrhosis, and endocrine dysfunction.

2. **Bone Abnormalities**: Such as osteopenia and osteoporosis.

3. **Endocrine Dysfunction**: Including diabetes and hypothyroidism due to iron deposition.

4. **Growth Delays**: Particularly in children with severe forms of thalassemia.

**Prevention**

**Primary Prevention**:

1. **Genetic Counseling**: For individuals with a family history or in regions with high prevalence, to understand risks and reproductive options.

**Secondary Prevention**:

1. **Prenatal Screening**: To identify thalassemia in at-risk pregnancies and provide early management.

2. **Newborn Screening**: Early detection to initiate treatment and improve outcomes.

**Tertiary Prevention**:

1. **Regular Monitoring**: For patients receiving transfusions to manage iron levels and prevent complications.

2. **Education**: To inform patients and families about disease management and preventive measures.

Effective management of thalassemia involves a combination of supportive care, specific treatments, and preventive strategies to improve quality of life and reduce complications. Advances in research continue to enhance treatment options and offer hope for future cures.

**E. Hereditary acquired anemia:**

**Hereditary acquired anemia** refers to an anemia condition that arises from genetic or inherited factors affecting red blood cell production or function, as opposed to acquired anemia due to external factors like nutrient deficiencies or chronic diseases. Here's a detailed look at various types of hereditary anemia, including their introduction, pathophysiology, epidemiology, symptoms, complications, diagnosis, treatment, and prevention.

**1. Hereditary Anemia Overview**

**Introduction**: Hereditary anemia encompasses various genetic disorders affecting red blood cells' production, structure, or function. These disorders are inherited in an autosomal dominant or recessive pattern and lead to chronic anemia due to abnormal red blood cell morphology or production.

**2. Pathophysiology**

**Common Hereditary Anemias**:

1. **Sickle Cell Anemia**:
   a. **Genetic Mutation**: Mutation in the HBB gene leads to abnormal hemoglobin S (HbS) that causes red blood cells to sickle under low oxygen conditions.
   b. **Mechanism**: Sickle-shaped cells cause vaso-occlusive crises, hemolysis, and chronic anemia.

2. **Thalassemia**:
   a. **Alpha Thalassemia**: Caused by mutations in alpha-globin genes, leading to imbalanced hemoglobin production.
   b. **Beta Thalassemia**: Caused by mutations in the beta-globin gene, leading to ineffective erythropoiesis and excess alpha chains.

3. **Hereditary Spherocytosis**:
   a. **Genetic Defects**: Defects in red blood cell membrane proteins (e.g., spectrin, ankyrin) lead to spherical, rigid RBCs that are prematurely destroyed.

4. **Hereditary Elliptocytosis**:
   a. **Genetic Mutations**: Defects in the red blood cell membrane proteins (e.g., spectrin) cause red blood cells to assume an elliptical shape, leading to hemolysis.

5. **G6PD Deficiency**:
   a. **Genetic Mutation**: Mutations in the G6PD gene impair the enzyme's function, leading to oxidative stress and hemolysis.

**3. Epidemiology**

a. **Sickle Cell Anemia**: Common in sub-Saharan Africa, the Middle East, Mediterranean regions, and India. Approximately 1 in 365 African-American births in the U.S.

b. **Thalassemia**: Common in the Mediterranean Basin, the Middle East, Central Asia, and parts of Africa and South Asia. Carrier rates vary by region.

c. **Hereditary Spherocytosis and Elliptocytosis**: More common in Northern European populations. Spherocytosis has a prevalence of about 1 in 2,000 individuals.

d. **G6PD Deficiency**: Common in regions with high malaria prevalence, including parts of Africa, the Middle East, and Southeast Asia. About 400 million people globally are affected.

## 4. Symptoms and Complications

**Symptoms:**

a. **Sickle Cell Anemia**: Painful crises, anemia, jaundice, organ damage, and susceptibility to infections.

b. **Thalassemia**: Fatigue, pallor, bone deformities, splenomegaly, and growth retardation.

c. **Hereditary Spherocytosis**: Anemia, jaundice, splenomegaly, and gallstones.

d. **Hereditary Elliptocytosis**: Mild to moderate anemia and an increased risk of hemolysis.

e. **G6PD Deficiency**: Acute hemolytic episodes triggered by infections, certain drugs, or fava beans.

**Complications:**

a. **Sickle Cell Anemia**: Stroke, acute chest syndrome, organ failure, and delayed growth.

b. **Thalassemia**: Iron overload, organ damage, and endocrine dysfunction.

c. **Hereditary Spherocytosis**: Splenomegaly, gallstones, and risk of anemia-related complications.

d. **Hereditary Elliptocytosis**: Chronic anemia and increased hemolysis.

e. **G6PD Deficiency**: Acute hemolysis, potential renal failure, and hemolytic anemia crisis.

## 5. Diagnosis

**Diagnostic Tests**:

a. **Complete Blood Count (CBC)**: Reveals anemia and abnormal red blood cell indices.

b. **Peripheral Blood Smear**: Identifies characteristic cell shapes and sizes.

c. **Hemoglobin Electrophoresis**: For diagnosing sickle cell anemia and thalassemia.

d. **Genetic Testing**: Confirms specific genetic mutations associated with various hereditary anemias.

e. **Osmotic Fragility Test**: For hereditary spherocytosis.

f. **Enzyme Assays**: For G6PD deficiency to assess enzyme activity.

**Additional Tests**:

a. **Bone Marrow Biopsy**: In cases where anemia etiology is unclear or to assess erythropoiesis.

b. **Prenatal Testing**: Includes chorionic villus sampling or amniocentesis for at-risk pregnancies.

## 6. Treatment

**Supportive Care**:

a. **Transfusions**: To manage severe anemia and complications in conditions like sickle cell anemia and thalassemia.

b. **Iron Chelation Therapy**: For patients receiving frequent transfusions to prevent iron overload.

**Specific Treatments**:

a. **Sickle Cell Anemia**:

       i.    **Hydroxyurea**: Increases fetal hemoglobin (HbF) levels and reduces complications.

       ii.   **Bone Marrow Transplant**: Potentially curative for some patients.

  b. **Thalassemia**:

       i.    **Regular Blood Transfusions**: For managing severe cases.

       ii.   **Iron Chelation**: To manage iron overload from transfusions.

       iii.  **Bone Marrow Transplant**: Potentially curative in selected cases.

  c. **Hereditary Spherocytosis and Elliptocytosis**:

       i.    **Splenectomy**: To reduce hemolysis and improve anemia, particularly in severe cases.

  d. **G6PD Deficiency**:

       i.    **Avoidance of Triggers**: Avoidance of known oxidative stressors and certain medications.

**Emerging Therapies**:

  a. **Gene Therapy**: Research is ongoing for potential cures through gene editing and modification.

  b. **New Medications**: Developing drugs to modify disease course and improve management.

## 7. Complications

  a. **Sickle Cell Anemia**: Chronic pain, stroke, acute chest syndrome, and organ failure.

  b. **Thalassemia**: Iron overload, endocrine dysfunction, and organ damage.

  c. **Hereditary Spherocytosis**: Anemia-related complications and risk of gallstones.

  d. **Hereditary Elliptocytosis**: Chronic anemia and hemolysis.

  e. **G6PD Deficiency**: Acute hemolytic crises and potential renal issues.

## 8. Prevention

**Primary Prevention**:

a. **Genetic Counseling**: For couples with a family history or living in regions where these conditions are prevalent.

b. **Prenatal Screening**: To detect hereditary anemias early in at-risk pregnancies.

**Secondary Prevention**:

a. **Newborn Screening**: Early detection of hereditary anemia to start management early and prevent complications.

b. **Regular Monitoring**: For individuals at risk or diagnosed with hereditary anemia to manage symptoms and prevent complications.

**Tertiary Prevention**:

a. **Patient Education**: Providing information on disease management, avoiding triggers, and understanding treatment options.

b. **Support Services**: Access to support groups and resources for patients and families affected by hereditary anemia.

Effective management of hereditary acquired anemia involves understanding the specific type of anemia, providing supportive and specific treatments, and implementing preventive measures to enhance quality of life and reduce complications.

## F. Hemophilia:

**Introduction**

**Hemophilia** is a group of inherited bleeding disorders characterized by the inability of blood to clot properly due to deficiencies or abnormalities in specific clotting factors. This results in prolonged bleeding or spontaneous bleeding episodes, particularly into joints and muscles.

**Pathophysiology**

1. **Genetic Defects**:

a. **Hemophilia A**: Caused by a deficiency or dysfunction of clotting factor VIII (FVIII), an essential protein in the blood clotting cascade.

b. **Hemophilia B**: Caused by a deficiency or dysfunction of clotting factor IX (FIX), another crucial protein in the clotting cascade.

c. **Hemophilia C**: Caused by a deficiency of clotting factor XI (FXI). It is less common and usually less severe than types A and B.

2. **Impaired Coagulation Cascade**:

a. **Intrinsic Pathway**: Both Hemophilia A and B affect the intrinsic pathway of the clotting cascade, leading to prolonged activated partial thromboplastin time (aPTT) but normal prothrombin time (PT).

b. **Factor Deficiency**: The specific factor deficiency impairs the formation of fibrin clots, which are essential for stopping bleeding.

3. **Bleeding Tendency**:

a. **Spontaneous Bleeding**: Even minor injuries can lead to excessive bleeding. Internal bleeding into joints (hemarthrosis) and muscles is common.

b. **Delayed Hemostasis**: Clotting is inefficient, leading to prolonged bleeding times and difficulty stopping bleeding.

**Epidemiology**

1. **Prevalence**:

a. **Hemophilia A**: Affects approximately 1 in 5,000 male births.

b. **Hemophilia B**: Affects approximately 1 in 25,000 male births.

c. **Hemophilia C**: Less common, with varying prevalence depending on ethnicity and geography.

2. **Inheritance Pattern**:

a. **X-Linked Recessive**: Hemophilia A and B are inherited in an X-linked recessive pattern, meaning the condition predominantly affects males, while females are carriers.

b. **Autosomal Recessive**: Hemophilia C follows an autosomal recessive inheritance pattern and can affect both males and females.

**Symptoms and Complications**

**Symptoms:**

1. **Spontaneous Bleeding**: Frequent bleeding without an obvious cause, including nosebleeds and bleeding gums.
2. **Joint Bleeding**: Pain, swelling, and limited movement due to bleeding into joints (hemarthrosis).
3. **Muscle Bleeding**: Pain, swelling, and bruising in muscles.
4. **Bleeding After Surgery or Injury**: Prolonged bleeding following medical procedures or trauma.

**Complications:**

1. **Chronic Joint Damage**: Repeated joint bleeds can lead to hemophilic arthropathy, causing joint damage and arthritis.
2. **Inhibitors**: Some patients develop antibodies (inhibitors) against clotting factors, making treatment less effective.
3. **Internal Bleeding**: Risk of bleeding into organs or the central nervous system.
4. **Anemia**: Chronic bleeding can lead to iron deficiency anemia.

**Diagnosis**

**Diagnostic Tests:**

1. **Coagulation Profile:**

   a. **Activated Partial Thromboplastin Time (aPTT)**: Prolonged in Hemophilia A and B.

b. **Prothrombin Time (PT)**: Normal in Hemophilia A and B; may be prolonged in Hemophilia C.

c. **Bleeding Time**: Typically normal in hemophilia.

2. **Specific Factor Assays**:

    a. **Factor VIII Assay**: Diagnoses Hemophilia A.

    b. **Factor IX Assay**: Diagnoses Hemophilia B.

    c. **Factor XI Assay**: Diagnoses Hemophilia C.

3. **Genetic Testing**:

    a. **Mutation Analysis**: Identifies specific mutations in the genes coding for the clotting factors.

4. **Family History**:

    a. **Pedigree Analysis**: Helps identify carriers and affected individuals in families with a history of hemophilia.

**Treatment**

**Management Strategies**:

1. **Factor Replacement Therapy**:

    a. **Factor VIII Concentrates**: Used for Hemophilia A.

    b. **Factor IX Concentrates**: Used for Hemophilia B.

    c. **Factor XI Concentrates**: Used for Hemophilia C in some cases.

2. **Desmopressin (DDAVP)**:

    a. **Indication**: Used for mild Hemophilia A to stimulate the release of endogenous FVIII.

3. **Prophylactic Treatment**:

    a. **Regular Factor Infusions**: To prevent bleeding episodes and joint damage.

4. **Management of Inhibitors**:

    a. **Immune Tolerance Induction (ITI)**: For patients with inhibitors to reduce or eliminate the immune response against clotting factors.

b. **Bypassing Agents**: Such as activated prothrombin complex concentrate (aPCC) or recombinant activated factor VII (rFVIIa) for those with inhibitors.

5. **Gene Therapy**:

a. **Emerging Treatments**: Research is ongoing into gene therapy approaches to correct the genetic defects causing hemophilia.

**Emergency Management**:

1. **Treatment of Bleeding Episodes**: Immediate infusion of clotting factors to control bleeding.

2. **Supportive Care**: Pain management and rehabilitation for joint and muscle injuries.

**Complications**

1. **Joint Damage**: Chronic bleeding into joints can lead to joint deformity and arthritis.

2. **Inhibitor Development**: Development of antibodies against clotting factors can complicate treatment.

3. **Transfusion-Related Infections**: Risk of infections from blood products, although modern screening reduces this risk.

4. **Allergic Reactions**: Potential reactions to clotting factor concentrates.

**Prevention**

**Primary Prevention**:

1. **Genetic Counseling**: For families with a history of hemophilia to understand inheritance patterns and risks.

2. **Prenatal Testing**: To diagnose hemophilia in at-risk pregnancies.

**Secondary Prevention**:

1. **Early Diagnosis**: Newborn screening and early diagnosis to initiate treatment and prevent complications.

**Tertiary Prevention**:

1. **Regular Monitoring**: Ongoing assessment and treatment adjustments to manage symptoms and prevent complications.

2. **Education and Support**: For patients and families on managing hemophilia, including recognizing bleeding symptoms and understanding treatment options.

Effective management of hemophilia involves a comprehensive approach to treat bleeding episodes, prevent complications, and improve quality of life through specialized care and ongoing monitoring. Advances in research, including gene therapy, offer hope for future improvements in treatment and potential cures.

## ENDOCRINE SYSTEM

## A. Diabetes:

**Diabetes Mellitus** is a chronic metabolic disorder characterized by elevated blood glucose levels due to defects in insulin production, insulin action, or both. It affects various systems in the body and has significant implications for both hematological and endocrine health.

**Introduction**

Diabetes Mellitus is divided into two main types:

1. **Type 1 Diabetes (T1D)**: An autoimmune condition where the body's immune system attacks and destroys insulin-producing beta cells in the pancreas.

2. **Type 2 Diabetes (T2D)**: Characterized by insulin resistance and relative insulin deficiency, often associated with obesity and a sedentary lifestyle.

**Pathophysiology**

**Type 1 Diabetes**:

1. **Autoimmune Destruction**: The immune system erroneously targets and destroys beta cells in the pancreas, leading to little or no insulin production.

2. **Insulin Deficiency**: Lack of insulin prevents glucose uptake into cells, resulting in elevated blood glucose levels.

**Type 2 Diabetes**:

1. **Insulin Resistance**: Cells become less responsive to insulin, reducing glucose uptake.
2. **Beta-Cell Dysfunction**: Over time, beta cells fail to produce sufficient insulin to compensate for insulin resistance.
3. **Glucose Overproduction**: The liver may produce excess glucose, contributing to elevated blood glucose levels.

**Both Types**:

1. **Hyperglycemia**: Persistent high blood sugar levels cause various metabolic disturbances and damage to organs and tissues.

**Epidemiology**

1. **Global Prevalence**:
   a. **Type 1 Diabetes**: Affects approximately 5-10% of all diabetes cases. Typically presents in children and young adults but can occur at any age.
   b. **Type 2 Diabetes**: More common, accounting for about 90-95% of diabetes cases. Increasing prevalence due to rising obesity rates and sedentary lifestyles.
2. **Risk Factors**:
   a. **Type 1 Diabetes**: Genetic predisposition and autoimmune factors. No known modifiable risk factors.
   b. **Type 2 Diabetes**: Obesity, sedentary lifestyle, poor diet, family history, older age, and certain ethnic backgrounds (e.g., African, Hispanic, Asian).

**Symptoms and Complications**

**Symptoms**:

1. **Classic Symptoms**: Polyuria (frequent urination), polydipsia (excessive thirst), polyphagia (increased hunger), and unexplained weight loss.

2. **Other Symptoms**: Fatigue, blurred vision, and recurrent infections.

**Complications**:

1. **Short-Term Complications**:

    a. **Hypoglycemia**: Low blood sugar levels can cause symptoms such as shakiness, sweating, confusion, and in severe cases, loss of consciousness.

    b. **Diabetic Ketoacidosis (DKA)**: A serious condition characterized by high blood sugar, ketone production, and metabolic acidosis, commonly seen in Type 1 diabetes.

    c. **Hyperosmolar Hyperglycemic State (HHS)**: Severe hyperglycemia and dehydration, more common in Type 2 diabetes.

2. **Long-Term Complications**:

    a. **Cardiovascular Disease**: Increased risk of heart attack, stroke, and peripheral artery disease.

    b. **Neuropathy**: Nerve damage leading to pain, tingling, and loss of sensation, particularly in the feet and hands.

    c. **Retinopathy**: Damage to the blood vessels in the retina, potentially leading to blindness.

    d. **Nephropathy**: Kidney damage that can progress to chronic kidney disease and end-stage renal disease.

    e. **Foot Ulcers**: Increased risk of infections and ulcers, often due to poor circulation and neuropathy.

**Diagnosis**

**Diagnostic Tests:**

1. **Fasting Blood Glucose**: A fasting plasma glucose level of 126 mg/dL (7.0 mmol/L) or higher indicates diabetes.

2. **Oral Glucose Tolerance Test (OGTT)**: A 2-hour plasma glucose level of 200 mg/dL (11.1 mmol/L) or higher after consuming a glucose-rich drink.

3. **Hemoglobin A1c (HbA1c)**: An average blood glucose level over the past 2-3 months. An HbA1c level of 6.5% or higher indicates diabetes.

4. **Random Blood Glucose Test**: A plasma glucose level of 200 mg/dL (11.1 mmol/L) or higher, with symptoms of diabetes.

**Additional Tests**:

1. **Urinalysis**: To detect glucose and ketones in the urine.

2. **Lipid Profile**: To assess cardiovascular risk.

3. **Renal Function Tests**: To evaluate kidney function and detect early signs of nephropathy.

**Treatment**

**General Management**:

1. **Lifestyle Modifications**: Healthy diet, regular physical activity, weight management, and smoking cessation.

2. **Blood Glucose Monitoring**: Regular monitoring to manage blood glucose levels and adjust treatment as needed.

**Type 1 Diabetes**:

1. **Insulin Therapy**: Requires lifelong insulin injections or an insulin pump to regulate blood glucose levels.

2. **Continuous Glucose Monitoring (CGM)**: Helps in real-time monitoring of glucose levels and adjusting insulin therapy.

**Type 2 Diabetes**:

1. **Oral Medications**: Includes metformin, sulfonylureas, DPP-4 inhibitors, and SGLT2 inhibitors to improve insulin sensitivity or increase insulin secretion.

2. **Insulin Therapy**: May be required in advanced cases or when oral medications are insufficient.

**Emerging Therapies**:

1. **GLP-1 Receptor Agonists**: Enhance insulin secretion and reduce appetite.
2. **Bariatric Surgery**: For eligible patients with severe obesity to improve blood glucose control.
3. **Gene Therapy and Regenerative Medicine**: Research into potential cures and advanced treatment options.

**Complications**

1. **Cardiovascular Issues**: Increased risk of heart disease and stroke.
2. **Neuropathy**: Nerve damage leading to pain, numbness, and difficulty with movement.
3. **Retinopathy**: Vision impairment and potential blindness.
4. **Nephropathy**: Progressive kidney damage and failure.
5. **Foot Problems**: Infections and ulcers due to poor circulation and sensation.

**Prevention**

**Primary Prevention**:

1. **Healthy Lifestyle**: Emphasize a balanced diet, regular exercise, and maintaining a healthy weight.
2. **Genetic Counseling**: For families with a history of Type 1 diabetes to understand risk factors.

**Secondary Prevention**:

1. **Early Detection**: Regular screening for at-risk individuals to identify diabetes early and manage it effectively.
2. **Education**: Providing information on lifestyle changes and monitoring to prevent the onset of Type 2 diabetes.

**Tertiary Prevention**:

1. **Regular Monitoring**: Ongoing assessment to manage diabetes effectively and prevent complications.

2. **Patient Education**: Teaching patients about managing their condition, recognizing symptoms of complications, and adhering to treatment plans.

Managing diabetes effectively involves a combination of lifestyle modifications, medical treatment, and ongoing monitoring to prevent complications and improve quality of life. Advances in treatment and research continue to offer new opportunities for better management and potential future cures.

**Thyroid diseases:**

**Thyroid diseases** encompass a range of disorders affecting the thyroid gland, which plays a critical role in regulating metabolism, growth, and development. Thyroid diseases can impact various body systems, including the hematological and endocrine systems.

**Introduction**

**Thyroid Diseases:**

1. **Hypothyroidism**: A condition where the thyroid gland underproduces thyroid hormones.
2. **Hyperthyroidism**: A condition where the thyroid gland overproduces thyroid hormones.
3. **Thyroiditis**: Inflammation of the thyroid gland, which can be caused by autoimmune conditions or infections.
4. **Thyroid Cancer**: Malignant growths in the thyroid gland.

**Pathophysiology**

1. **Hypothyroidism**:
   a. **Primary Hypothyroidism**: The thyroid gland itself is dysfunctional, often due to autoimmune thyroiditis (Hashimoto's thyroiditis), iodine deficiency, or thyroid surgery.
   b. **Secondary Hypothyroidism**: Caused by insufficient thyroid-stimulating hormone (TSH) production from the pituitary gland.

c. **Tertiary Hypothyroidism**: Due to inadequate thyrotropin-releasing hormone (TRH) production from the hypothalamus.

2. **Hyperthyroidism:**

   a. **Graves' Disease**: An autoimmune disorder where antibodies stimulate the thyroid gland to produce excess thyroid hormones.

   b. **Toxic Nodular Goiter**: Hyperfunctioning nodules in the thyroid gland produce excess hormones.

   c. **Thyroiditis**: Inflammation of the thyroid can release stored thyroid hormones into the bloodstream, causing temporary hyperthyroidism.

3. **Thyroiditis:**

   a. **Hashimoto's Thyroiditis**: An autoimmune disorder where the immune system attacks the thyroid gland, leading to hypothyroidism.

   b. **Subacute Thyroiditis**: Often viral in origin, causing transient hyperthyroidism followed by hypothyroidism.

4. **Thyroid Cancer:**

   a. **Papillary Thyroid Cancer**: The most common form of thyroid cancer, typically slow-growing.

   b. **Follicular Thyroid Cancer**: More aggressive than papillary thyroid cancer.

   c. **Medullary Thyroid Cancer**: Arises from parafollicular C cells and can be associated with genetic syndromes.

   d. **Anaplastic Thyroid Cancer**: A rare and aggressive form of thyroid cancer.

**Epidemiology**

1. **Hypothyroidism:**

   a. Prevalence: Affects approximately 4-5% of the general population, with a higher prevalence in women and the elderly.

b. Autoimmune thyroiditis (Hashimoto's) is the most common cause.

2. **Hyperthyroidism**:

a. Prevalence: Affects about 1-2% of the general population, with a higher incidence in women and older adults.

b. Graves' disease is the most common cause.

3. **Thyroiditis**:

a. Prevalence varies by type; Hashimoto's thyroiditis is common worldwide, while subacute thyroiditis is less common.

4. **Thyroid Cancer**:

a. Incidence: The most common endocrine malignancy. Rates have increased over recent decades, partly due to improved detection.

**Symptoms and Complications**

**Hypothyroidism**:

1. **Symptoms**: Fatigue, weight gain, cold intolerance, constipation, dry skin, hair loss, and depression.

2. **Complications**: Cardiovascular issues (e.g., heart disease), myxedema (severe hypothyroidism), and impaired mental function.

**Hyperthyroidism**:

1. **Symptoms**: Weight loss, heat intolerance, palpitations, tremors, diarrhea, and anxiety.

2. **Complications**: Thyroid storm (a severe, life-threatening exacerbation of hyperthyroidism), osteoporosis, and atrial fibrillation.

**Thyroiditis**:

1. **Symptoms**: Symptoms vary by type but can include neck pain, fever, and symptoms of hypothyroidism or hyperthyroidism.

2. **Complications**: May progress to chronic hypothyroidism or lead to persistent thyroid dysfunction.

**Thyroid Cancer:**

1. **Symptoms**: Often asymptomatic, but can include a palpable neck lump, hoarseness, difficulty swallowing, and cervical lymphadenopathy.
2. **Complications**: Local invasion, metastasis, and complications from treatment (e.g., surgery-related vocal cord paralysis).

**Diagnosis**

**Diagnostic Tests:**

1. **Thyroid Function Tests:**
   a. **Thyroid-Stimulating Hormone (TSH)**: Elevated in hypothyroidism, suppressed in hyperthyroidism.
   b. **Free T4 and Free T3**: Elevated in hyperthyroidism, decreased in hypothyroidism.
2. **Autoimmune Markers:**
   a. **Anti-Thyroid Peroxidase Antibodies (Anti-TPO)**: Elevated in Hashimoto's thyroiditis.
   b. **Anti-Thyroglobulin Antibodies**: Can be elevated in autoimmune thyroid disorders.
3. **Thyroid Imaging:**
   a. **Ultrasound**: Evaluates thyroid nodules, cysts, and structural abnormalities.
   b. **Thyroid Scintigraphy**: Assesses thyroid function and identifies hyperfunctioning or non-functioning nodules.
4. **Fine Needle Aspiration (FNA) Biopsy:**
   a. **Indication**: For evaluation of thyroid nodules or suspected thyroid cancer.
5. **Thyroid Function Tests:**
   a. **T4 and T3 Levels**: Measure thyroid hormone levels in the blood.
6. **Genetic Testing:**
   a. **For Thyroid Cancer**: Certain genetic mutations may be identified.

**Treatment**

**Hypothyroidism**:

1. **Thyroid Hormone Replacement**:

    a. **Levothyroxine**: Synthetic T4, the standard treatment for hypothyroidism.

**Hyperthyroidism**:

1. **Antithyroid Medications**:

    a. **Methimazole** or **Propylthiouracil**: To inhibit thyroid hormone synthesis.

2. **Radioactive Iodine Therapy**:

    a. **Indication**: For patients with Graves' disease or toxic nodular goiter.

3. **Surgery**:

    a. **Thyroidectomy**: May be required for large goiters or cancer.

**Thyroiditis**:

1. **Treatment**:

    a. **Hashimoto's Thyroiditis**: Treated similarly to hypothyroidism with levothyroxine.

    b. **Subacute Thyroiditis**: May require anti-inflammatory medications or corticosteroids.

**Thyroid Cancer**:

1. **Surgery**:

    a. **Thyroidectomy**: Total or partial removal of the thyroid gland.

2. **Radioactive Iodine Therapy**:

    a. **Indication**: Post-surgery to destroy remaining cancer cells.

3. **Thyroid Hormone Therapy**:

    a. **Levothyroxine**: Used post-surgery to suppress TSH and reduce the risk of cancer recurrence.

**Complications**

1. **Hypothyroidism**: Cardiovascular issues, myxedema coma, and mental impairment.
2. **Hyperthyroidism**: Thyroid storm, osteoporosis, and cardiovascular problems.
3. **Thyroiditis**: Persistent thyroid dysfunction, including chronic hypothyroidism or hyperthyroidism.
4. **Thyroid Cancer**: Recurrence, metastasis, and complications from surgery or radiation therapy.

**Prevention**

**Primary Prevention**:

1. **Iodine Intake**: Ensure adequate iodine intake in areas where deficiency is common to prevent iodine deficiency-related thyroid disorders.
2. **Autoimmune Monitoring**: Genetic and environmental factors may predispose individuals to autoimmune thyroid disease.

**Secondary Prevention**:

1. **Regular Screening**: For individuals with risk factors (e.g., family history of thyroid disease) to detect thyroid disorders early.
2. **Management of Symptoms**: Early and effective treatment to prevent progression and complications.

**Tertiary Prevention**:

1. **Ongoing Monitoring**: Regular follow-up for individuals with thyroid disorders to manage treatment and prevent complications.
2. **Patient Education**: Teaching about symptoms of thyroid dysfunction and the importance of adherence to treatment plans.

Thyroid diseases require a multifaceted approach involving diagnosis, treatment, and regular monitoring to manage symptoms and prevent complications. Advances in understanding and treatment continue to improve outcomes and quality of life for individuals with thyroid disorders.

**B. Disorders of sex hormones:**

**Disorders of sex hormones** affect the endocrine system and can have significant implications for reproductive health, development, and overall well-being. These disorders can impact both males and females, leading to various clinical presentations and health concerns.

**Introduction**

**Sex Hormones**:

1. **Estrogens**: Primarily produced in the ovaries in females and in smaller amounts in males.
2. **Progesterone**: Produced mainly in the ovaries, particularly during the menstrual cycle and pregnancy.
3. **Testosterone**: Produced mainly in the testes in males and in smaller amounts in females.
4. **Luteinizing Hormone (LH)** and **Follicle-Stimulating Hormone (FSH)**: Regulate reproductive functions in both males and females.

**Common Disorders**:

1. **Hypogonadism**: Reduced hormone production.
2. **Polycystic Ovary Syndrome (PCOS)**: A common endocrine disorder in females.
3. **Premature Ovarian Insufficiency (POI)**: Early loss of ovarian function.
4. **Andropause**: Age-related decline in testosterone levels in males.
5. **Hyperprolactinemia**: Elevated prolactin levels affecting reproductive function.

**Pathophysiology**

1. **Hypogonadism**:
   a. **Primary Hypogonadism**: Dysfunction in the gonads (ovaries or testes) leading to insufficient hormone production.

b. **Secondary Hypogonadism**: Dysfunction in the pituitary gland or hypothalamus affecting the release of gonadotropins (LH and FSH), thus impacting gonadal function.

2. **Polycystic Ovary Syndrome (PCOS)**:

   a. **Insulin Resistance**: Elevated insulin levels can stimulate ovarian androgen production.

   b. **Elevated Androgens**: Higher levels of male hormones (e.g., testosterone) disrupt normal ovarian function.

3. **Premature Ovarian Insufficiency (POI)**:

   a. **Autoimmune Attack**: The immune system attacks ovarian tissues.

   b. **Genetic Mutations**: Some genetic conditions can lead to early loss of ovarian function.

   c. **Chromosomal Abnormalities**: Such as Turner syndrome.

4. **Andropause**:

   a. **Testosterone Decline**: Gradual decrease in testosterone levels with age, affecting various bodily functions.

5. **Hyperprolactinemia**:

   a. **Prolactin-Secreting Pituitary Tumor (Prolactinoma)**: Causes excessive prolactin secretion.

   b. **Medications**: Certain drugs can increase prolactin levels.

**Epidemiology**

1. **Hypogonadism**:

   a. **Primary Hypogonadism**: Affects both males and females, with causes ranging from genetic conditions to autoimmune diseases.

   b. **Secondary Hypogonadism**: Affects both genders and can be due to pituitary or hypothalamic disorders.

2. **Polycystic Ovary Syndrome (PCOS)**:

   a. Prevalence: Affects 6-12% of women of reproductive age. It is one of the most common endocrine disorders in women.

3. **Premature Ovarian Insufficiency (POI)**:

   a. Prevalence: Affects about 1% of women under 40 years of age.

4. **Andropause**:

   a. Prevalence: Affects a significant percentage of men over 50 years of age, with varying degrees of symptom severity.

5. **Hyperprolactinemia**:

   a. Prevalence: Prolactinomas account for approximately 30% of all pituitary tumors.

**Symptoms and Complications**

**Hypogonadism**:

1. **Symptoms**: Infertility, delayed puberty, reduced libido, erectile dysfunction in males, and irregular menstruation or amenorrhea in females.

2. **Complications**: Osteoporosis, cardiovascular disease, and impaired cognitive function.

**Polycystic Ovary Syndrome (PCOS)**:

1. **Symptoms**: Irregular menstrual cycles, acne, hirsutism (excessive hair growth), and infertility.

2. **Complications**: Type 2 diabetes, cardiovascular disease, endometrial hyperplasia, and increased risk of endometrial cancer.

**Premature Ovarian Insufficiency (POI)**:

1. **Symptoms**: Irregular or absent menstrual periods, infertility, and symptoms of menopause (e.g., hot flashes).

2. **Complications**: Osteoporosis, cardiovascular disease, and reduced quality of life.

**Andropause**:

1. **Symptoms**: Decreased libido, erectile dysfunction, fatigue, and mood changes.

2. **Complications**: Osteoporosis, increased body fat, and decreased muscle mass.

**Hyperprolactinemia**:

1. **Symptoms**: Galactorrhea (unexplained milk production), amenorrhea, and infertility in women; decreased libido and erectile dysfunction in men.
2. **Complications**: Vision problems (if a large pituitary tumor), bone density loss due to prolonged low estrogen levels in women.

**Diagnosis**

**Diagnostic Tests**:

1. **Hormone Levels**:
    a. **Sex Hormones**: Measure levels of estrogens, progesterone, testosterone, and others.
    b. **Gonadotropins**: LH and FSH levels to assess pituitary function.
    c. **Prolactin**: Elevated levels suggest hyperprolactinemia.
2. **Imaging**:
    a. **Ultrasound**: For ovarian cysts and PCOS.
    b. **CT/MRI**: To evaluate pituitary tumors or structural abnormalities.
3. **Genetic Testing**:
    a. **For Genetic Conditions**: Such as Turner syndrome or certain mutations associated with POI.
4. **Pituitary Function Tests**:
    a. **Dynamic Testing**: To assess pituitary hormone production and response.

**Treatment**

**Hypogonadism**:

1. **Hormone Replacement Therapy**:
    a. **Estrogen/Progesterone**: For females to induce menstrual cycles and prevent osteoporosis.

b. **Testosterone**: For males to improve libido, energy, and muscle mass.

**Polycystic Ovary Syndrome (PCOS)**:

1. **Lifestyle Modifications**: Weight loss, diet, and exercise to improve insulin sensitivity.
2. **Medications**:
   a. **Metformin**: To manage insulin resistance.
   b. **Oral Contraceptives**: To regulate menstrual cycles and reduce androgens.
   c. **Anti-Androgens**: Such as spironolactone to manage hirsutism.

**Premature Ovarian Insufficiency (POI)**:

1. **Hormone Replacement Therapy**: Estrogen and progesterone to manage menopausal symptoms and prevent osteoporosis.
2. **Fertility Treatments**: Options such as egg donation for those seeking pregnancy.

**Andropause**:

1. **Testosterone Replacement Therapy**: To address symptoms and improve quality of life.
2. **Lifestyle Changes**: Exercise and diet improvements to manage weight and muscle mass.

**Hyperprolactinemia**:

1. **Medications**:
   a. **Dopamine Agonists**: Such as cabergoline or bromocriptine to lower prolactin levels and shrink prolactin-secreting tumors.
2. **Surgery**: May be needed for large tumors or if medication is ineffective.

**Complications**

**Hypogonadism**: Osteoporosis, cardiovascular issues, and diminished quality of life. **Polycystic Ovary Syndrome (PCOS)**: Long-term risks include type 2 diabetes, cardiovascular disease, and endometrial cancer. **Premature Ovarian**

**Insufficiency (POI)**: Increased risk of osteoporosis and cardiovascular disease. **Andropause**: Osteoporosis and decreased muscle mass, potentially impacting overall health and physical function. **Hyperprolactinemia**: Vision issues (with large tumors), bone density loss due to low estrogen levels.

**Prevention**

**Primary Prevention**:

1. **Healthy Lifestyle**: Maintain a healthy weight, balanced diet, and regular exercise to prevent insulin resistance and related disorders.
2. **Regular Screening**: For individuals with a family history of endocrine disorders or those at risk.

**Secondary Prevention**:

1. **Early Diagnosis**: Regular check-ups and hormone assessments to detect abnormalities early and initiate treatment.
2. **Management of Symptoms**: Effective treatment of symptoms to prevent progression and complications.

**Tertiary Prevention**:

1. **Ongoing Monitoring**: Regular follow-up to manage treatment, monitor for complications, and adjust therapies as needed.
2. **Patient Education**: Informing patients about managing their condition, recognizing symptoms, and adhering to treatment plans.

Effective management of sex hormone disorders involves a comprehensive approach including diagnosis, treatment, and regular monitoring to improve quality of life and prevent complications. Advances in research and treatment continue to enhance the ability to manage these conditions effectively.


**Multiple-Choice Questions (Objective)**

1. Which of the following is NOT a type of anemia?
    a) Iron Deficiency Anemia

b) Vitamin B12 Deficiency Anemia

c) Acute Lymphoblastic Leukemia

d) Aplastic Anemia

2. What is the primary cause of Iron Deficiency Anemia?

a) Lack of Vitamin B12

b) Lack of Iron

c) Genetic Mutation

d) Infection

3. Which type of leukemia is characterized by the presence of the Philadelphia chromosome?

a) Acute Lymphoblastic Leukemia (ALL)

b) Acute Myeloid Leukemia (AML)

c) Chronic Lymphocytic Leukemia (CLL)

d) Chronic Myeloid Leukemia (CML)

4. What characterizes Hodgkin Lymphoma?

a) Overproduction of abnormal WBCs

b) Presence of Reed-Sternberg cells

c) Bone marrow failure

d) Increased platelet count

5. Which hormone is produced by the pancreas to regulate blood sugar levels?

a) Insulin

b) Cortisol

c) Thyroxine

d) Adrenaline

6. What is the primary function of the thyroid gland?

a) Regulate metabolism

b) Control blood sugar

c) Produce red blood cells

d) Filter waste from the blood

7. Which gland produces hormones like oxytocin and antidiuretic hormone (ADH)?

   a) Thyroid Gland

   b) Parathyroid Glands

   c) Posterior Pituitary

   d) Adrenal Glands

8. What is the primary symptom of iron deficiency?

   a) Fatigue

   b) Weight gain

   c) Insomnia

   d) Hyperactivity

9. Which test measures the amount of stored iron in the body?

   a) Complete Blood Count (CBC)

   b) Serum Ferritin

   c) Serum Iron

   d) Total Iron-Binding Capacity (TIBC)

10. What causes megaloblastic anemia?

   a) Iron Deficiency

   b) Vitamin B12 and Folate Deficiency

   c) Excessive Red Blood Cell Production

   d) Bone Marrow Failure

11. Which genetic mutation causes sickle cell anemia?

   a) Mutation in the HBB gene

   b) Mutation in the G6PD gene

   c) Mutation in the CFTR gene

   d) Mutation in the BRCA1 gene

12. Which type of thalassemia results from mutations in the HBB gene?

   a) Alpha Thalassemia

   b) Beta Thalassemia

c) Gamma Thalassemia

d) Delta Thalassemia

13. What is the primary treatment for hemophilia A?

a) Platelet Transfusion

b) Factor VIII Concentrates

c) Iron Supplements

d) Bone Marrow Transplant

14. Which type of diabetes is characterized by autoimmune destruction of beta cells in the pancreas?

a) Type 1 Diabetes

b) Type 2 Diabetes

c) Gestational Diabetes

d) Insipidus Diabetes

15. What is the primary cause of hyperthyroidism in Graves' disease?

a) Iodine Deficiency

b) Autoimmune Stimulation of the Thyroid

c) Pituitary Tumor

d) Thyroid Cancer

16. Which hormone is primarily responsible for regulating sleep-wake cycles?

a) Insulin

b) Cortisol

c) Melatonin

d) Thyroxine

17. What is the hallmark symptom of hypothyroidism?

a) Weight Loss

b) Weight Gain

c) Increased Appetite

d) Increased Heart Rate

18. What condition is associated with the presence of Reed-Sternberg cells?

a) Non-Hodgkin Lymphoma

b) Hodgkin Lymphoma

c) Multiple Myeloma

d) Polycythemia Vera

19. What complication is common in both sickle cell anemia and thalassemia?

a) Iron Overload

b) Excessive Bleeding

c) Increased Platelet Count

d) Elevated Blood Sugar

20. Which hormone is produced by the adrenal glands to help regulate blood pressure?

a) Insulin

b) Cortisol

c) Aldosterone

d) Thyroxine

**Short Answer Type Questions (Subjective)**

1. What are the primary causes of iron deficiency anemia?

2. Describe the pathophysiology of sickle cell anemia.

3. Explain the difference between acute and chronic leukemias.

4. What are the symptoms and complications of polycythemia vera?

5. How does the hypothalamus regulate the endocrine system?

6. What is the role of the parathyroid glands in calcium regulation?

7. Describe the symptoms and treatment of megaloblastic anemia.

8. What are the diagnostic criteria for diabetes mellitus?

9. Explain the complications associated with untreated hyperthyroidism.

10. What is the significance of Reed-Sternberg cells in diagnosing lymphoma?

11. How does hemophilia affect the blood clotting process?

12. Describe the epidemiology of beta thalassemia.

13. What are the primary functions of cortisol in the body?

14. How does hyperprolactinemia affect reproductive health?

15. What are the treatment options for hypothyroidism?

16. Explain the role of insulin in glucose metabolism.

17. What are the common symptoms of iron deficiency?

18. How is Graves' disease diagnosed and treated?

19. Describe the long-term complications of untreated diabetes.

20. What are the risk factors for developing thyroid cancer?


**Long Answer Type Questions (Subjective)**

1. Discuss the pathophysiology, symptoms, diagnosis, and treatment of iron deficiency anemia.

2. Describe the genetic and molecular basis of sickle cell anemia, including its epidemiology, complications, and management strategies.

3. Explain the different types of leukemia, their pathophysiology, symptoms, diagnostic approaches, and treatment options.

4. Discuss the endocrine regulation of metabolism, focusing on the roles of the thyroid gland and adrenal glands.

5. Describe the pathophysiology, diagnosis, and treatment of polycystic ovary syndrome (PCOS).

6. Explain the impact of diabetes mellitus on the hematological and endocrine systems, including short-term and long-term complications.

7. Discuss the role of hormone replacement therapy in managing endocrine disorders such as hypothyroidism and hypogonadism.

8. Describe the pathophysiology, symptoms, and treatment of hemophilia, including the complications associated with this condition.

9. Explain the mechanisms of thyroid hormone regulation and the clinical manifestations of hyperthyroidism and hypothyroidism.

10.Discuss the interactions between hematological diseases and endocrine disorders, providing examples of how these systems influence each other.

**Answer Key for MCQ Questions**

1.  c) Acute Lymphoblastic Leukemia
2.  b) Lack of Iron
3.  d) Chronic Myeloid Leukemia (CML)
4.  b) Presence of Reed-Sternberg cells
5.  a) Insulin
6.  a) Regulate metabolism
7.  c) Posterior Pituitary
8.  a) Fatigue
9.  b) Serum Ferritin
10.b) Vitamin B12 and Folate Deficiency
11.a) Mutation in the HBB gene
12.b) Beta Thalassemia
13.b) Factor VIII Concentrates
14.a) Type 1 Diabetes
15.b) Autoimmune Stimulation of the Thyroid
16.c) Melatonin
17.b) Weight Gain
18.b) Hodgkin Lymphoma
19.a) Iron Overload
20.c) Aldosterone

# CHAPTER – 5

## NERVOUS SYSTEM AND GASTRO INTESTINE SYSTEM

Nervous System:

The nervous system is a complex network responsible for transmitting signals between different parts of the body. It plays a crucial role in regulating and coordinating body functions, including perception, movement, cognition, and homeostasis.

## Components

1. **Central Nervous System (CNS)**: Consists of the brain and spinal cord.
    a. **Brain**: The control center for cognitive functions, emotions, and sensory processing.
    b. **Spinal Cord**: Acts as a conduit for signals between the brain and the rest of the body; also coordinates reflexes.
2. **Peripheral Nervous System (PNS)**: Includes all nerves outside the CNS. It is divided into:
    a. **Somatic Nervous System**: Controls voluntary movements and transmits sensory information from the skin, muscles, and joints.
    b. **Autonomic Nervous System (ANS)**: Regulates involuntary functions, such as heart rate, digestion, and respiratory rate. It is further divided into:
        i. **Sympathetic Division**: Prepares the body for stress-related activities ("fight or flight" response).
        ii. **Parasympathetic Division**: Promotes relaxation and recovery ("rest and digest" response).

**Functions**

1. **Sensory Input**: Gathering information from sensory receptors.
2. **Integration**: Processing and interpreting sensory information to make decisions.
3. **Motor Output**: Sending commands to muscles and glands to elicit responses.

**Gastrointestinal (GI) System:**

**Overview**

The GI system is responsible for the digestion and absorption of nutrients, as well as the elimination of waste. It is a continuous tube running from the mouth to the anus.

**Components**

1. **Mouth**: Where digestion begins with mechanical breakdown (chewing) and chemical breakdown (saliva).
2. **Esophagus**: A muscular tube that transports food from the mouth to the stomach through peristalsis.
3. **Stomach**: Performs both mechanical and chemical digestion. It secretes gastric acid and enzymes to break down food into chyme.
4. **Small Intestine**: Consists of three parts—duodenum, jejunum, and ileum. It is the primary site for nutrient absorption. Enzymes from the pancreas and bile from the liver aid in digestion.
5. **Large Intestine**: Includes the cecum, colon, and rectum. It absorbs water and electrolytes, forming and storing feces.
6. **Rectum and Anus**: The final part of the GI tract where feces are stored and eventually expelled.

**Functions**

1. **Ingestion**: Taking in food and liquids.
2. **Digestion**: Breaking down food into absorbable units.
3. **Absorption**: Transporting nutrients from the digestive tract into the bloodstream.
4. **Excretion**: Eliminating waste products from the body.

**Interactions Between Nervous and GI Systems**

The nervous system and the GI system are closely interconnected. The **enteric nervous system** (ENS), often referred to as the "second brain," regulates gastrointestinal functions independently of the CNS but is influenced by it. This network controls gut motility, enzyme secretion, and blood flow, and responds to stress, emotions, and various stimuli through the vagus nerve and other pathways.

Understanding the interplay between these systems is essential for comprehending how the body maintains homeostasis and responds to internal and external changes.

**NERVOUS SYSTEM**

1. **EPILEPSY**

Epilepsy is a neurological disorder characterized by recurrent, unprovoked seizures due to abnormal electrical activity in the brain. These seizures can vary in intensity and presentation, ranging from brief and nearly undetectable to prolonged and convulsive.

**Introduction**

Epilepsy is one of the most common neurological disorders, affecting people of all ages. It can result from various underlying causes, including genetic factors, brain injuries, infections, and developmental disorders.

**Pathophysiology**

Epilepsy occurs when there is a disruption in the normal electrical activity of the brain, leading to excessive and synchronous neuronal firing. This can result from:

a. **Genetic Mutations**: Certain genes involved in ion channel function, neurotransmitter receptors, and other neuronal processes may be mutated.

b. **Structural Brain Abnormalities**: Tumors, congenital malformations, and scars from previous brain injuries can disrupt normal brain activity.

c. **Metabolic Disturbances**: Conditions like hypoglycemia, electrolyte imbalances, and inborn errors of metabolism can provoke seizures.

d. **Infections**: Encephalitis, meningitis, and other infections can cause inflammation and damage to the brain, leading to seizures.

e. **Autoimmune Disorders**: Autoimmune processes can target neuronal tissues and disrupt normal brain function.

**Epidemiology**

a. **Prevalence**: Epilepsy affects approximately 50 million people worldwide, making it one of the most prevalent neurological conditions.

b. **Age Distribution**: It can occur at any age but is most commonly diagnosed in childhood, adolescence, and in individuals over 60.

c. **Gender**: It affects both males and females equally, although certain types of epilepsy may be more common in one gender.

**Symptoms and Complications**

a. **Symptoms**:

1. **Seizures**: The primary symptom of epilepsy, which can be of various types:

    i. **Generalized Seizures**: Affect both hemispheres of the brain and can include tonic-clonic (grand mal), absence (petit mal), myoclonic, and atonic seizures.

ii. **Focal Seizures**: Originate in one area of the brain and can be simple (without loss of consciousness) or complex (with altered consciousness).

2. **Auras**: Sensory, motor, or psychic sensations that precede a seizure.

3. **Postictal State**: Confusion, fatigue, and other symptoms following a seizure.

b. **Complications**:

1. **Injury**: Due to falls, accidents, or self-harm during seizures.

2. **Status Epilepticus**: A medical emergency where seizures last longer than five minutes or occur back-to-back without recovery in between.

3. **Sudden Unexpected Death in Epilepsy (SUDEP)**: Unexplained death in individuals with epilepsy, thought to be related to respiratory or cardiac dysfunction during seizures.

4. **Psychosocial Issues**: Anxiety, depression, and social stigma.

**Diagnosis**

a. **Medical History and Physical Examination**: Detailed patient history and neurological examination.

b. **Electroencephalogram (EEG)**: Records electrical activity in the brain and helps identify abnormal patterns associated with epilepsy.

c. **Neuroimaging**: MRI or CT scans to detect structural abnormalities in the brain.

d. **Blood Tests**: To rule out metabolic causes or infections.

e. **Video Monitoring**: For capturing and analyzing seizure activity.

**Treatment**

a. **Medications**: Antiepileptic drugs (AEDs) are the mainstay of treatment and include:

i. **Phenytoin**

ii. **Carbamazepine**

iii. **Valproate**

iv. **Lamotrigine**

v. **Levetiracetam**

vi. **Topiramate**

b. **Surgery**: For patients with refractory epilepsy, surgical options like lobectomy, lesionectomy, or corpus callosotomy may be considered.

c. **Vagus Nerve Stimulation (VNS)**: A device implanted to stimulate the vagus nerve and reduce seizure frequency.

d. **Ketogenic Diet**: High-fat, low-carbohydrate diet that can help control seizures in some patients.

e. **Lifestyle Modifications**: Avoiding seizure triggers, maintaining a regular sleep schedule, and stress management.

## Prevention

a. **Prenatal Care**: Ensuring good prenatal care to prevent brain injuries and infections in newborns.

b. **Injury Prevention**: Using helmets and safety measures to prevent head injuries.

c. **Vaccinations**: Protecting against infections like meningitis and encephalitis.

d. **Early Treatment**: Managing underlying conditions that can lead to epilepsy, such as febrile seizures in children.

## Epilepsy and the Gastrointestinal System:

While epilepsy primarily affects the nervous system, it can have various impacts on the gastrointestinal (GI) system, both as direct complications of seizures and as side effects of treatment.

## GI Symptoms and Complications

a. **Nausea and Vomiting**: Common side effects of antiepileptic drugs (AEDs) like phenytoin, valproate, and carbamazepine.

b. **Dyspepsia and Gastric Ulcers**: Chronic use of AEDs can lead to gastrointestinal discomfort and ulcers.

c. **Diarrhea or Constipation**: Some AEDs can alter bowel habits.

d. **Pancreatitis**: Valproate has been associated with pancreatitis, which is inflammation of the pancreas.

**GI Impact of Seizures**

a. **Aspiration**: During a seizure, especially tonic-clonic seizures, there is a risk of aspiration of stomach contents into the lungs, leading to aspiration pneumonia.

b. **Esophageal Injuries**: Seizure activity can sometimes cause spasms or injuries to the esophagus.

**Managing GI Complications**

a. **Medication Adjustments**: Switching to AEDs with fewer GI side effects.

b. **Supportive Care**: Using antiemetics for nausea and proton pump inhibitors (PPIs) or H2 blockers for gastric ulcer prevention.

c. **Dietary Modifications**: Adjusting diet to manage symptoms like diarrhea or constipation.

d. **Monitoring and Early Intervention**: Regular monitoring for signs of pancreatitis and other serious GI complications.

**Preventive Measures for GI Issues**

a. **Regular Monitoring**: Routine blood tests to monitor liver and pancreatic function in patients on AEDs.

b. **Hydration and Nutrition**: Ensuring adequate hydration and a balanced diet to support GI health.

c. **Patient Education**: Informing patients about potential GI side effects and encouraging them to report symptoms early.

## 2. PARKINSON'S DISEASE

Parkinson's disease (PD) is a progressive neurodegenerative disorder that primarily affects movement control. It results from the loss of dopamine-producing neurons in the substantia nigra, a region of the brain involved in regulating movement.

**Introduction**

Parkinson's disease is characterized by motor symptoms such as tremors, rigidity, bradykinesia (slowness of movement), and postural instability. It also has non-motor symptoms that can significantly impact quality of life.

**Pathophysiology**

The primary pathological feature of Parkinson's disease is the degeneration of dopaminergic neurons in the substantia nigra pars compacta. This leads to a depletion of dopamine in the striatum, which is crucial for coordinating smooth and balanced muscle movements. The exact cause of neuronal loss is not fully understood but is believed to involve a combination of genetic and environmental factors. The accumulation of Lewy bodies, which are abnormal aggregates of the protein alpha-synuclein, is a hallmark of PD and contributes to neuronal dysfunction and death.

**Epidemiology**

a. **Prevalence**: Parkinson's disease affects approximately 1% of the population over the age of 60, with incidence increasing with age.

b. **Age Distribution**: Most commonly diagnosed in people over 60, but early-onset Parkinson's can occur before the age of 50.

c. **Gender**: Men are slightly more likely to develop Parkinson's disease than women.

**Symptoms and Complications**

a. **Motor Symptoms**:

    i. **Tremor**: Often starts in a limb, usually the hand or fingers. Characteristic "pill-rolling" tremor at rest.

ii. **Bradykinesia**: Slowness of movement, making everyday tasks difficult and time-consuming.

iii. **Rigidity**: Muscle stiffness that can occur in any part of the body, leading to pain and a reduced range of motion.

iv. **Postural Instability**: Impaired balance and coordination, increasing the risk of falls.

b. **Non-Motor Symptoms**:

i. **Cognitive Impairment**: Memory problems, difficulty concentrating, and eventually, dementia in some patients.

ii. **Mood Disorders**: Depression, anxiety, and apathy.

iii. **Autonomic Dysfunction**: Issues with blood pressure regulation, bladder control, and sexual function.

iv. **Sleep Disorders**: Insomnia, restless legs syndrome, and REM sleep behavior disorder.

c. **Complications**:

i. **Falls and Injuries**: Due to impaired balance and coordination.

ii. **Swallowing Difficulties**: Leading to aspiration pneumonia and malnutrition.

iii. **Immobility**: Resulting in muscle atrophy, joint problems, and pressure sores.

iv. **Cognitive Decline**: Progressing to dementia in advanced stages.

**Diagnosis**

a. **Clinical Evaluation**: Diagnosis is primarily based on medical history and neurological examination. The presence of at least two of the cardinal motor symptoms (tremor, bradykinesia, rigidity) is required.

b. **Imaging**: MRI or CT scans are used to rule out other conditions, while DaTscan (dopamine transporter scan) can help confirm the diagnosis by showing reduced dopamine function in the brain.

c. **Response to Dopaminergic Medication**: A significant improvement in symptoms with dopaminergic medication can support the diagnosis of PD.

**Treatment**

a. **Medications**:

    i. **Levodopa**: The most effective treatment, converted to dopamine in the brain. Often combined with carbidopa to prevent peripheral conversion of levodopa.

    ii. **Dopamine Agonists**: Mimic dopamine effects in the brain (e.g., pramipexole, ropinirole).

    iii. **MAO-B Inhibitors**: Reduce the breakdown of brain dopamine (e.g., selegiline, rasagiline).

    iv. **COMT Inhibitors**: Prolong the effect of levodopa (e.g., entacapone).

    v. **Anticholinergics**: Help control tremor and rigidity (e.g., trihexyphenidyl).

    vi. **Amantadine**: Provides mild relief of symptoms and reduces dyskinesias.

b. **Surgical Treatments**:

    i. **Deep Brain Stimulation (DBS)**: Electrodes implanted in the brain to deliver electrical impulses that reduce motor symptoms.

    ii. **Lesioning Procedures**: Thalamotomy or pallidotomy to destroy small parts of the brain causing symptoms.

c. **Supportive Therapies**:

    i. **Physical Therapy**: Improves mobility, flexibility, and balance.

    ii. **Occupational Therapy**: Helps maintain independence in daily activities.

    iii. **Speech Therapy**: Assists with speech and swallowing difficulties.

iv. **Psychological Support**: Counseling and support groups for mental health.

**Complications and Management**

a. **Motor Fluctuations**: Adjusting medication schedules and doses to manage "on-off" periods and dyskinesias.

b. **Cognitive Decline**: Cholinesterase inhibitors for dementia, cognitive behavioral therapy, and support for caregivers.

c. **Psychiatric Symptoms**: Antidepressants, antipsychotics (with caution), and counseling.

d. **Autonomic Dysfunction**: Medications and lifestyle changes for blood pressure management, bladder control, and sexual dysfunction.

**Prevention**

Currently, there is no known way to prevent Parkinson's disease, but certain lifestyle choices may reduce the risk or delay the onset:

a. **Regular Exercise**: May help maintain motor function and slow disease progression.

b. **Healthy Diet**: A diet rich in antioxidants, omega-3 fatty acids, and a Mediterranean diet may be beneficial.

c. **Avoiding Toxins**: Reducing exposure to environmental toxins such as pesticides and heavy metals.

d. **Monitoring and Managing Health Conditions**: Keeping other health conditions such as cardiovascular diseases, diabetes, and hypertension under control.

**Parkinson's Disease and the Gastrointestinal System:**

Gastrointestinal symptoms are common in Parkinson's disease and can significantly affect the quality of life. These symptoms often result from both the disease itself and the side effects of medications.

**GI Symptoms and Complications**

a. **Constipation**: One of the most common non-motor symptoms, due to slowed colonic transit and impaired autonomic function.

b. **Gastroparesis**: Delayed gastric emptying leading to nausea, vomiting, and bloating.

c. **Dysphagia**: Difficulty swallowing, increasing the risk of aspiration and pneumonia.

d. **Drooling (Sialorrhea)**: Due to impaired swallowing and reduced spontaneous swallowing.

e. **Weight Loss**: Resulting from difficulty eating, swallowing problems, and increased energy expenditure due to tremors.

## Managing GI Symptoms

a. **Dietary Adjustments**: High-fiber diet, adequate hydration, and small, frequent meals to manage constipation and gastroparesis.

b. **Medications**: Laxatives, stool softeners, and prokinetic agents for managing constipation and gastroparesis.

c. **Swallowing Therapy**: Speech and swallowing therapy to improve dysphagia.

d. **Botulinum Toxin Injections**: For managing severe drooling.

## Preventive Measures for GI Issues

a. **Regular Monitoring**: Early identification and management of GI symptoms through regular follow-ups.

b. **Hydration and Fiber Intake**: Ensuring adequate water and fiber intake to prevent constipation.

c. **Exercise**: Encouraging physical activity to stimulate bowel movements.

d. **Medication Review**: Regularly reviewing medications to adjust for those contributing to GI side effects.

3. **STROKE**

A stroke, also known as a cerebrovascular accident (CVA), occurs when the blood supply to a part of the brain is interrupted or reduced, preventing brain tissue from getting the oxygen and nutrients it needs. Brain cells begin to die within minutes, leading to significant neurological damage.

**Introduction**

Strokes are medical emergencies that require immediate treatment to minimize brain damage and improve outcomes. They are a leading cause of disability and death worldwide.

**Pathophysiology**

There are two main types of strokes:

1. **Ischemic Stroke**: Caused by a blockage in an artery supplying blood to the brain. This can result from:
    a. **Thrombotic Stroke**: Formation of a blood clot within a cerebral artery.
    b. **Embolic Stroke**: A blood clot or other debris forms away from the brain, often in the heart, and is swept through the bloodstream to lodge in narrower brain arteries.
2. **Hemorrhagic Stroke**: Caused by the rupture of a blood vessel in the brain, leading to bleeding within or around the brain. This can result from:
    a. **Intracerebral Hemorrhage**: Bleeding within the brain tissue.
    b. **Subarachnoid Hemorrhage**: Bleeding in the space between the brain and the surrounding membrane.

**Epidemiology**

   a. **Prevalence**: Stroke is a leading cause of death and disability worldwide. Approximately 1 in 4 adults over the age of 25 will have a stroke in their lifetime.
   b. **Age Distribution**: While strokes can occur at any age, the risk increases significantly with age.

c. **Gender**: Strokes are slightly more common in men, but women tend to have worse outcomes and a higher mortality rate.

**Symptoms and Complications**

a. **Symptoms**:

    i.   **Sudden Numbness or Weakness**: Especially on one side of the body.

    ii.   **Confusion**: Trouble speaking or understanding speech.

    iii.   **Visual Disturbances**: Trouble seeing in one or both eyes.

    iv.   **Difficulty Walking**: Dizziness, loss of balance, or coordination.

    v.   **Severe Headache**: Especially if accompanied by vomiting or altered consciousness (more common in hemorrhagic stroke).

b. **Complications**:

    i.   **Permanent Disability**: Paralysis, loss of muscle movement, difficulty talking or swallowing, memory loss, and cognitive impairments.

    ii.   **Secondary Complications**: Pneumonia, urinary tract infections, deep vein thrombosis, and bedsores due to immobility.

    iii.   **Recurrent Stroke**: Increased risk of having another stroke.

    iv.   **Death**: Stroke is a leading cause of mortality.

**Diagnosis**

a. **Medical History and Physical Examination**: Initial assessment to identify stroke symptoms.

b. **Imaging Tests**:

    i.   **CT Scan**: Quickly distinguishes between ischemic and hemorrhagic stroke.

    ii.   **MRI**: Provides detailed images of brain tissue and blood vessels.

c. **Blood Tests**: To determine blood clotting status, blood sugar levels, and other stroke-related factors.

d. **Electrocardiogram (ECG)**: To detect heart problems that might have caused the stroke.

e. **Carotid Ultrasound**: To check for narrowing or blockages in the carotid arteries.

**Treatment**

a. **Ischemic Stroke**:

    i. **Thrombolytic Therapy**: Intravenous administration of tissue plasminogen activator (tPA) to dissolve the clot, if administered within 3 to 4.5 hours of symptom onset.

    ii. **Mechanical Thrombectomy**: Surgical removal of the clot using a stent retriever, effective within 24 hours of symptom onset in certain patients.

    iii. **Antiplatelet Agents and Anticoagulants**: To prevent further clot formation (e.g., aspirin, clopidogrel, warfarin).

b. **Hemorrhagic Stroke**:

    i. **Surgical Interventions**: To repair the ruptured blood vessel or remove accumulated blood.

    ii. **Blood Pressure Management**: Using medications to control high blood pressure.

    iii. **Coagulation Therapy**: To manage blood clotting, especially if the patient is on anticoagulant medication.

c. **Rehabilitation**: Intensive physical, occupational, and speech therapy to regain lost functions and promote independence.

**Prevention**

a. **Lifestyle Modifications**:

    i. **Healthy Diet**: Reducing salt, saturated fats, and cholesterol intake.

    ii. **Regular Exercise**: At least 150 minutes of moderate-intensity aerobic activity per week.

    iii. **Weight Management**: Maintaining a healthy weight.

iv. **Smoking Cessation**: Avoiding tobacco use.

v. **Alcohol Moderation**: Limiting alcohol consumption.

b. **Medical Management**:

i. **Blood Pressure Control**: Using medications and lifestyle changes to maintain healthy blood pressure levels.

ii. **Cholesterol Management**: Statins and other medications to control cholesterol levels.

iii. **Diabetes Management**: Tight control of blood sugar levels.

iv. **Antithrombotic Therapy**: Aspirin or other antiplatelet/anticoagulant medications for at-risk individuals.

## Stroke and the Gastrointestinal System

Strokes can impact the gastrointestinal (GI) system directly and indirectly, leading to various complications.

## GI Symptoms and Complications

a. **Dysphagia**: Difficulty swallowing, which can lead to aspiration pneumonia, malnutrition, and dehydration.

b. **Gastroesophageal Reflux Disease (GERD)**: Increased risk due to impaired swallowing and altered esophageal motility.

c. **Constipation**: Common due to immobility, dehydration, and medication side effects.

d. **Incontinence**: Loss of bowel control, either constipation or fecal incontinence, due to neurological damage.

## Managing GI Symptoms

a. **Dysphagia Management**:

i. **Swallowing Therapy**: Exercises and techniques to improve swallowing.

ii. **Dietary Modifications**: Adjusting food texture and consistency to reduce choking risk.

iii. **Tube Feeding**: For severe dysphagia, temporary or permanent feeding tubes may be necessary.

b. **Constipation Management**:

i. **Dietary Adjustments**: High-fiber diet and adequate hydration.

ii. **Medications**: Laxatives or stool softeners as needed.

iii. **Physical Activity**: Encouraging mobility to stimulate bowel movements.

c. **GERD Management**:

i. **Medications**: Proton pump inhibitors (PPIs) or H2 blockers.

ii. **Lifestyle Changes**: Elevating the head of the bed, avoiding large meals, and reducing acidic foods.

**Preventive Measures for GI Issues**

a. **Early Assessment and Intervention**: Regular monitoring for signs of dysphagia, GERD, and constipation.

b. **Hydration and Nutrition**: Ensuring adequate fluid and nutrient intake.

c. **Multidisciplinary Approach**: Involving dietitians, speech therapists, and occupational therapists in the care plan.

## 4. PSYCHIATRIC DISORDERS

Psychiatric disorders encompass a wide range of mental health conditions that affect mood, thinking, and behavior. These disorders can manifest in various forms, impacting the nervous system and gastrointestinal (GI) system.

**Pathophysiology:**

**Nervous System**

a. **Neurotransmitter Imbalance:** Many psychiatric disorders are associated with imbalances in neurotransmitters such as serotonin, dopamine, and norepinephrine.

b. **Neuroinflammation:** Chronic inflammation in the brain can contribute to the development of psychiatric disorders.

c. **Genetic Factors:** Hereditary factors can predispose individuals to psychiatric conditions.

**Gastrointestinal System**

a. **Gut-Brain Axis:** There is a bidirectional communication system between the gut and the brain. Dysbiosis (an imbalance in gut microbiota) can influence brain function and contribute to psychiatric symptoms.

b. **Inflammation:** Chronic inflammation in the GI tract can lead to changes in the central nervous system, contributing to psychiatric disorders.

**Epidemiology**

Psychiatric disorders are prevalent worldwide, affecting people of all ages and backgrounds. Specific prevalence rates vary by disorder:

a. **Depression:** Affects over 264 million people globally.

b. **Anxiety Disorders:** Affect approximately 284 million people.

c. **Bipolar Disorder:** Affects about 45 million people.

d. **Schizophrenia:** Affects about 20 million people.

**Symptoms and Complications:**

**Nervous System**

a. **Mood Disorders:** Depression, mania, mood swings.

b. **Anxiety Disorders:** Excessive worry, panic attacks, phobias.

c. **Psychotic Disorders:** Hallucinations, delusions, disorganized thinking.

d. **Cognitive Impairments:** Memory loss, difficulty concentrating.

**Gastrointestinal System**

a. **GI Symptoms:** Nausea, vomiting, diarrhea, constipation, abdominal pain.

b. **Behavioral Symptoms:** Changes in appetite, eating disorders (anorexia, bulimia).

c. **Emotional Symptoms:** Stress, anxiety, depression linked to GI distress.

**Diagnosis**

a. **Clinical Assessment:** Detailed history and examination to identify symptoms.

b. **Psychiatric Evaluation:** Interviews, questionnaires, and standardized assessment tools.

c. **Laboratory Tests:** Blood tests to rule out other conditions.

d. **Imaging Studies:** MRI, CT scans to assess brain structure and function.

e. **Endoscopy/Colonoscopy:** To examine GI tract for underlying issues.

**Treatment:**

**Nervous System**

a. **Pharmacotherapy:** Antidepressants, antipsychotics, mood stabilizers, anxiolytics.

b. **Psychotherapy:** Cognitive-behavioral therapy (CBT), psychodynamic therapy, counseling.

c. **Lifestyle Changes:** Exercise, diet, sleep hygiene.

d. **Alternative Therapies:** Mindfulness, meditation, yoga.

**Gastrointestinal System**

a. **Medications:** Antidepressants, antianxiety medications, probiotics, antacids.

b. **Dietary Management:** High-fiber diet, avoiding trigger foods, regular meals.

c. **Behavioral Therapy:** Techniques to manage stress and anxiety, biofeedback.

d. **Surgery:** In severe cases of GI disorders contributing to psychiatric symptoms.

**Complications**

a. **Chronic Psychiatric Conditions:** Long-term disability, reduced quality of life.

b. **Comorbid Physical Conditions:** Increased risk of cardiovascular disease, diabetes.

c. **Substance Abuse:** Higher likelihood of alcohol and drug misuse.

d. **Social and Occupational Impairment:** Difficulty maintaining relationships and employment.

**Prevention**

a. **Early Intervention:** Prompt treatment of psychiatric and GI symptoms.

b. **Healthy Lifestyle:** Regular exercise, balanced diet, adequate sleep.

c. **Stress Management:** Techniques such as mindfulness, relaxation exercises.

d. **Regular Medical Check-ups:** Monitoring and managing health conditions.

e. **Education and Awareness:** Promoting mental health awareness and reducing stigma.

## 5. DEPRESSION

Depression, or major depressive disorder (MDD), is a common and serious medical illness that negatively affects how you feel, the way you think, and how you act. It causes feelings of sadness and/or a loss of interest in activities once enjoyed. It can lead to a variety of emotional and physical problems and can decrease a person's ability to function at work and at home.

**Introduction**

Depression is a complex mood disorder with various contributing factors, including genetic, biochemical, environmental, and psychological components. It is characterized by persistent feelings of sadness and a lack of interest or pleasure in previously rewarding or enjoyable activities.

**Pathophysiology**

The exact pathophysiology of depression is not fully understood, but it involves several mechanisms:

1. **Neurotransmitter Imbalance**: Depression has been linked to imbalances in neurotransmitters such as serotonin, norepinephrine, and dopamine, which are involved in mood regulation.

2. **Neuroplasticity**: Reduced neuroplasticity and changes in brain structure, particularly in the hippocampus and prefrontal cortex, have been observed in depressed individuals.

3. **Inflammation**: Elevated levels of inflammatory markers and cytokines are found in some individuals with depression, suggesting a role for inflammation in the disease process.

4. **Genetic Factors**: There is a hereditary component, with multiple genes contributing to the susceptibility to depression.

5. **HPA Axis Dysregulation**: Hyperactivity of the hypothalamic-pituitary-adrenal (HPA) axis, leading to increased levels of cortisol, is commonly found in depressed patients.

**Epidemiology**

a. **Prevalence**: Depression affects more than 264 million people worldwide. It is one of the leading causes of disability globally.

b. **Age Distribution**: Can occur at any age but typically starts in late adolescence to mid-20s.

c. **Gender**: Women are more likely than men to experience depression. The lifetime risk is approximately 10-25% for women and 5-12% for men.

**Symptoms and Complications**

a. **Symptoms** (must be present for at least two weeks):

   i. Persistent sad, anxious, or "empty" mood.

   ii. Loss of interest or pleasure in most or all activities.

   iii. Significant weight loss or gain, or decrease or increase in appetite.

   iv. Insomnia or hypersomnia.

   v. Psychomotor agitation or retardation.

   vi. Fatigue or loss of energy.

   vii. Feelings of worthlessness or excessive guilt.

   viii. Difficulty thinking, concentrating, or making decisions.

   ix. Recurrent thoughts of death or suicide, or a suicide attempt.

b. **Complications**:
   i. **Suicidal Behavior**: Increased risk of suicidal thoughts and actions.
   ii. **Substance Abuse**: Higher likelihood of substance use disorders.
   iii. **Chronic Diseases**: Worsening of chronic conditions such as diabetes, cardiovascular disease, and arthritis.
   iv. **Impaired Functioning**: Significant impact on personal, social, and occupational functioning.
   v. **Sleep Disturbances**: Chronic insomnia or sleep disorders.

**Diagnosis**

a. **Clinical Interview**: Diagnosis is primarily based on the patient's history and clinical presentation. A thorough psychiatric evaluation is performed.

b. **Standardized Questionnaires**: Tools like the Beck Depression Inventory (BDI), Patient Health Questionnaire (PHQ-9), and Hamilton Depression Rating Scale (HDRS) can help assess the severity of depression.

c. **Medical Examination**: To rule out underlying medical conditions that may mimic depressive symptoms, such as thyroid disorders, anemia, and vitamin deficiencies.

**Treatment**

a. **Medications**:
   1. **Antidepressants**:
      i. Selective serotonin reuptake inhibitors (SSRIs) (e.g., fluoxetine, sertraline).
      ii. Serotonin-norepinephrine reuptake inhibitors (SNRIs) (e.g., venlafaxine, duloxetine).
      iii. Tricyclic antidepressants (TCAs) (e.g., amitriptyline, nortriptyline).
      iv. Monoamine oxidase inhibitors (MAOIs) (e.g., phenelzine, tranylcypromine).
      v. Atypical antidepressants (e.g., bupropion, mirtazapine).

b. **Psychotherapy**:

1. **Cognitive Behavioral Therapy (CBT)**: Helps patients identify and change negative thought patterns and behaviors.
2. **Interpersonal Therapy (IPT)**: Focuses on improving interpersonal relationships and communication skills.
3. **Psychodynamic Therapy**: Explores unconscious processes and unresolved conflicts.

c. **Lifestyle Modifications**:

1. **Regular Exercise**: Physical activity can improve mood and reduce symptoms.
2. **Healthy Diet**: Balanced nutrition can support overall mental health.
3. **Sleep Hygiene**: Establishing regular sleep patterns and improving sleep quality.

d. **Other Treatments**:

1. **Electroconvulsive Therapy (ECT)**: Used for severe depression that does not respond to other treatments.
2. **Transcranial Magnetic Stimulation (TMS)**: A non-invasive procedure that uses magnetic fields to stimulate nerve cells in the brain.
3. **Light Therapy**: Especially effective for seasonal affective disorder (SAD).

**Prevention**

a. **Early Intervention**: Addressing symptoms early and providing appropriate treatment to prevent worsening.
b. **Stress Management**: Techniques such as mindfulness, relaxation exercises, and stress reduction strategies.
c. **Social Support**: Strong support networks, including family, friends, and support groups.

d. **Education and Awareness**: Increasing awareness about depression and reducing stigma associated with mental health issues.

**Depression and the Gastrointestinal System:**

Depression can significantly affect the gastrointestinal (GI) system, and conversely, GI issues can contribute to the development or exacerbation of depressive symptoms.

**GI Symptoms and Complications**

a. **Irritable Bowel Syndrome (IBS)**: A common comorbidity with depression, characterized by abdominal pain, bloating, and altered bowel habits.

b. **Appetite Changes**: Depression can cause increased or decreased appetite, leading to weight changes.

c. **Gastroesophageal Reflux Disease (GERD)**: Higher prevalence in individuals with depression, potentially due to altered eating habits and increased stress.

d. **Constipation or Diarrhea**: Commonly associated with both depression and antidepressant use.

**Managing GI Symptoms**

a. **Dietary Adjustments**: High-fiber diet, adequate hydration, and avoiding trigger foods for IBS and GERD.

b. **Medications**:

   1. Probiotics and antispasmodics for IBS.

   2. Antacids, H2 blockers, or proton pump inhibitors for GERD.

   3. Laxatives or stool softeners for constipation.

c. **Behavioral Interventions**: Stress management techniques, such as relaxation exercises and biofeedback.

**Preventive Measures for GI Issues**

a. **Healthy Diet and Exercise**: Maintaining a balanced diet and regular physical activity.

b. **Routine Medical Check-ups**: Regular monitoring for early detection and management of GI symptoms.

c. **Psychological Support**: Counseling or therapy to address the psychological components of GI disorders.

## 6. SCHIZOPHRENIA

Schizophrenia is a chronic, severe mental disorder that affects how a person thinks, feels, and behaves. Individuals with schizophrenia may seem like they have lost touch with reality, which can be distressing for them and for those around them. Schizophrenia can also have significant impacts on the gastrointestinal (GI) system, often due to the side effects of medications and the lifestyle associated with managing a chronic mental illness.

**Pathophysiology:**

**Nervous System**

1. **Neurotransmitter Dysregulation:** Abnormalities in dopamine pathways are central to schizophrenia, particularly hyperactivity in the mesolimbic pathway and hypoactivity in the prefrontal cortex.

2. **Neurodevelopmental Hypothesis:** Schizophrenia may arise from disruptions in brain development during prenatal and early life stages.

3. **Genetic Factors:** A significant genetic component exists, with multiple genes implicated in increasing susceptibility to schizophrenia.

4. **Structural Brain Abnormalities:** Reduced gray matter volume in the brain, enlarged ventricles, and abnormalities in hippocampal and prefrontal areas.

**Gastrointestinal System**

a. **Gut-Brain Axis:** Increasing evidence suggests that gut microbiota dysbiosis may contribute to the pathophysiology of schizophrenia.

b. **Inflammation:** Systemic inflammation and elevated levels of inflammatory markers have been noted in schizophrenia, potentially influencing both brain and gut health.

c. **Medication Effects:** Antipsychotic medications can lead to various GI issues, including weight gain, metabolic syndrome, and altered gut motility.

**Epidemiology**

a. **Prevalence:** Schizophrenia affects approximately 1% of the global population.

b. **Onset:** Typically manifests in late adolescence to early adulthood, with males often presenting earlier than females.

c. **Risk Factors:** Family history, prenatal exposure to infections or malnutrition, urban upbringing, and cannabis use during adolescence.

**Symptoms and Complications:**

**Nervous System**

a. **Positive Symptoms:** Hallucinations, delusions, thought disorders, movement disorders.

b. **Negative Symptoms:** Reduced expression of emotions, lack of pleasure, difficulty beginning and sustaining activities, reduced speaking.

c. **Cognitive Symptoms:** Impaired executive function, attention, working memory.

**Gastrointestinal System**

a. **GI Symptoms:** Constipation, diarrhea, bloating, abdominal pain, nausea.

b. **Metabolic Issues:** Weight gain, increased risk of diabetes and cardiovascular diseases due to antipsychotic medications.

c. **Nutritional Deficiencies:** Poor diet and reduced appetite, leading to potential vitamin and mineral deficiencies.

**Diagnosis**

a. **Clinical Assessment:** Detailed patient history and symptom evaluation.

b. **Psychiatric Evaluation:** Structured interviews and use of standardized diagnostic tools like the DSM-5 or ICD-10 criteria.

c. **Neuroimaging:** MRI or CT scans to rule out other conditions and to observe brain structural abnormalities.

d. **Laboratory Tests:** Blood tests to exclude other medical causes of symptoms and to monitor the side effects of medications.

**Treatment:**

**Nervous System**

a. **Pharmacotherapy:** Antipsychotics (first-generation and second-generation), mood stabilizers, antidepressants.

b. **Psychotherapy:** Cognitive-behavioral therapy (CBT), supportive therapy, family therapy.

c. **Psychosocial Interventions:** Social skills training, vocational rehabilitation, community support programs.

d. **Lifestyle Changes:** Regular physical activity, healthy diet, and adequate sleep.

**Gastrointestinal System**

a. **Medications:** Probiotics, laxatives, antidiarrheals, and medications to manage metabolic side effects.

b. **Dietary Management:** Balanced diet rich in fiber, regular meal schedules, and avoiding foods that trigger GI symptoms.

c. **Behavioral Therapy:** Stress management techniques, education on healthy eating habits.

**Complications**

a. **Chronic Psychiatric Symptoms:** Persistent and severe symptoms can lead to significant disability.

b. **Physical Health Issues:** Increased risk of cardiovascular diseases, diabetes, and other metabolic disorders.

c. **Substance Abuse:** Higher likelihood of alcohol and drug misuse, often as a form of self-medication.

d. **Social and Occupational Impairment:** Difficulty maintaining relationships, education, and employment.

e. **Suicide Risk:** Increased risk of suicide compared to the general population.

**Prevention**

a. **Early Intervention:** Identifying and treating symptoms early can improve long-term outcomes.

b. **Genetic Counseling:** For individuals with a family history of schizophrenia.

c. **Healthy Lifestyle:** Regular exercise, balanced diet, and stress management techniques.

d. **Avoiding Substance Use:** Particularly cannabis and other recreational drugs during adolescence.

e. **Regular Medical Check-ups:** Monitoring physical health and managing medication side effects.

f. **Education and Awareness:** Promoting mental health awareness and reducing stigma.

## 7. ALZHEIMER'S DISEASE

Alzheimer's disease (AD) is a progressive neurodegenerative disorder that primarily affects memory, thinking skills, and behavior. It is the most common cause of dementia, accounting for 60-70% of cases.

**Introduction**

Alzheimer's disease gradually destroys brain cells, leading to cognitive decline and memory loss. It impacts daily functioning and eventually interferes with the ability to carry out simple tasks.

**Pathophysiology**

The exact cause of Alzheimer's disease is not fully understood, but it involves several key pathological changes in the brain:

1. **Amyloid Plaques**: Abnormal deposits of beta-amyloid protein form plaques between neurons.
2. **Neurofibrillary Tangles**: Twisted fibers of tau protein accumulate inside neurons, disrupting cell transport systems.
3. **Neuronal Loss**: Progressive death of nerve cells (neurons) leads to brain shrinkage (atrophy) over time, especially in the hippocampus and cortex.
4. **Neurotransmitter Disruption**: Decreased levels of neurotransmitters, including acetylcholine, which is crucial for memory and learning.
5. **Inflammation and Oxidative Stress**: Chronic inflammation and oxidative damage contribute to neuronal dysfunction and death.

**Epidemiology**

a. **Prevalence**: Alzheimer's disease affects millions of people worldwide, with numbers expected to rise as the population ages.
b. **Age Distribution**: Most common in older adults, with risk increasing significantly after the age of 65.
c. **Gender**: Women are more likely to develop Alzheimer's disease compared to men, partly due to their longer lifespan.

**Symptoms and Complications**

a. **Early Symptoms**:
    i. Mild memory loss, especially of recent events.
    ii. Difficulty performing familiar tasks.
    iii. Problems with language (aphasia).
    iv. Disorientation to time and place.
    v. Poor judgment.
    vi. Changes in mood or behavior.
b. **Advanced Symptoms**:
    i. Severe memory loss, including forgetting names of family members or familiar objects.
    ii. Inability to recognize faces or places.

    iii.    Difficulty speaking, swallowing, and walking.

    iv.    Behavioral changes, including agitation, aggression, and hallucinations.

    v.    Dependency on others for daily care.

c. **Complications**:

    i.    **Progressive Cognitive Decline**: Loss of ability to function independently.

    ii.    **Medical Complications**: Increased risk of infections, falls, and fractures.

    iii.    **Behavioral and Psychological Symptoms**: Agitation, anxiety, depression, and sleep disturbances.

    iv.    **End-Stage Complications**: Complete loss of ability to communicate, respond to surroundings, and control movement.

## Diagnosis

a. **Clinical Evaluation**: Based on medical history, symptoms, and cognitive tests to assess memory, language, and problem-solving abilities.

b. **Neuropsychological Testing**: Detailed assessment of cognitive function, including memory, attention, and executive function.

c. **Brain Imaging**: MRI or CT scans to detect changes in brain structure and rule out other causes of dementia.

d. **Biomarkers**: Tests for beta-amyloid and tau proteins in cerebrospinal fluid or imaging techniques (e.g., PET scans) to identify characteristic changes in the brain.

## Treatment

a. **Medications**:

    i.    **Cholinesterase Inhibitors**: Donepezil, rivastigmine, galantamine to improve symptoms by increasing acetylcholine levels.

ii. **Memantine**: NMDA receptor antagonist that regulates glutamate activity in the brain, improving symptoms and slowing progression.

b. **Symptomatic Treatment**:

i. **Behavioral Interventions**: Cognitive stimulation therapy, reality orientation therapy to improve quality of life and reduce behavioral symptoms.

ii. **Psychological Support**: Counseling for patients and caregivers to cope with the emotional and practical challenges of the disease.

c. **Experimental Therapies**:

i. **Immunotherapy**: Targeting beta-amyloid or tau proteins to reduce their accumulation in the brain.

ii. **Gene Therapy and Stem Cell Therapy**: Investigational approaches to repair or regenerate damaged neurons.

## Complications and Management

a. **Care Planning**: Long-term care planning to address safety, medical needs, and financial considerations.

b. **Support Services**: Accessing community resources, support groups, and respite care for caregivers.

c. **Advance Directives**: Documenting preferences for medical care and end-of-life decisions.

## Prevention

a. **Healthy Lifestyle Choices**:

i. **Physical Activity**: Regular exercise to improve cardiovascular health and reduce risk of cognitive decline.

ii. **Healthy Diet**: Mediterranean-style diet rich in fruits, vegetables, whole grains, and lean proteins.

iii. **Mental Stimulation**: Engaging in intellectually stimulating activities, such as reading, puzzles, and social interactions.

iv. **Management of Chronic Conditions**: Controlling hypertension, diabetes, and other vascular risk factors that may contribute to dementia risk.

v. **Social Engagement**: Maintaining social connections and participating in social activities.

b. **Research**: Participation in clinical trials to explore new treatments and preventive strategies.

**Alzheimer's Disease and the Gastrointestinal System:**

While Alzheimer's disease primarily affects the brain, it can indirectly impact the gastrointestinal (GI) system through several mechanisms:

**GI Symptoms and Complications**

a. **Dysphagia**: Difficulty swallowing, leading to aspiration pneumonia and malnutrition.

b. **Weight Loss**: Due to decreased appetite, forgetfulness of meals, or difficulty in chewing and swallowing.

c. **Constipation**: Common in Alzheimer's patients due to decreased physical activity, medications, and changes in routine.

d. **Incontinence**: Loss of bowel or bladder control, which can lead to embarrassment and social withdrawal.

**Managing GI Symptoms**

a. **Dietary Modifications**: Soft or pureed foods, smaller and more frequent meals, and adequate hydration.

b. **Behavioral Interventions**: Assistance with eating, reminders to use the restroom, and establishing a regular toileting schedule.

c. **Medications**: Laxatives or stool softeners for constipation, anticholinergic medications for urinary incontinence.

**Preventive Measures for GI Issues**

a. **Routine Monitoring**: Regular assessment of swallowing function, bowel habits, and nutritional status.

b. **Hydration and Nutrition**: Ensuring adequate fluid intake and a balanced diet rich in fiber and nutrients.

c. **Physical Activity**: Encouraging mobility and regular exercise to promote GI motility.

# GASTROINTESTINAL SYSTEM

## 1. PEPTIC ULCER

A peptic ulcer is a sore that develops on the lining of the stomach, small intestine, or esophagus, typically caused by infection with Helicobacter pylori bacteria or prolonged use of nonsteroidal anti-inflammatory drugs (NSAIDs). It can affect both the nervous system and gastrointestinal (GI) system due to its impact on stress levels and the gut-brain axis.

**Pathophysiology:**

**Nervous System**

a. **Stress Response:** Chronic stress can increase stomach acid production and decrease blood flow to the stomach lining, predisposing to ulcer formation.

b. **Neuroendocrine Factors:** Imbalances in neurotransmitters and hormones (such as cortisol) under stress can contribute to gastric acid secretion and mucosal defense mechanisms.

**Gastrointestinal System**

a. **H. pylori Infection:** Primary cause in many cases, leading to inflammation and weakening of the protective mucous layer of the stomach or duodenum.

b. **NSAID Use:** These medications inhibit prostaglandin synthesis, which normally helps protect the stomach lining, increasing susceptibility to ulcers.

c. **Acid and Pepsin:** Excessive acid production and presence of pepsin can erode the mucosal barrier, leading to ulcer formation.

**Epidemiology**

a. **Prevalence:** Common worldwide, affecting millions of people annually.

b. **Risk Factors:** H. pylori infection, NSAID use, smoking, excessive alcohol consumption, and stress.

c. **Age and Gender:** More common in older adults, and men are generally affected more than women.

**Symptoms and Complications:**

**Nervous System**

a. **Stress-Related Symptoms:** Anxiety, irritability, insomnia, which can exacerbate ulcer symptoms.

b. **Psychological Impact:** Chronic pain and discomfort affecting mood and daily activities.

**Gastrointestinal System**

a. **Symptoms:** Burning pain in the abdomen, especially between meals or at night, bloating, nausea, vomiting, and loss of appetite.

b. **Complications:** Bleeding ulcers can lead to anemia, perforation of the stomach or intestine, and gastric outlet obstruction.

**Diagnosis**

a. **Clinical Assessment:** Detailed history and physical examination.

b. **Endoscopy:** Direct visualization of the ulcer and biopsy for H. pylori testing.

c. **Laboratory Tests:** Blood tests for H. pylori antibodies or stool antigen.

d. **Imaging:** X-rays or CT scans if perforation or obstruction is suspected.

**Treatment:**

**Nervous System**

a. **Stress Management:** Relaxation techniques, counseling, and lifestyle changes to reduce stress levels.

b. **Medications:** Proton pump inhibitors (PPIs) to reduce acid production, and antacids to neutralize stomach acid.

**Gastrointestinal System**

a. **Eradication of H. pylori:** Antibiotics (e.g., clarithromycin, amoxicillin, metronidazole) in combination with PPIs.

b. **NSAID Management:** Limiting or discontinuing NSAID use if possible, or using gastroprotective agents alongside.

**Complications**

a. **Bleeding:** Leading to iron deficiency anemia and requiring transfusions.

b. **Perforation:** Ulcer penetration through the stomach or intestinal wall, causing severe abdominal pain and requiring emergency surgery.

c. **Obstruction:** Swelling and scarring can narrow the pylorus or duodenum, blocking food passage.

**Prevention**

a. **H. pylori Screening and Treatment:** Testing and treating infected individuals, particularly in high-risk populations.

b. **NSAID Use:** Limiting NSAID use, using the lowest effective dose, or adding gastroprotective agents.

c. **Lifestyle Modifications:** Avoiding smoking, alcohol, and managing stress through relaxation techniques and regular exercise.

d. **Dietary Changes:** Eating smaller, more frequent meals, and avoiding spicy foods and irritants.

## 2. INFLAMMATORY BOWEL DISEASES

Inflammatory bowel diseases (IBD) are chronic inflammatory conditions of the gastrointestinal (GI) tract, primarily encompassing Crohn's disease and ulcerative colitis. These conditions involve periods of active inflammation followed by periods of remission.

**Introduction**

IBD is characterized by inflammation of the GI tract, which can lead to severe diarrhea, abdominal pain, fatigue, weight loss, and malnutrition. The exact cause of IBD is not fully understood, but it involves a complex interplay of genetic, environmental, and immunological factors.

**Pathophysiology**

1. **Immune Response**: Dysregulation of the immune system leads to an inappropriate inflammatory response against normal gut flora or dietary antigens.
2. **Genetic Predisposition**: Family history plays a significant role, with certain genetic mutations (e.g., NOD2) increasing susceptibility.
3. **Environmental Factors**: Factors such as diet, smoking, infections, and antibiotics may trigger or exacerbate inflammation.
4. **Microbiota Dysbiosis**: Imbalance in the gut microbiota composition may contribute to inflammation.
5. **Epithelial Barrier Dysfunction**: Impaired intestinal barrier function allows antigens to penetrate and trigger immune responses.

**Epidemiology**

a. **Prevalence**: IBD affects millions of people worldwide, with varying prevalence depending on geographic location and ethnic background.
b. **Age Distribution**: Typically diagnosed in young adults, but can occur at any age, including childhood and older adulthood.
c. **Gender**: Similar incidence in men and women, with some variations in disease behavior.

**Symptoms and Complications**

a. **Symptoms**:
   i. **Diarrhea**: Often bloody and persistent.
   ii. **Abdominal Pain**: Cramping and discomfort, often located in the lower abdomen.
   iii. **Weight Loss**: Due to malabsorption and reduced appetite.
   iv. **Fatigue**: Chronic inflammation and anemia can lead to persistent tiredness.

v. **Fever**: Inflammation and infection may cause fever during disease flares.

vi. **Extraintestinal Manifestations**: Joint pain, skin rashes, and eye inflammation.

b. **Complications**:

i. **Intestinal Strictures**: Narrowing of the bowel lumen due to chronic inflammation, leading to bowel obstruction.

ii. **Fistulas**: Abnormal connections between different parts of the intestine or between the intestine and other organs.

iii. **Abscesses**: Collection of pus within the abdomen or around the anus.

iv. **Perforation**: Rare but serious complication where the intestinal wall develops a hole.

v. **Malnutrition**: Poor absorption of nutrients due to intestinal inflammation and diarrhea.

vi. **Increased Risk of Colorectal Cancer**: Particularly in long-standing and severe cases of ulcerative colitis.

**Diagnosis**

a. **Medical History and Physical Examination**: Detailed history of symptoms, family history, and physical assessment.

b. **Laboratory Tests**: Blood tests to assess inflammation (e.g., CRP, ESR), anemia, and nutritional deficiencies.

c. **Stool Tests**: To rule out infections and assess for occult blood.

d. **Imaging Studies**:

i. **Endoscopy and Biopsy**: Direct visualization of the bowel mucosa and collection of tissue samples for histological examination.

ii. **CT Scan or MRI**: Imaging of the abdomen to assess for complications such as strictures or abscesses.

e. **Colonoscopy**: Allows for a detailed examination of the entire colon and terminal ileum.

**Treatment**

a. **Medications**:

    i. **Anti-inflammatory Agents**:

        1. **Aminosalicylates**: Mesalamine, sulfasalazine.

        2. **Corticosteroids**: Prednisone, budesonide for acute flares.

    ii. **Immunomodulators**: Azathioprine, 6-mercaptopurine, methotrexate to modulate the immune response.

    iii. **Biologic Therapies**: TNF-alpha inhibitors (e.g., infliximab, adalimumab), integrin antagonists (e.g., vedolizumab), and interleukin inhibitors (e.g., ustekinumab) to target specific inflammatory pathways.

b. **Nutritional Therapy**: Enteral nutrition or dietary modifications to manage symptoms and promote healing.

c. **Surgery**: Resection of diseased bowel segments in severe cases of complications or refractory disease.

d. **Supportive Therapies**: Symptomatic relief with antidiarrheal medications, pain management, and nutritional supplements.

**Complications and Management**

a. **Monitoring and Surveillance**: Regular follow-up to monitor disease activity, assess for complications, and adjust treatment as needed.

b. **Psychosocial Support**: Counseling and support groups to help cope with the chronic nature of the disease and its impact on daily life.

c. **Vaccinations**: Ensuring up-to-date vaccinations, especially against influenza and pneumococcus, due to increased infection risk with immunosuppressive therapies.

**Prevention**

a. **Smoking Cessation**: Smoking is a significant risk factor for Crohn's disease exacerbations.

b. **Healthy Diet**: Low in processed foods and rich in fruits, vegetables, and whole grains.

c. **Medication Adherence**: Taking prescribed medications as directed to maintain disease remission.

d. **Early Intervention**: Prompt diagnosis and initiation of treatment to prevent complications and disease progression.

## 3. JAUNDICE, HEPATITIS (A, B, C, D, E, F)

Jaundice and hepatitis are conditions that affect the liver and can have systemic effects on both the nervous system and gastrointestinal (GI) system. They are caused by various viruses (A, B, C, D, E) and other factors, impacting liver function and overall health.

**Pathophysiology:**

**Nervous System**

a. **Neurological Manifestations:** Hepatitis viruses can cause neurological complications such as encephalopathy due to liver dysfunction (hepatic encephalopathy).

b. **Metabolic Disturbances:** Liver dysfunction affects metabolism of neurotransmitters and toxins, impacting brain function.

c. **Viral Invasion:** Direct invasion of viruses into the central nervous system can lead to neurological symptoms.

**Gastrointestinal System**

a. **Liver Function:** Hepatitis viruses primarily affect liver function, impairing bile production and metabolism of nutrients.

b. **GI Symptoms:** Nausea, vomiting, abdominal pain, and changes in appetite are common.

c. **Malabsorption:** Impaired bile flow can lead to malabsorption of fats and fat-soluble vitamins.

**Epidemiology**

a. **Hepatitis A:** Transmitted through contaminated food or water, common in regions with poor sanitation.

b. **Hepatitis B:** Transmitted through blood, sexual contact, or from mother to child during childbirth.

c. **Hepatitis C:** Transmitted through blood, primarily via injecting drug use or unsafe medical practices.

d. **Hepatitis D:** Occurs only in individuals infected with hepatitis B.

e. **Hepatitis E:** Transmitted through contaminated water, particularly in developing countries.

**Symptoms and Complications:**

**Nervous System**

a. **Neurological Symptoms:** Confusion, disorientation, behavioral changes (hepatic encephalopathy).

b. **Peripheral Neuropathy:** Tingling, numbness, or weakness due to metabolic disturbances.

**Gastrointestinal System**

a. **Jaundice:** Yellowing of the skin and eyes due to elevated bilirubin levels.

b. **GI Symptoms:** Abdominal pain, nausea, vomiting, diarrhea, and loss of appetite.

c. **Complications:** Acute liver failure, cirrhosis, and increased risk of liver cancer (especially with chronic hepatitis B and C).

**Diagnosis**

a. **Clinical Assessment:** History of risk factors (e.g., travel history, exposure to infected individuals).

b. **Laboratory Tests:** Blood tests for liver enzymes, bilirubin levels, and specific viral markers (e.g., hepatitis B surface antigen, hepatitis C antibodies).

c. **Imaging Studies:** Ultrasound, CT scan, or MRI to evaluate liver structure and detect complications.

d. **Liver Biopsy:** To assess liver tissue for inflammation, fibrosis, or cancer.

**Treatment:**

**Nervous System**

a. **Supportive Care:** Management of neurological symptoms with medications to reduce ammonia levels (e.g., lactulose).

b. **Monitoring:** Regular assessment of mental status and neurological function.

**Gastrointestinal System**

a. **Antiviral Therapy:** Depending on the virus (e.g., interferon, direct-acting antivirals for hepatitis B and C).

b. **Symptomatic Treatment:** Medications to relieve nausea, pain, and other GI symptoms.

c. **Liver Transplant:** For severe cases of acute liver failure or end-stage liver disease.

**Complications**

a. **Chronic Hepatitis:** Progression to chronic infection with ongoing liver damage.

b. **Cirrhosis:** Scarring of the liver tissue, leading to impaired liver function and potential liver failure.

c. **Liver Cancer:** Increased risk of hepatocellular carcinoma, especially with chronic hepatitis B and C infections.

d. **Neurological Complications:** Permanent cognitive impairment in severe cases of hepatic encephalopathy.

**Prevention**

a. **Vaccination:** Hepatitis A and B vaccines are available and recommended for prevention.

b. **Safe Practices:** Avoiding sharing needles, practicing safe sex, and ensuring safe food and water sources (especially for hepatitis A and E).

c. **Screening:** Testing individuals at risk (e.g., healthcare workers, those with multiple sexual partners) for hepatitis B and C.

d. **Education:** Promoting awareness about transmission routes and preventive measures in communities at risk.

## 4. ALCOHOLIC LIVER DISEASE

Alcoholic liver disease (ALD) refers to liver damage caused by excessive alcohol consumption over time. It encompasses a spectrum of conditions, ranging from fatty liver to alcoholic hepatitis and cirrhosis.

**Introduction**

ALD develops when the liver is unable to effectively metabolize alcohol, leading to liver inflammation, damage to liver cells, and eventually, scarring (fibrosis) and cirrhosis. It is a major cause of liver-related morbidity and mortality worldwide.

**Pathophysiology**

1. **Metabolism of Alcohol**: Alcohol is primarily metabolized in the liver by enzymes such as alcohol dehydrogenase (ADH) and cytochrome P450 2E1 (CYP2E1). These enzymes convert alcohol into toxic byproducts, including acetaldehyde, which can damage liver cells.

2. **Inflammatory Response**: Chronic alcohol consumption triggers an inflammatory response in the liver, leading to the release of cytokines and activation of immune cells.

3. **Oxidative Stress**: Alcohol metabolism generates reactive oxygen species (ROS) and oxidative stress, contributing to liver cell injury and apoptosis.

4. **Fat Accumulation**: Initially, alcohol consumption leads to fat accumulation in the liver (fatty liver or steatosis). Continued alcohol abuse can progress to inflammation (alcoholic hepatitis) and fibrosis (cirrhosis).

5. **Genetic and Environmental Factors**: Genetic predisposition, nutritional status, and concurrent liver diseases (e.g., viral hepatitis) can influence the development and severity of ALD.

**Epidemiology**

a. **Prevalence**: ALD is a leading cause of liver disease globally, with prevalence varying by region and patterns of alcohol consumption.

b. **Gender Differences**: Men are more likely than women to develop ALD, although women may be more susceptible to liver damage at lower levels of alcohol consumption.

c. **Alcohol Consumption Patterns**: Chronic heavy drinking over many years significantly increases the risk of developing ALD.

**Symptoms and Complications**

a. **Symptoms**:

   i. **Fatty Liver**: Often asymptomatic but may present with mild discomfort or fatigue.

   ii. **Alcoholic Hepatitis**: Jaundice, abdominal pain, nausea, vomiting, fever, and potentially hepatic encephalopathy (confusion, altered mental status).

   iii. **Cirrhosis**: Fatigue, weakness, jaundice, fluid retention (edema, ascites), easy bruising, and gastrointestinal bleeding.

b. **Complications**:

   i. **Portal Hypertension**: Increased pressure in the portal vein leading to complications such as varices (esophageal or gastric), ascites, and hepatic encephalopathy.

ii. **Hepatorenal Syndrome**: Impaired kidney function due to severe liver damage.

iii. **Hepatocellular Carcinoma**: Increased risk of liver cancer, particularly in individuals with cirrhosis.

**Diagnosis**

a. **Medical History and Physical Examination**: Inquire about alcohol consumption history and symptoms suggestive of liver disease.

b. **Laboratory Tests**:

i. **Liver Function Tests**: Assess liver enzymes (AST, ALT), bilirubin levels, albumin, and coagulation profile.

ii. **Serologic Tests**: Exclude other causes of liver disease, such as viral hepatitis (HBV, HCV).

c. **Imaging Studies**:

i. **Ultrasound**: Evaluate liver size, texture, and presence of steatosis or cirrhosis.

ii. **CT Scan or MRI**: Assess for liver structure, nodules, and extent of fibrosis.

d. **Liver Biopsy**: Gold standard for confirming the presence and severity of liver inflammation, fibrosis, or cirrhosis.

**Treatment**

a. **Abstinence from Alcohol**: The most critical aspect of treatment to prevent further liver damage and improve outcomes.

b. **Nutritional Support**: Ensure adequate nutrition, including vitamins (especially B-complex) and minerals, to support liver function and promote healing.

c. **Medications**:

i. **Corticosteroids**: Used in severe cases of alcoholic hepatitis to reduce inflammation.

ii. **Pentoxifylline**: Anti-inflammatory agent that may be used as an alternative in alcoholic hepatitis.

iii. **Ursodeoxycholic Acid**: May be beneficial in certain cases of cholestatic liver injury.

d. **Management of Complications**:

i. **Ascites**: Diuretics (e.g., spironolactone, furosemide), paracentesis for fluid removal, and sodium restriction.

ii. **Hepatic Encephalopathy**: Lactulose to promote bowel movements and reduce ammonia levels.

iii. **Variceal Bleeding**: Endoscopic band ligation, beta-blockers, or transjugular intrahepatic portosystemic shunt (TIPS) placement.

**Complications and Management**

a. **Regular Monitoring**: Serial liver function tests, imaging studies, and clinical assessments to monitor disease progression and response to treatment.

b. **Liver Transplantation**: Considered in severe cases of cirrhosis or liver failure that do not respond to medical therapy.

**Prevention**

a. **Moderation or Abstinence**: Limit alcohol consumption to recommended levels (if drinking) or abstain from alcohol entirely.

b. **Education and Counseling**: Raise awareness about the risks of alcohol abuse and promote healthy lifestyle choices.

c. **Screening and Early Intervention**: Identify individuals at risk of developing ALD and provide counseling and support to reduce alcohol intake.

**Multiple-Choice Questions (Objective)**

1. What is the main division of the nervous system responsible for processing sensory information?

    a) Peripheral Nervous System (PNS)

    b) Central Nervous System (CNS)

    c) Autonomic Nervous System (ANS)

    d) Somatic Nervous System

2. Which part of the brain is involved in voluntary movements and balance?

    a) Cerebrum

    b) Brainstem

    c) Cerebellum

    d) Spinal Cord

3. What type of neurons transmit information from sensory receptors to the CNS?

    a) Motor (efferent) neurons

    b) Sensory (afferent) neurons

    c) Interneurons

    d) Glial cells

4. The "fight or flight" response is regulated by which division of the autonomic nervous system?

    a) Somatic Nervous System

    b) Parasympathetic Nervous System

    c) Sympathetic Nervous System

    d) Central Nervous System

5. Which neurotransmitter is primarily associated with Parkinson's disease due to its decreased levels?

    a) Serotonin

    b) Dopamine

c) Acetylcholine

d) GABA

6. What is the primary pathological feature of Alzheimer's disease?

    a) Amyloid plaques and neurofibrillary tangles

    b) Loss of motor neurons

    c) Demyelination of neurons

    d) Increased dopamine levels

7. Which condition is characterized by recurrent, unprovoked seizures?

    a) Parkinson's disease

    b) Stroke

    c) Epilepsy

    d) Schizophrenia

8. Which of the following is NOT a symptom of Parkinson's disease?

    a) Bradykinesia

    b) Tremor

    c) Rigidity

    d) Euphoria

9. In which part of the gastrointestinal tract does most nutrient absorption occur?

    a) Stomach

    b) Large intestine

    c) Small intestine

    d) Esophagus

10. What enzyme is primarily responsible for metabolizing alcohol in the liver?

    a) Lactase

    b) Amylase

    c) Alcohol dehydrogenase (ADH)

    d) Pepsin

11. Which hepatitis virus is primarily transmitted through contaminated water?

a) Hepatitis A

b) Hepatitis B

c) Hepatitis C

d) Hepatitis D

12. Which part of the brain controls involuntary functions like breathing and heart rate?

a) Cerebrum

b) Cerebellum

c) Brainstem

d) Spinal cord

13. Which condition involves inflammation of the GI tract and includes Crohn's disease and ulcerative colitis?

a) Peptic ulcer disease

b) Irritable bowel syndrome (IBS)

c) Inflammatory bowel disease (IBD)

d) Gastroesophageal reflux disease (GERD)

14. Which symptom is common in both epilepsy and Parkinson's disease?

a) Seizures

b) Tremor

c) Bradykinesia

d) Hallucinations

15. What is the primary treatment goal for epilepsy?

a) Increase dopamine levels

b) Reduce inflammation

c) Control seizures

d) Enhance neuroplasticity

16. Which neurotransmitter is often targeted in the treatment of depression?

a) Dopamine

b) Serotonin

c) Acetylcholine

d) Glutamate

17. What is the primary function of bile produced by the liver?

a) Break down carbohydrates

b) Neutralize stomach acid

c) Aid in fat digestion

d) Produce insulin

18. What condition is characterized by yellowing of the skin and eyes due to elevated bilirubin levels?

a) Cirrhosis

b) Jaundice

c) Hepatitis

d) Pancreatitis

19. What complication is associated with long-term use of nonsteroidal anti-inflammatory drugs (NSAIDs)?

a) Increased neurotransmitter levels

b) Peptic ulcers

c) Decreased liver enzymes

d) Improved GI motility

20. What is the main preventive measure for hepatitis B?

a) Avoiding alcohol

b) Safe food practices

c) Vaccination

d) Antiviral medications

**Short Answer Type Questions (Subjective)**

1. Explain the primary functions of the central nervous system (CNS).

2. Describe the role of the cerebellum in the nervous system.

3. What are the differences between the sympathetic and parasympathetic nervous systems?

4. How do neurotransmitters affect brain function?

5. Discuss the pathophysiology of Parkinson's disease.

6. What are the main symptoms and complications of epilepsy?

7. Describe the digestive process in the small intestine.

8. Explain the role of Helicobacter pylori in the development of peptic ulcers.

9. What are the risk factors for developing alcoholic liver disease (ALD)?

10. How does chronic hepatitis lead to cirrhosis?

11. What is hepatic encephalopathy, and how does it affect the nervous system?

12. Describe the role of the gut-brain axis in psychiatric disorders.

13. What are the common symptoms of Alzheimer's disease in its early stages?

14. How can inflammatory bowel diseases (IBD) be managed?

15. What are the preventive measures for hepatitis A?

16. Explain the impact of stress on the development of peptic ulcers.

17. Discuss the role of neurotransmitter imbalance in depression.

18. How does jaundice develop, and what are its primary causes?

19. Describe the complications associated with advanced liver cirrhosis.

20. What are the treatment options for managing gastroesophageal reflux disease (GERD)?


**Long Answer Type Questions (Subjective)**

1. Discuss the structure and functions of the central and peripheral nervous systems, highlighting their key differences.

2. Explain the pathophysiology, symptoms, and treatment options for Parkinson's disease.

3. Describe the various stages of Alzheimer's disease and the associated neurological changes.

4. Discuss the role of the gut-brain axis in the development of psychiatric disorders and its implications for treatment.

5. Explain the process of diagnosing and managing peptic ulcer disease, including the role of Helicobacter pylori.

6. Describe the pathophysiology of inflammatory bowel diseases (IBD) and the current treatment approaches.

7. Discuss the epidemiology, symptoms, and complications of hepatitis B and C, and explain the available preventive measures.

8. Explain the impact of alcohol on the liver, including the development and progression of alcoholic liver disease (ALD).

9. Describe the neurological and gastrointestinal complications associated with chronic liver disease and their management.

10. Discuss the mechanisms of action, side effects, and clinical use of antiepileptic drugs (AEDs) in the treatment of epilepsy.

**Answer Key for MCQ Questions**

1. b) Central Nervous System (CNS)

2. c) Cerebellum

3. b) Sensory (afferent) neurons

4. c) Sympathetic Nervous System

5. b) Dopamine

6. a) Amyloid plaques and neurofibrillary tangles

7. c) Epilepsy

8. d) Euphoria

9. c) Small intestine

10. c) Alcohol dehydrogenase (ADH)

11. a) Hepatitis A

12. c) Brainstem

13. c) Inflammatory bowel disease (IBD)

14.b) Tremor

15.c) Control seizures

16.b) Serotonin

17.c) Aid in fat digestion

18.b) Jaundice

19.b) Peptic ulcers

20.c) Vaccination

# CHAPTER – 6

## DISEASE OF BONES AND JOINT AND CANCER

**INTRODUCTION:**

**Diseases of Bones and Joints:**

1. **Osteoporosis:**
   a. **Definition**: A condition characterized by weakened bones that are more susceptible to fractures. It occurs when the body loses too much bone mass or makes too little bone.
   b. **Risk Factors**: Age, gender (more common in women), family history, low body weight, smoking, excessive alcohol consumption, and certain medications.
   c. **Symptoms**: Often asymptomatic until a fracture occurs. Common fractures occur in the spine, hip, and wrist.
   d. **Diagnosis**: Bone density tests (DEXA scans), X-rays.
   e. **Treatment**: Medications like bisphosphonates, hormone replacement therapy, calcium and vitamin D supplements, and lifestyle changes including exercise and diet.

2. **Rheumatoid Arthritis (RA):**
   a. **Definition**: An autoimmune disorder that primarily affects the joints, causing inflammation, pain, and eventual joint damage.
   b. **Risk Factors**: Gender (more common in women), family history, age, and smoking.
   c. **Symptoms**: Joint pain, swelling, stiffness, and reduced joint mobility. Often affects joints symmetrically.
   d. **Diagnosis**: Clinical examination, blood tests (rheumatoid factor, anti-CCP antibodies), and imaging studies.

e. **Treatment**: Disease-modifying antirheumatic drugs (DMARDs), biologics, NSAIDs, and corticosteroids.

3. **Osteoarthritis (OA)**:

   a. **Definition**: The most common form of arthritis, characterized by the degeneration of cartilage in the joints.

   b. **Risk Factors**: Age, joint injury, obesity, genetics, and repetitive stress on joints.

   c. **Symptoms**: Joint pain, stiffness, and swelling. Typically affects weight-bearing joints like the knees, hips, and spine.

   d. **Diagnosis**: Clinical examination, X-rays, MRI.

   e. **Treatment**: Pain management with NSAIDs, physical therapy, weight management, and joint replacement surgery in severe cases.

4. **Gout**:

   a. **Definition**: A form of inflammatory arthritis caused by the accumulation of uric acid crystals in the joints.

   b. **Risk Factors**: High purine diet, obesity, genetic predisposition, and certain medications.

   c. **Symptoms**: Sudden and severe pain, redness, and swelling in the affected joint, often the big toe.

   d. **Diagnosis**: Joint fluid analysis, blood tests to measure uric acid levels, and imaging.

   e. **Treatment**: Medications to lower uric acid levels, pain relief, dietary changes, and lifestyle modifications.

**Cancer:**

1. **Breast Cancer**:

   a. **Definition**: Cancer that forms in the cells of the breasts. It can occur in both men and women but is far more common in women.

   b. **Risk Factors**: Gender, age, family history, genetic mutations (e.g., BRCA1, BRCA2), and lifestyle factors.

c. **Symptoms**: Lump in the breast, changes in breast shape or size, skin changes, and discharge from the nipple.

d. **Diagnosis**: Mammography, ultrasound, biopsy, and MRI.

e. **Treatment**: Surgery, radiation therapy, chemotherapy, hormone therapy, and targeted therapies.

2. **Lung Cancer**:

a. **Definition**: Cancer that originates in the lungs, often due to smoking or exposure to carcinogens.

b. **Risk Factors**: Smoking, exposure to secondhand smoke, environmental pollutants, and genetic factors.

c. **Symptoms**: Persistent cough, chest pain, breathlessness, and coughing up blood.

d. **Diagnosis**: Chest X-ray, CT scan, bronchoscopy, and biopsy.

e. **Treatment**: Surgery, radiation therapy, chemotherapy, targeted therapy, and immunotherapy.

3. **Prostate Cancer**:

a. **Definition**: Cancer that forms in the prostate gland, which is part of the male reproductive system.

b. **Risk Factors**: Age, family history, race (more common in African American men), and certain genetic mutations.

c. **Symptoms**: Difficulty urinating, blood in urine, pelvic pain, and erectile dysfunction.

d. **Diagnosis**: PSA blood test, digital rectal exam, biopsy, and imaging studies.

e. **Treatment**: Surgery, radiation therapy, hormone therapy, and chemotherapy.

4. **Colorectal Cancer**:

a. **Definition**: Cancer that begins in the colon or rectum, part of the large intestine.

b. **Risk Factors**: Age, family history, inflammatory bowel disease, diet high in red or processed meats, and smoking.

c. **Symptoms**: Changes in bowel habits, blood in stool, abdominal pain, and weight loss.

d. **Diagnosis**: Colonoscopy, stool tests, and imaging studies.

e. **Treatment**: Surgery, chemotherapy, radiation therapy, and targeted therapy.

## DISEASE OF BONES AND JOINTS

### A. Rheumatoid arthritis:

**Introduction**

Rheumatoid arthritis (RA) is a chronic, systemic autoimmune disorder that primarily affects the joints. It is characterized by inflammation of the synovial membrane, leading to joint damage and deformities. RA can also affect other organs and systems in the body, making it a complex and potentially debilitating condition.

**Pathophysiology**

1. **Immune System Dysfunction**: RA involves the immune system attacking the synovial membrane (the lining of the joints). This immune response leads to inflammation and damage.

2. **Inflammatory Cascade**: The inflammation results in the release of cytokines (e.g., tumor necrosis factor-alpha, interleukin-1, and interleukin-6) and other inflammatory mediators that promote further joint damage.

3. **Synovial Hyperplasia**: The synovium thickens and becomes inflamed, forming a pannus (an abnormal tissue growth) that erodes cartilage and bone.

4. **Joint Damage**: Over time, the destruction of cartilage and bone leads to joint deformities, pain, and loss of function.

**Epidemiology**

1. **Prevalence**: RA affects approximately 1% of the global population.

2. **Gender**: Women are more commonly affected than men, with a ratio of about 2-3:1.

3. **Age**: RA can occur at any age but is most commonly diagnosed between the ages of 30 and 60.

4. **Genetics**: There is a genetic predisposition to RA, with certain genetic markers like the HLA-DR4 allele being associated with increased risk.

5. **Environmental Factors**: Smoking is a known environmental risk factor that can trigger RA in genetically predisposed individuals.

**Symptoms and Complications**

1. **Symptoms**:

   a. **Joint Pain and Swelling**: Commonly affects the small joints of the hands and feet.

   b. **Morning Stiffness**: Lasts for more than an hour and is often worse in the morning.

   c. **Fatigue and General Malaise**: Systemic symptoms like fatigue and a feeling of general unwellness.

   d. **Joint Deformities**: Over time, affected joints may become deformed and lose function.

   e. **Systemic Manifestations**: RA can also cause symptoms in other organs, including the lungs, heart, and eyes.

2. **Complications**:

   a. **Joint Deformities**: Progressive damage can lead to joint deformities such as ulnar deviation and swan-neck deformities.

   b. **Bone Loss**: Increased risk of osteoporosis and bone fractures due to chronic inflammation.

   c. **Cardiovascular Disease**: Higher risk of developing heart disease due to inflammation.

d. **Lung Disease**: RA can lead to interstitial lung disease and pleuritis.

e. **Infections**: Immunosuppressive treatments increase susceptibility to infections.

**Diagnosis**

1. **Clinical Evaluation**: Based on symptoms, medical history, and physical examination.

2. **Laboratory Tests**:

    a. **Rheumatoid Factor (RF)**: An antibody present in many RA patients but not exclusively.

    b. **Anti-Cyclic Citrullinated Peptide (Anti-CCP)**: More specific for RA and helps in early diagnosis.

    c. **Erythrocyte Sedimentation Rate (ESR) and C-Reactive Protein (CRP)**: Indicators of inflammation.

3. **Imaging Studies**:

    a. **X-rays**: Can reveal joint damage, erosion, and deformities.

    b. **Ultrasound**: Useful for detecting early inflammatory changes and synovitis.

    c. **MRI**: Provides detailed images of joint structures and can detect early inflammatory changes.

**Treatment**

1. **Medications**:

    a. **Disease-Modifying Antirheumatic Drugs (DMARDs)**: Methotrexate, sulfasalazine, and leflunomide to slow disease progression.

    b. **Biologic DMARDs**: TNF inhibitors (e.g., etanercept, infliximab), IL-6 inhibitors (e.g., tocilizumab), and other targeted therapies.

    c. **Nonsteroidal Anti-Inflammatory Drugs (NSAIDs)**: For pain relief and inflammation reduction.

d. **Corticosteroids**: Short-term use to manage severe inflammation.

2. **Physical Therapy**: Helps maintain joint function and mobility.

3. **Surgical Interventions**: Joint replacement or repair may be necessary in advanced cases.

## Complications

1. **Joint Deformities**: Progressive damage can lead to significant joint deformities affecting function.

2. **Osteoporosis**: Increased risk due to chronic inflammation and steroid use.

3. **Cardiovascular Problems**: Higher risk of heart disease and related complications.

4. **Infections**: Increased risk due to immunosuppressive treatments.

## Prevention

1. **Early Diagnosis and Treatment**: Prompt treatment can help prevent or minimize joint damage.

2. **Lifestyle Modifications**:

   a. **Smoking Cessation**: Reducing the risk of developing RA.

   b. **Healthy Diet**: Anti-inflammatory diets may help manage symptoms.

   c. **Regular Exercise**: Maintains joint function and overall health.

3. **Regular Monitoring**: Ongoing evaluation and management by a healthcare provider to prevent complications and adjust treatment as needed.

## B. Osteoporosis:

## Introduction

Osteoporosis is a metabolic bone disorder characterized by reduced bone mass and deterioration of bone tissue, leading to increased bone fragility and susceptibility to fractures. It is often termed a "silent disease" because it progresses without symptoms until a fracture occurs.

**Pathophysiology**

1. **Bone Remodeling Imbalance**: Osteoporosis results from an imbalance between bone resorption and bone formation. Osteoclasts (cells that break down bone) become more active or osteoblasts (cells that build bone) become less active, leading to decreased bone density.

2. **Bone Microarchitecture**: The loss of bone mass affects the microarchitecture of bone tissue, making bones more porous and less structurally sound.

3. **Hormonal Changes**: In postmenopausal women, decreased estrogen levels contribute to increased osteoclast activity and bone loss. In men, reduced testosterone levels can similarly affect bone density.

**Epidemiology**

1. **Prevalence**: Osteoporosis affects approximately 1 in 3 women and 1 in 5 men over the age of 50.

2. **Gender**: Women are more commonly affected due to postmenopausal hormonal changes, which lead to faster bone loss.

3. **Age**: The risk of osteoporosis increases with age, as bone density naturally decreases.

4. **Genetics**: Family history of osteoporosis or fractures increases risk.

5. **Lifestyle Factors**: Factors such as physical inactivity, smoking, and excessive alcohol consumption contribute to the risk.

**Symptoms and Complications**

1. **Symptoms**:
   a. Often asymptomatic until a fracture occurs.
   b. Possible early signs include back pain, loss of height, and a stooped posture.

2. **Complications**:

a. **Fractures**: Common sites include the spine, hip, and wrist. Fragility fractures occur with minimal trauma.

b. **Kyphosis**: Compression fractures in the spine can lead to a forward-bending posture.

c. **Chronic Pain**: Fractures and deformities can lead to chronic pain and reduced mobility.

d. **Functional Impairment**: Increased risk of falls and reduced ability to perform daily activities.

**Diagnosis**

1. **Bone Density Testing**:

   a. **Dual-Energy X-ray Absorptiometry (DXA)**: The most common and reliable method for measuring bone mineral density (BMD). T-scores from DXA scans are used to diagnose osteoporosis.

2. **Clinical Evaluation**:

   a. **Medical History**: Includes risk factors, family history, and previous fractures.

   b. **Physical Examination**: Identifies height loss, spinal deformities, and other physical signs of osteoporosis.

3. **Laboratory Tests**:

   a. **Serum Calcium and Vitamin D Levels**: To rule out secondary causes of bone loss.

   b. **Bone Turnover Markers**: Can indicate the rate of bone resorption and formation.

**Treatment**

1. **Medications**:

   a. **Bisphosphonates**: Alendronate, risedronate, and zoledronic acid inhibit bone resorption.

   b. **Selective Estrogen Receptor Modulators (SERMs)**: Raloxifene mimics estrogen's effects on bones.

c. **Hormone Replacement Therapy (HRT)**: Estrogen therapy, though used less frequently due to risks.

d. **Parathyroid Hormone Analogues**: Teriparatide stimulates bone formation.

e. **Denosumab**: A monoclonal antibody that inhibits osteoclast activity.

2. **Lifestyle Modifications**:

   a. **Diet**: Adequate intake of calcium and vitamin D.

   b. **Exercise**: Weight-bearing and muscle-strengthening exercises to improve bone strength and balance.

   c. **Fall Prevention**: Measures to reduce the risk of falls, such as home safety modifications and balance training.

3. **Surgical Interventions**:

   a. **Fracture Repair**: Surgery may be needed to repair severe fractures.

## Complications

1. **Fractures**: High risk of fractures due to reduced bone strength, leading to potential disability and decreased quality of life.

2. **Decreased Mobility**: Fractures and pain can limit physical activity and independence.

3. **Chronic Pain**: Persistent pain from fractures or deformities.

4. **Increased Risk of Falls**: Impaired balance and mobility can lead to more frequent falls.

## Prevention

1. **Bone Health**:

   a. **Diet**: Ensure adequate intake of calcium (1,000-1,200 mg/day) and vitamin D (800-1,000 IU/day).

   b. **Exercise**: Engage in regular weight-bearing and resistance exercises to strengthen bones and improve balance.

2. **Lifestyle Changes**:
   a. **Avoid Smoking**: Smoking accelerates bone loss.
   b. **Limit Alcohol Consumption**: Excessive alcohol can affect bone health and increase fracture risk.
3. **Medications**: For individuals at high risk, medications may be used to prevent bone loss before significant damage occurs.
4. **Regular Screening**: DXA scans for those at risk or over the age of 65 to monitor bone density.

Osteoporosis is a manageable condition, especially with early detection and a proactive approach to treatment and prevention. Addressing risk factors and maintaining bone health through lifestyle choices and appropriate medical interventions can significantly reduce the impact of osteoporosis.

## C. Gout:

### Introduction

Gout is a type of inflammatory arthritis characterized by sudden and severe pain, redness, and swelling in the affected joints, most commonly the big toe. It is caused by the deposition of monosodium urate crystals in the joints due to high levels of uric acid in the blood.

### Pathophysiology

1. **Hyperuricemia**: Gout develops when there is an excessive amount of uric acid in the blood, a condition known as hyperuricemia. Uric acid is a byproduct of purine metabolism, and its excess can result from overproduction or reduced excretion.
2. **Crystal Formation**: High levels of uric acid lead to the formation of monosodium urate crystals, which precipitate in the joints and surrounding tissues.
3. **Inflammatory Response**: The presence of these crystals triggers a strong inflammatory response from the immune system, leading to pain, redness,

and swelling. The body's immune cells, particularly neutrophils, are recruited to the site, exacerbating inflammation.

**Epidemiology**

1. **Prevalence**: Gout affects approximately 1-4% of adults in Western countries. It is becoming increasingly common due to rising obesity rates and changes in diet.

2. **Gender**: More common in men, with a 3:1 ratio compared to women, largely due to differences in uric acid metabolism and excretion.

3. **Age**: Typically manifests in middle-aged adults, with the risk increasing with age.

4. **Genetics**: Family history of gout can increase the risk, suggesting a genetic predisposition.

**Symptoms and Complications**

1. **Symptoms**:

    a. **Acute Attack**: Sudden onset of intense pain, swelling, redness, and warmth in the affected joint, often the big toe (podagra). Attacks can last from a few days to a couple of weeks.

    b. **Intercritical Periods**: Periods between acute attacks where symptoms subside but may recur.

    c. **Chronic Gout**: If untreated, gout can lead to chronic joint pain and the development of tophi (deposits of urate crystals under the skin).

2. **Complications**:

    a. **Tophaceous Gout**: Formation of tophi, which can cause joint damage and deformities.

    b. **Kidney Stones**: Elevated uric acid levels can lead to the formation of uric acid stones in the kidneys.

    c. **Joint Damage**: Repeated attacks can lead to permanent joint damage and loss of function.

d. **Infection**: Joint inflammation can increase the risk of secondary bacterial infections.

**Diagnosis**

1. **Clinical Evaluation**: Diagnosis is based on symptoms, medical history, and physical examination.

2. **Laboratory Tests**:

    a. **Serum Uric Acid**: Elevated levels indicate hyperuricemia but are not definitive for gout.

    b. **Joint Fluid Analysis**: The most definitive test. Synovial fluid from the affected joint is analyzed under polarized light microscopy to identify urate crystals.

    c. **Blood Tests**: To rule out other conditions and assess kidney function.

3. **Imaging Studies**:

    a. **X-rays**: May show joint damage or tophi in chronic cases but are not used for initial diagnosis.

    b. **Ultrasound**: Can detect urate crystals and early changes in the joints.

    c. **CT Scan**: Used in certain cases to detect urate crystal deposits.

**Treatment**

1. **Acute Attack Management**:

    a. **Nonsteroidal Anti-Inflammatory Drugs (NSAIDs)**: Such as ibuprofen or naproxen, to reduce pain and inflammation.

    b. **Colchicine**: Effective for acute gout attacks and can also be used for prophylaxis.

    c. **Corticosteroids**: Such as prednisone, can be used when NSAIDs or colchicine are not suitable.

2. **Long-Term Management**:

    a. **Urate-Lowering Therapy**:

- **Allopurinol**: Reduces uric acid production.
- **Febuxostat**: Another option for lowering uric acid levels.
- **Probenecid**: Increases uric acid excretion by the kidneys.

b. **Lifestyle Changes**: Dietary modifications to reduce purine intake (e.g., avoiding red meat, shellfish, and alcohol), weight management, and adequate hydration.

c. **Medication Adherence**: Ongoing urate-lowering therapy to prevent future attacks and manage hyperuricemia.

## Complications

1. **Tophaceous Deposits**: Can lead to chronic pain and joint deformities.
2. **Renal Complications**: Risk of uric acid nephrolithiasis (kidney stones) and potential kidney damage.
3. **Recurrent Attacks**: Failure to manage uric acid levels can lead to frequent and severe attacks.

## Prevention

1. **Dietary Modifications**:
   a. **Reduce Purine Intake**: Limit consumption of high-purine foods like red meats, organ meats, and certain seafood.
   b. **Limit Alcohol**: Especially beer and spirits, which can increase uric acid levels.
   c. **Increase Fluid Intake**: Helps dilute uric acid and prevent kidney stones.
2. **Maintain Healthy Weight**: Reducing body weight can lower uric acid levels and reduce the risk of gout attacks.
3. **Regular Monitoring**: For individuals with hyperuricemia or previous gout attacks, regular monitoring and management of uric acid levels are crucial to prevent complications.

Gout is a manageable condition with appropriate treatment and lifestyle adjustments. Early intervention and adherence to treatment plans can significantly improve outcomes and quality of life for individuals with gout.

**PRINCIPLES OF CANCER**

**A. Classification of cancer:**

**Introduction**

Cancer is a group of diseases characterized by uncontrolled cell growth and spread to other parts of the body. The classification of cancer is crucial for diagnosis, treatment, and understanding the disease's behavior. Classification is typically based on the type of tissue from which the cancer originates, the cancer's molecular and genetic characteristics, and its stage and grade.

**Pathophysiology**

1. **Genetic Mutations**: Cancer begins with genetic mutations in a cell's DNA. These mutations can be inherited or acquired due to environmental factors or lifestyle choices.
2. **Uncontrolled Growth**: Mutations disrupt normal cell cycle control, leading to uncontrolled cell proliferation.
3. **Angiogenesis**: Tumors stimulate the growth of new blood vessels to supply nutrients and oxygen, which supports their growth and spread.
4. **Metastasis**: Cancer cells can invade surrounding tissues and spread to distant organs through the bloodstream or lymphatic system.

**Epidemiology**

1. **Prevalence**: Cancer is a leading cause of morbidity and mortality worldwide. The prevalence varies by type, with breast, lung, prostate, and colorectal cancers being the most common.
2. **Gender**: Incidence rates vary by gender, with prostate cancer being more common in men and breast cancer more common in women.

3. **Age**: Cancer risk generally increases with age, though some cancers can occur in younger populations.

4. **Risk Factors**: Includes genetic predisposition, lifestyle factors (e.g., smoking, diet, alcohol consumption), environmental exposures, and infections (e.g., HPV in cervical cancer).

**Classification of Cancer**

1. **By Tissue Origin**:

    a. **Carcinomas**: Cancers that originate in epithelial tissues. Common types include:

        i. **Adenocarcinomas**: Originating from glandular tissues (e.g., breast, prostate).

        ii. **Squamous Cell Carcinomas**: Originating from squamous epithelium (e.g., skin, lungs).

    b. **Sarcomas**: Cancers arising from connective tissues such as bone, muscle, and fat. Examples include:

        i. **Osteosarcoma**: Bone cancer.

        ii. **Leiomyosarcoma**: Smooth muscle cancer.

    c. **Leukemias**: Cancers of the blood and bone marrow. Examples include:

        i. **Acute Myeloid Leukemia (AML)**.

        ii. **Chronic Lymphocytic Leukemia (CLL)**.

    d. **Lymphomas**: Cancers of the lymphatic system. Examples include:

        i. **Hodgkin Lymphoma**.

        ii. **Non-Hodgkin Lymphoma**.

    e. **Melanomas**: Cancers originating from melanocytes (pigment-producing cells). The most common type is:

        i. **Cutaneous Melanoma**.

2. **By Molecular and Genetic Characteristics**:

a. **Oncogenes**: Genes that, when mutated or overexpressed, drive cancer progression (e.g., HER2 in breast cancer).

b. **Tumor Suppressor Genes**: Genes that normally inhibit cancer development but are inactivated in cancer (e.g., TP53, BRCA1/2).

c. **Genomic Alterations**: Includes chromosomal translocations (e.g., BCR-ABL in chronic myeloid leukemia), gene amplifications, and mutations.

3. **By Stage and Grade**:

a. **Stage**: Indicates the extent of cancer spread.

    i. **Stage I**: Localized cancer.

    ii. **Stage II**: Regional spread to nearby tissues or lymph nodes.

    iii. **Stage III**: Extensive regional spread.

    iv. **Stage IV**: Distant metastasis.

b. **Grade**: Refers to the appearance of cancer cells under a microscope.

    i. **Grade 1**: Well-differentiated (cells look similar to normal cells).

    ii. **Grade 2**: Moderately differentiated.

    iii. **Grade 3**: Poorly differentiated (cells look less like normal cells).

    iv. **Grade 4**: Undifferentiated (cells look very abnormal).

## Symptoms and Complications

1. **Symptoms**: Vary depending on the type and location of cancer but can include unexplained weight loss, persistent pain, fatigue, changes in skin or bowel habits, and abnormal bleeding.

2. **Complications**:

a. **Local Effects**: Pain, obstruction, or dysfunction in the affected organ.

b. **Metastasis**: Spread to distant organs can lead to organ failure or additional symptoms.

c. **Treatment-Related Effects**: Side effects of chemotherapy, radiation therapy, and surgery can include nausea, hair loss, immunosuppression, and secondary cancers.

**Diagnosis**

1. **Imaging Studies**:

   a. **X-rays**: Useful for detecting bone tumors and some other cancers.

   b. **CT Scans**: Provide detailed cross-sectional images to assess tumor size and spread.

   c. **MRI**: Useful for imaging soft tissues and detecting brain and spinal tumors.

   d. **PET Scans**: Evaluate cancer metabolism and detect metastasis.

2. **Biopsy**:

   a. **Histopathology**: Examination of tissue samples to determine cancer type and grade.

   b. **Needle Biopsy**: For sampling tissue from a suspicious area.

   c. **Surgical Biopsy**: Involves removing a larger tissue sample.

3. **Laboratory Tests**:

   a. **Blood Tests**: To detect tumor markers and assess overall health.

   b. **Molecular Testing**: To identify genetic mutations and guide targeted therapy.

**Treatment**

1. **Surgery**: Removal of the tumor and surrounding tissue. Often used for localized cancers.

2. **Radiation Therapy**: Uses high-energy radiation to kill cancer cells and shrink tumors.

3. **Chemotherapy**: Systemic treatment using drugs to kill or inhibit cancer cell growth.

4. **Targeted Therapy**: Drugs or substances that specifically target cancer cells with particular genetic changes.

5. **Immunotherapy**: Boosts the body's immune system to fight cancer cells.

6. **Hormone Therapy**: Used for cancers that are hormone-sensitive, such as breast and prostate cancer.

**Complications**

1. **Treatment Side Effects**: Include nausea, fatigue, immunosuppression, and risk of infections.

2. **Disease Progression**: Local or distant spread of cancer can worsen prognosis and quality of life.

3. **Secondary Cancers**: Risk of developing new cancers as a result of treatment or due to genetic predispositions.

**Prevention**

1. **Lifestyle Modifications**:
   a. **Healthy Diet**: High in fruits, vegetables, and whole grains, and low in processed foods.
   b. **Regular Exercise**: Reduces the risk of several cancers.
   c. **Avoid Smoking**: Smoking is a major risk factor for various cancers.
   d. **Limit Alcohol**: Reducing alcohol intake can decrease cancer risk.

2. **Screening**: Regular screenings for cancers with known early detection methods (e.g., mammograms for breast cancer, colonoscopy for colorectal cancer).

3. **Vaccination**: Vaccines for cancer-related infections, such as HPV vaccination for cervical cancer and hepatitis B vaccination for liver cancer.

4. **Genetic Counseling**: For individuals with a family history of cancer, genetic testing and counseling can help assess risk and guide preventive measures.

**B. Etiology of cancer:**

**Introduction**

The etiology of cancer refers to the underlying causes and risk factors that contribute to the development of cancer. Understanding the etiology is crucial for prevention, early detection, and treatment. Cancer arises from complex interactions between genetic, environmental, and lifestyle factors.

**Pathophysiology**

1. **Genetic Mutations**: Cancer begins with mutations in the DNA of cells. These mutations can be inherited or acquired. They affect genes that control cell growth and division, leading to uncontrolled proliferation.

   a. **Oncogenes**: Mutated genes that promote cell growth and division (e.g., RAS, MYC).

   b. **Tumor Suppressor Genes**: Genes that normally inhibit cell growth but are inactivated in cancer (e.g., TP53, BRCA1/2).

   c. **DNA Repair Genes**: Mutations in genes responsible for repairing DNA damage can lead to cancer (e.g., MLH1, MSH2).

2. **Epigenetic Changes**: Alterations in gene expression without changes to the DNA sequence, such as DNA methylation and histone modification, can contribute to cancer development.

3. **Cellular Mechanisms**:

   a. **Apoptosis**: Defects in programmed cell death can allow damaged cells to survive and proliferate.

   b. **Angiogenesis**: Tumors stimulate the growth of new blood vessels to supply nutrients and support growth.

   c. **Metastasis**: Cancer cells acquire the ability to invade surrounding tissues and spread to distant sites.

**Epidemiology**

1. **Genetic Factors**: Inherited genetic mutations can increase cancer risk. Examples include mutations in BRCA1/BRCA2 (breast and ovarian cancer) and APC (colorectal cancer).

2. **Environmental Exposures**:

   a. **Carcinogens**: Substances that cause cancer (e.g., tobacco smoke, asbestos, certain chemicals).

   b. **Radiation**: Exposure to ionizing radiation (e.g., X-rays, radon) increases cancer risk.

   c. **Infections**: Certain viruses and bacteria are linked to cancer (e.g., HPV in cervical cancer, Hepatitis B/C in liver cancer).

3. **Lifestyle Factors**:

   a. **Diet**: High-fat, low-fiber diets, and consumption of processed foods can increase risk.

   b. **Alcohol**: Excessive alcohol intake is linked to several cancers (e.g., breast, liver).

   c. **Physical Activity**: Lack of exercise is associated with increased cancer risk.

4. **Socioeconomic Factors**: Access to healthcare, education, and lifestyle choices influenced by socioeconomic status can impact cancer risk.

**Symptoms and Complications**

1. **Symptoms**: Vary depending on the type and stage of cancer. Common symptoms include unexplained weight loss, persistent pain, changes in skin or bowel habits, and abnormal bleeding.

2. **Complications**:

   a. **Local Effects**: Pain, obstruction, or dysfunction in the affected organ.

   b. **Metastasis**: Spread of cancer to distant organs can lead to additional symptoms and complications.

c. **Treatment-Related Complications**: Side effects from cancer treatments, such as nausea, hair loss, immunosuppression, and increased risk of secondary cancers.

**Diagnosis**

1. **Clinical Evaluation**: Initial assessment based on symptoms and physical examination.
2. **Imaging Studies**:
    a. **X-rays, CT Scans, MRI, PET Scans**: To visualize tumors and assess their extent.
3. **Biopsy**:
    a. **Histopathology**: Examination of tissue samples to determine cancer type and grade.
4. **Laboratory Tests**:
    a. **Blood Tests**: To identify tumor markers and assess overall health.
    b. **Genetic Testing**: To identify hereditary mutations and guide treatment.
5. **Molecular Testing**: To determine specific genetic and molecular characteristics of the cancer, guiding targeted therapy.

**Treatment**

1. **Surgery**: Removal of the tumor and surrounding tissue.
2. **Radiation Therapy**: Uses high-energy radiation to kill cancer cells and shrink tumors.
3. **Chemotherapy**: Systemic treatment with drugs to kill or inhibit cancer cell growth.
4. **Targeted Therapy**: Drugs or substances that specifically target cancer cells with particular genetic changes.
5. **Immunotherapy**: Stimulates the body's immune system to recognize and destroy cancer cells.

6. **Hormone Therapy**: For cancers sensitive to hormones (e.g., breast, prostate).

**Complications**

1. **Treatment Side Effects**: Include nausea, fatigue, immunosuppression, and risk of infections.
2. **Disease Progression**: Local or distant spread of cancer can worsen prognosis and quality of life.
3. **Secondary Cancers**: Risk of developing new cancers as a result of treatment or genetic predisposition.

**Prevention**

1. **Lifestyle Modifications**:
    a. **Healthy Diet**: High in fruits, vegetables, and whole grains, and low in processed foods.
    b. **Regular Exercise**: Reduces the risk of several cancers.
    c. **Avoid Smoking**: Tobacco is a major risk factor for many cancers.
    d. **Limit Alcohol**: Reducing alcohol intake decreases cancer risk.
2. **Screening**: Regular screenings for cancers with known early detection methods (e.g., mammograms, colonoscopy).
3. **Vaccination**: Vaccines for cancer-related infections (e.g., HPV vaccine for cervical cancer, hepatitis B vaccine for liver cancer).
4. **Genetic Counseling**: For individuals with a family history of cancer, genetic testing and counseling can help assess risk and guide preventive measures.

**C. Pathogenesis of cancer:**

**Introduction**

The pathogenesis of cancer involves the complex processes through which normal cells transform into cancerous cells. This transformation is driven by a series of genetic, epigenetic, and environmental changes that disrupt normal cellular processes and lead to uncontrolled cell growth and spread.

**Pathophysiology**

1. **Genetic Alterations**:

   a. **Oncogenes**: Genes that, when mutated or overexpressed, drive cancer progression by promoting cell growth and division. Examples include RAS, MYC, and HER2.

   b. **Tumor Suppressor Genes**: Genes that normally inhibit cell growth. Mutations or loss of function in these genes (e.g., TP53, BRCA1/BRCA2) allow cells to grow uncontrollably.

   c. **DNA Repair Genes**: Defects in genes responsible for repairing DNA damage (e.g., MLH1, MSH2) lead to accumulation of mutations and cancer development.

2. **Cellular Mechanisms**:

   a. **Cell Cycle Dysregulation**: Disruption in the regulatory mechanisms of the cell cycle leads to unchecked cell division.

   b. **Apoptosis**: Defective apoptosis allows damaged or abnormal cells to evade programmed cell death and continue to proliferate.

   c. **Angiogenesis**: Tumors secrete growth factors (e.g., VEGF) that stimulate the formation of new blood vessels to supply the growing tumor with nutrients and oxygen.

   d. **Metastasis**: Cancer cells acquire the ability to invade surrounding tissues and spread to distant sites through the bloodstream or lymphatic system.

3. **Microenvironment Interactions**:

   a. **Inflammation**: Chronic inflammation in tissues can create an environment conducive to cancer development. Inflammatory cells release cytokines and growth factors that promote tumor growth.

b. **Immune Evasion**: Cancer cells can evade immune surveillance through various mechanisms, including the expression of immune checkpoint proteins (e.g., PD-L1) that inhibit immune response.

**Epidemiology**

1. **Genetic Predisposition**: Some individuals inherit genetic mutations that increase cancer risk (e.g., BRCA1/2 mutations in breast and ovarian cancer).

2. **Environmental Factors**: Exposure to carcinogens (e.g., tobacco smoke, asbestos) and physical agents (e.g., radiation) can lead to genetic mutations and cancer development.

3. **Lifestyle Factors**: Diet, physical activity, and alcohol consumption can influence cancer risk by affecting cellular processes and promoting mutations.

4. **Infections**: Certain infections are linked to cancer development (e.g., HPV in cervical cancer, hepatitis B/C in liver cancer).

**Symptoms and Complications**

1. **Symptoms**: Symptoms vary depending on the cancer type and stage. Common symptoms include:
   a. **Local Symptoms**: Pain, swelling, and functional impairment in the affected organ.
   b. **Systemic Symptoms**: Unexplained weight loss, fatigue, fever, and night sweats.

2. **Complications**:
   a. **Local Complications**: Tumor growth can cause obstruction or damage to surrounding tissues.
   b. **Metastasis**: Spread of cancer to distant organs can lead to organ dysfunction and further complications.

c. **Treatment-Related Complications**: Side effects from treatments such as chemotherapy, radiation, and surgery include nausea, immunosuppression, and risk of secondary cancers.

**Diagnosis**

1. **Clinical Evaluation**: Initial assessment involves a thorough medical history and physical examination to identify symptoms and potential cancer signs.

2. **Imaging Studies**:

   a. **X-rays, CT Scans, MRI, PET Scans**: Used to visualize tumors, assess their size, and determine the extent of spread.

3. **Biopsy**:

   a. **Histopathology**: Examination of tissue samples to identify cancer type, grade, and other characteristics.

4. **Laboratory Tests**:

   a. **Blood Tests**: To detect tumor markers and assess overall health.

   b. **Genetic and Molecular Testing**: Identifies specific mutations and molecular alterations that can guide treatment decisions.

**Treatment**

1. **Surgery**: Removal of the tumor and surrounding tissue to eliminate localized cancer.

2. **Radiation Therapy**: Uses high-energy radiation to kill cancer cells and shrink tumors.

3. **Chemotherapy**: Systemic treatment with drugs to kill or inhibit the growth of cancer cells throughout the body.

4. **Targeted Therapy**: Drugs that specifically target genetic mutations or molecular pathways involved in cancer growth.

5. **Immunotherapy**: Enhances the body's immune response to recognize and attack cancer cells.

6. **Hormone Therapy**: Used for cancers that are hormone-sensitive (e.g., breast and prostate cancers).

**Complications**

1. **Treatment Side Effects**: Include nausea, fatigue, immunosuppression, and increased risk of infections.
2. **Disease Progression**: Continued tumor growth and metastasis can lead to worsening symptoms and reduced quality of life.
3. **Secondary Cancers**: Risk of developing new cancers as a result of treatment or genetic predisposition.

**Prevention**

1. **Lifestyle Changes**:
   a. **Healthy Diet**: A diet rich in fruits, vegetables, and whole grains while limiting processed foods and red meats.
   b. **Regular Exercise**: Helps reduce the risk of several cancers.
   c. **Avoid Tobacco**: Reduces the risk of cancers associated with smoking.
   d. **Limit Alcohol**: Reduces cancer risk, particularly for cancers of the digestive tract.
2. **Screening and Early Detection**:
   a. **Regular Screenings**: For cancers with established screening methods (e.g., mammograms, colonoscopies).
3. **Vaccination**:
   a. **HPV Vaccine**: Reduces the risk of cervical and other cancers associated with HPV.
   b. **Hepatitis B Vaccine**: Reduces the risk of liver cancer.
4. **Genetic Counseling**: For individuals with a family history of cancer, genetic testing and counseling can help assess risk and guide preventive measures.

**Multiple-Choice Questions (Objective)**

1. What is the most common symptom of osteoporosis until a fracture occurs?

   a) Joint pain

   b) Bone pain

   c) Often asymptomatic

   d) Muscle cramps

2. Which test is commonly used to diagnose osteoporosis?

   a) MRI

   b) Bone density test (DEXA scan)

   c) CT scan

   d) Ultrasound

3. What is the primary cause of rheumatoid arthritis (RA)?

   a) Bacterial infection

   b) Autoimmune disorder

   c) Viral infection

   d) Genetic mutation

4. Which medication is commonly used to manage rheumatoid arthritis?

   a) Antibiotics

   b) DMARDs

   c) Antivirals

   d) Diuretics

5. What characterizes osteoarthritis (OA)?

   a) Autoimmune disorder

   b) Inflammatory bowel disease

   c) Degeneration of cartilage in joints

   d) Overproduction of bone tissue

6. Which joint is most commonly affected by gout?

   a) Knee

b) Shoulder

c) Big toe

d) Elbow

7. What is a significant risk factor for lung cancer?

   a) High-fat diet

   b) Smoking

   c) Excessive alcohol consumption

   d) Lack of exercise

8. Which diagnostic tool is primarily used for detecting breast cancer?

   a) Ultrasound

   b) Mammography

   c) CT scan

   d) MRI

9. What is the main function of bisphosphonates in osteoporosis treatment?

   a) Increase bone resorption

   b) Decrease bone formation

   c) Inhibit bone resorption

   d) Promote bone remodeling

10. What hormone deficiency is primarily associated with osteoporosis in postmenopausal women?

   a) Insulin

   b) Estrogen

   c) Testosterone

   d) Cortisol

11. What type of cells are primarily affected in leukemia?

   a) Epithelial cells

   b) Red blood cells

   c) White blood cells

   d) Muscle cells

12. Which type of cancer is characterized by the formation of tumors in glandular tissues?

    a) Carcinomas

    b) Sarcomas

    c) Leukemias

    d) Adenocarcinomas

13. What is the role of tumor suppressor genes in cancer development?

    a) Promote cell growth

    b) Inhibit cell growth

    c) Repair DNA mutations

    d) Stimulate angiogenesis

14. Which cancer is commonly associated with the BRCA1 and BRCA2 genetic mutations?

    a) Lung cancer

    b) Prostate cancer

    c) Breast cancer

    d) Colorectal cancer

15. What is the primary treatment method for localized prostate cancer?

    a) Chemotherapy

    b) Radiation therapy

    c) Surgery

    d) Immunotherapy

16. Which cancer treatment uses high-energy radiation to kill cancer cells?

    a) Chemotherapy

    b) Targeted therapy

    c) Immunotherapy

    d) Radiation therapy

17. What is a common symptom of colorectal cancer?

    a) Persistent cough

b) Changes in bowel habits

c) Joint pain

d) Skin rash

18. Which lifestyle change can significantly reduce the risk of developing osteoporosis?

a) Smoking cessation

b) High-protein diet

c) Increased alcohol consumption

d) Regular exercise

19. What is the main purpose of hormone therapy in cancer treatment?

a) Stimulate immune response

b) Increase cell proliferation

c) Inhibit hormone-sensitive cancer growth

d) Enhance chemotherapy effects

20. Which condition is characterized by chronic inflammation and damage to the synovial membrane of joints?

a) Osteoarthritis

b) Gout

c) Rheumatoid arthritis

d) Osteoporosis

**Short Answer Type Questions (Subjective)**

1. What are the primary risk factors for developing osteoporosis?

2. Describe the pathophysiology of rheumatoid arthritis.

3. How is osteoarthritis diagnosed and managed?

4. Explain the role of uric acid in the development of gout.

5. What are the common symptoms and complications of lung cancer?

6. How is breast cancer typically diagnosed?

7. What lifestyle modifications can help manage osteoporosis?

8.  What are the treatment options for rheumatoid arthritis?

9.  Describe the pathophysiology of cancer metastasis.

10. What are the key differences between sarcomas and carcinomas?

11. How does smoking contribute to the development of lung cancer?

12. What are the common diagnostic tools used for colorectal cancer?

13. Explain the role of bisphosphonates in the treatment of osteoporosis.

14. What are the genetic factors involved in the development of breast cancer?

15. Describe the symptoms and complications of prostate cancer.

16. How is hormone therapy used in the treatment of breast cancer?

17. What are the primary causes of chronic kidney disease?

18. How is gout diagnosed and treated?

19. What are the primary prevention strategies for reducing the risk of colorectal cancer?

20. Describe the role of the immune system in the pathogenesis of cancer.


**Long Answer Type Questions (Subjective)**

1.  Discuss the classification of cancer based on tissue origin, including examples of each type.

2.  Explain the pathogenesis of rheumatoid arthritis and its impact on joint function and overall health.

3.  Describe the pathophysiology, symptoms, diagnosis, and treatment options for osteoporosis.

4.  Discuss the etiology, symptoms, diagnosis, and management of lung cancer.

5.  Explain the principles of cancer treatment, including surgery, chemotherapy, radiation therapy, targeted therapy, and immunotherapy.

6.  Describe the epidemiology, pathophysiology, diagnosis, and treatment of prostate cancer.

7.  Discuss the role of genetic and environmental factors in the development of cancer.

8. Explain the symptoms, complications, and management of chronic obstructive pulmonary disease (COPD).

9. Describe the diagnostic process and treatment options for colorectal cancer.

10. Discuss the prevention and management strategies for gout, including lifestyle modifications and medication.

**Answer Key for MCQ Questions**

1. c) Often asymptomatic
2. b) Bone density test (DEXA scan)
3. b) Autoimmune disorder
4. b) DMARDs
5. c) Degeneration of cartilage in joints
6. c) Big toe
7. b) Smoking
8. b) Mammography
9. c) Inhibit bone resorption
10. b) Estrogen
11. c) White blood cells
12. d) Adenocarcinomas
13. b) Inhibit cell growth
14. c) Breast cancer
15. c) Surgery
16. d) Radiation therapy
17. b) Changes in bowel habits
18. d) Regular exercise
19. c) Inhibit hormone-sensitive cancer growth
20. c) Rheumatoid arthritis

# CHAPTER – 7

## INFECTION AND SEXUALLY TRANSMITTED DISEASES

**INTRODUCTION:**

Infection and sexually transmitted diseases (STDs) encompass a broad range of conditions caused by pathogenic microorganisms. Here's a detailed introduction:

**Infection:**

**1. Definition:** Infection occurs when pathogenic microorganisms (bacteria, viruses, fungi, or parasites) invade and multiply within the body, leading to disease. The immune system usually defends against these invaders, but sometimes the pathogens overcome this defense and cause illness.

**2. Types of Infections:**

    a. **Bacterial Infections:** Caused by bacteria such as *Streptococcus*, *Staphylococcus*, and *Escherichia coli*. Examples include strep throat, tuberculosis, and urinary tract infections.

    b. **Viral Infections:** Caused by viruses like influenza, HIV, and hepatitis viruses. Examples include the common cold, HIV/AIDS, and hepatitis B and C.

    c. **Fungal Infections:** Caused by fungi such as *Candida* and *Aspergillus*. Examples include athlete's foot, ringworm, and candidiasis.

    d. **Parasitic Infections:** Caused by parasites like protozoa, helminths, and ectoparasites (e.g., lice, ticks). Examples include malaria (protozoa), hookworm (helminth), and scabies (ectoparasite).

**3. Transmission Routes:**

a. **Direct Contact:** Physical contact with infected individuals or their bodily fluids.

b. **Indirect Contact:** Contact with contaminated surfaces or objects.

c. **Airborne:** Inhalation of droplets containing pathogens.

d. **Vector-borne:** Transmission through vectors like mosquitoes (e.g., malaria).

e. **Fecal-oral:** Ingestion of contaminated food or water.

**4. Prevention and Control:**

a. **Vaccination:** Immunization against certain infectious diseases (e.g., measles, influenza).

b. **Hygiene:** Hand washing, sanitizing surfaces, and safe food handling.

c. **Safe Practices:** Using barriers (e.g., condoms), and safe practices in healthcare settings.

d. **Antimicrobial Medications:** Antibiotics, antivirals, antifungals, and antiparasitics as appropriate.

**Sexually Transmitted Diseases (STDs):**

**1. Definition:** STDs, also known as sexually transmitted infections (STIs), are infections transmitted primarily through sexual contact. They can also be transmitted through non-sexual means, such as from mother to child during childbirth or through blood transfusions.

**2. Common STDs:**

a. **Chlamydia:** Caused by *Chlamydia trachomatis*, often asymptomatic but can lead to pelvic inflammatory disease (PID) if untreated.

b. **Gonorrhea:** Caused by *Neisseria gonorrhoeae*, can cause urethritis, cervicitis, and PID.

c. **Syphilis:** Caused by *Treponema pallidum*, has primary, secondary, latent, and tertiary stages with varied symptoms.

d. **Herpes Simplex Virus (HSV):** Causes oral and genital herpes, characterized by painful sores.

e. **Human Papillomavirus (HPV):** Can cause genital warts and is associated with cervical and other cancers.

f. **Human Immunodeficiency Virus (HIV):** Leads to AIDS and compromises the immune system.

g. **Hepatitis B and C:** Affect the liver and can lead to chronic liver disease and cancer.

3. **Transmission:** STDs are primarily spread through:

a. Vaginal, anal, or oral sex.

b. Sharing of contaminated needles.

c. Direct contact with infectious lesions or bodily fluids.

4. **Symptoms:** Symptoms vary depending on the infection but can include:

a. Painful urination.

b. Unusual discharge from the genitalia.

c. Sores or ulcers in the genital area.

d. Itching or irritation.

5. **Diagnosis:**

a. **Laboratory Tests:** Including blood tests, urine tests, and cultures.

b. **Physical Examination:** To identify symptoms and signs of infection.

c. **Imaging:** In some cases, to assess the extent of disease or complications.

6. **Treatment:**

a. **Antibiotics:** For bacterial STDs (e.g., chlamydia, gonorrhea, syphilis).

b. **Antiviral Medications:** For viral STDs (e.g., HSV, HIV).

c. **Supportive Care:** For managing symptoms and complications.

7. **Prevention:**

a. **Safe Sex Practices:** Using condoms and reducing the number of sexual partners.

b. **Regular Screening:** Especially for high-risk individuals.

c. **Vaccination:** For HPV and hepatitis B.

**8. Public Health Considerations:**

a. **Education:** Raising awareness about prevention and symptoms.

b. **Access to Healthcare:** Ensuring availability of testing and treatment.

c. **Contact Tracing:** Identifying and notifying sexual partners to prevent spread.

## INFECTIOUS DISEASES

## MENINGITIS

**Introduction:**

Meningitis is an inflammation of the protective membranes (meninges) covering the brain and spinal cord. This condition can be caused by infections with viruses, bacteria, fungi, or parasites, as well as by non-infectious factors such as certain drugs or autoimmune diseases. Meningitis can lead to serious health complications and requires prompt medical attention.

**Pathophysiology**

1. **Entry and Spread:** Pathogens can enter the central nervous system (CNS) through the bloodstream, direct extension from nearby infected areas (e.g., sinusitis or otitis media), or through direct inoculation (e.g., trauma or surgery).

2. **Immune Response:** The body's immune response to the invading pathogen leads to inflammation of the meninges. This response includes the release of inflammatory mediators, increased permeability of the blood-brain barrier, and recruitment of immune cells.

3. **Cerebral Edema:** Inflammation can cause cerebral edema, increasing intracranial pressure. This can lead to decreased cerebral blood flow and potential damage to brain tissue.

4. **Neuronal Damage**: Persistent inflammation can result in neuronal damage and dysfunction, contributing to the neurological symptoms associated with meningitis.

**Epidemiology**

1. **Bacterial Meningitis**: Commonly caused by *Streptococcus pneumoniae*, *Neisseria meningitidis*, *Haemophilus influenzae*, and *Listeria monocytogenes*. Incidence varies by region and population, with higher rates in developing countries and certain high-risk groups.

2. **Viral Meningitis**: Often caused by enteroviruses, herpes simplex virus, varicella-zoster virus, and mumps virus. It is more common than bacterial meningitis but generally less severe.

3. **Fungal Meningitis**: Caused by fungi such as *Cryptococcus neoformans*, particularly in immunocompromised individuals.

4. **Parasitic Meningitis**: Rare, caused by parasites like *Naegleria fowleri*.

**Symptoms**

1. **General Symptoms**: Fever, headache, stiff neck, photophobia (sensitivity to light), and altered mental status.

2. **Bacterial Meningitis**: Symptoms are often more severe and can progress rapidly, including nausea, vomiting, seizures, and coma.

3. **Viral Meningitis**: Symptoms are usually milder and may include fever, headache, and neck stiffness, often resolving without specific treatment.

**Diagnosis**

1. **Clinical Evaluation**: Assessment of symptoms and physical examination, including checking for signs of meningeal irritation (e.g., Kernig's sign, Brudzinski's sign).

2. **Lumbar Puncture (Spinal Tap)**: Analysis of cerebrospinal fluid (CSF) to identify the presence of pathogens, inflammatory cells, and changes in CSF chemistry (e.g., glucose and protein levels).

3. **Microbiological Tests**: Gram stain, culture, polymerase chain reaction (PCR), and antigen detection tests on CSF samples.
4. **Imaging**: CT or MRI scans to assess for complications or to rule out other conditions.

**Treatment**

1. **Bacterial Meningitis**: Prompt empirical antibiotic therapy, adjusted based on the identified pathogen and its susceptibility. Common antibiotics include ceftriaxone, vancomycin, and ampicillin.
2. **Viral Meningitis**: Primarily supportive care, including hydration, pain management, and antiviral therapy if a specific virus is identified (e.g., acyclovir for herpes simplex virus).
3. **Fungal Meningitis**: Antifungal medications such as amphotericin B and flucytosine.
4. **Parasitic Meningitis**: Specific antiparasitic treatments depending on the causative organism.
5. **Supportive Care**: Management of symptoms, including fever control, hydration, and addressing complications such as seizures or increased intracranial pressure.

**Complications**

1. **Neurological Sequelae**: Hearing loss, cognitive deficits, motor impairments, and seizures.
2. **Hydrocephalus**: Accumulation of cerebrospinal fluid leading to increased intracranial pressure.
3. **Septic Shock**: Particularly in severe bacterial meningitis, can lead to multi-organ failure.
4. **Death**: Meningitis can be fatal, especially if not treated promptly and appropriately.

**Prevention**

1. **Vaccination**:

a. **Haemophilus influenzae type b (Hib)**: Vaccine for children.

b. **Pneumococcal Vaccines**: PCV13 and PPSV23 for children, adults, and high-risk groups.

c. **Meningococcal Vaccines**: MenACWY and MenB vaccines for adolescents and high-risk populations.

2. **Prophylactic Antibiotics**: For close contacts of individuals with meningococcal or Hib meningitis.

3. **Public Health Measures**:

a. **Hand Hygiene**: Regular handwashing to reduce the spread of infections.

b. **Safe Practices**: Avoiding close contact with infected individuals and using protective measures during outbreaks.

4. **Environmental Controls**: Reducing overcrowding and improving living conditions to decrease transmission risk.

## TYPHOID

### Introduction

Typhoid fever is a systemic bacterial infection caused by *Salmonella enterica* serotype Typhi (commonly referred to as *Salmonella Typhi*). The disease is characterized by prolonged fever, gastrointestinal disturbances, and systemic involvement. It is primarily transmitted through the ingestion of contaminated food and water and is a significant public health problem in developing countries.

### Pathophysiology

1. **Ingestion and Entry**: *Salmonella Typhi* is ingested through contaminated food or water and survives the acidic environment of the stomach.

2. **Invasion and Dissemination**: The bacteria penetrate the intestinal mucosa, enter the bloodstream, and are carried to various organs, including the liver, spleen, and bone marrow.

3. **Immune Response**: The host immune system responds, leading to the release of inflammatory cytokines. The bacteria can survive and replicate within macrophages, facilitating their spread.

4. **Biliary Excretion and Reinfection**: The bacteria are excreted into the biliary system and re-enter the intestines, leading to reinfection and shedding in feces.

**Epidemiology**

1. **Geographic Distribution**: Typhoid fever is endemic in many developing countries, particularly in South Asia, Southeast Asia, and sub-Saharan Africa.

2. **Incidence**: There are an estimated 11–20 million cases and 128,000–161,000 deaths annually worldwide.

3. **Risk Factors**: Poor sanitation, lack of clean drinking water, and overcrowding contribute to the spread of typhoid fever. Travelers to endemic areas are also at risk.

**Symptoms**

1. **Early Symptoms (1-2 weeks)**: Gradual onset of high fever, malaise, headache, and abdominal pain.

2. **Progressive Symptoms**: Sustained high fever, hepatosplenomegaly (enlarged liver and spleen), rose-colored spots on the abdomen, and relative bradycardia.

3. **Gastrointestinal Symptoms**: Diarrhea or constipation, nausea, vomiting, and abdominal distension.

**Diagnosis**

1. **Clinical Evaluation**: Based on symptoms and epidemiological context (travel history, contact with known cases).

2. **Laboratory Tests**:

    a. **Blood Culture**: The most definitive test, particularly during the first week of illness.

b. **Bone Marrow Culture**: More sensitive than blood culture and useful in chronic cases.

c. **Stool and Urine Cultures**: Useful in later stages of the disease.

d. **Serological Tests**: Widal test, though less specific and sensitive compared to cultures.

3. **Molecular Tests**: PCR for rapid and specific detection of *Salmonella Typhi* DNA.

**Treatment**

1. **Antibiotic Therapy**:

   a. **First-line**: Fluoroquinolones (e.g., ciprofloxacin) for non-resistant strains.

   b. **Second-line**: Third-generation cephalosporins (e.g., ceftriaxone) and azithromycin for resistant strains.

   c. **MDR and XDR Typhoid**: Multi-drug resistant (MDR) and extensively drug-resistant (XDR) strains require alternative treatment regimens.

2. **Supportive Care**: Hydration, antipyretics for fever, and nutritional support.

**Complications**

1. **Intestinal Perforation**: Can lead to peritonitis, a life-threatening condition requiring surgical intervention.

2. **Sepsis and Septic Shock**: Systemic infection leading to multiple organ dysfunction.

3. **Neuropsychiatric Symptoms**: Delirium, confusion, and other mental status changes.

4. **Chronic Carrier State**: Persistent excretion of bacteria in stool, posing a risk of transmission to others.

5. **Relapse**: Recurrence of symptoms after apparent recovery, often requiring additional treatment.

**Prevention**

1. **Vaccination**:

   a. **Typhoid Conjugate Vaccine (TCV)**: Recommended for children in endemic areas.

   b. **Oral Live-Attenuated Vaccine (Ty21a)**: Taken in capsule form.

   c. **Vi Capsular Polysaccharide Vaccine**: Injectable form, recommended for travelers.

2. **Sanitation and Hygiene**:

   a. **Safe Drinking Water**: Use of purified or boiled water.

   b. **Proper Sewage Disposal**: To prevent contamination of water supplies.

   c. **Hand Hygiene**: Regular handwashing with soap and clean water.

3. **Food Safety**:

   a. **Safe Food Handling**: Proper cooking and storage of food.

   b. **Avoiding Raw Foods**: Particularly in endemic areas where contamination is likely.

4. **Education and Awareness**: Public health campaigns to promote hygiene and vaccination, especially in high-risk areas.

**LEPROSY**

**Introduction**

Tuberculosis (TB) is a contagious bacterial infection caused by *Mycobacterium tuberculosis*. It primarily affects the lungs (pulmonary TB) but can also affect other parts of the body (extrapulmonary TB). TB is a major global health problem, causing significant morbidity and mortality, especially in developing countries.

**Pathophysiology**

1. **Infection and Spread**: *Mycobacterium tuberculosis* is transmitted via airborne droplets when an infected person coughs, sneezes, or talks. Inhaled bacteria reach the alveoli of the lungs.

2. **Immune Response**: Macrophages engulf the bacteria but may fail to destroy them, leading to the formation of granulomas (tubercles) to contain the infection.

3. **Latent TB Infection**: In most cases, the immune system controls the infection, leading to a latent TB infection (LTBI), where the bacteria remain dormant without causing symptoms.

4. **Active TB Disease**: If the immune system becomes weakened, the bacteria can reactivate, causing active TB disease with symptomatic and transmissible infection.

**Epidemiology**

1. **Global Distribution**: TB is found worldwide, with the highest prevalence in sub-Saharan Africa, Southeast Asia, and Eastern Europe.

2. **Incidence**: The World Health Organization (WHO) estimates around 10 million new TB cases and 1.4 million TB-related deaths annually.

3. **Risk Factors**: HIV infection, diabetes, malnutrition, smoking, and close contact with TB patients increase the risk of developing TB.

**Symptoms and Complications**

1. **Pulmonary TB**:
    a. **Symptoms**: Persistent cough (lasting more than three weeks), hemoptysis (coughing up blood), chest pain, fatigue, weight loss, night sweats, and fever.

2. **Extrapulmonary TB**:
    a. **Symptoms**: Depend on the affected organ; can include lymphadenopathy, pleuritic chest pain, abdominal pain, bone and joint pain, and neurological symptoms.

3. **Complications**:
    a. **Respiratory Failure**: Due to extensive lung damage.
    b. **Miliary TB**: Disseminated TB causing widespread infection in multiple organs.

c. **TB Meningitis**: Infection of the meninges leading to severe neurological complications.

d. **Pericarditis**: TB infection of the pericardium causing pericardial effusion and tamponade.

**Diagnosis**

1. **Clinical Evaluation**: Assessment of symptoms and medical history, including exposure to TB.

2. **Microbiological Tests**:

    a. **Sputum Microscopy**: Acid-fast bacilli (AFB) staining.

    b. **Culture**: Gold standard for TB diagnosis, though it takes several weeks.

    c. **Nucleic Acid Amplification Tests (NAATs)**: Rapid and specific detection of *M. tuberculosis* DNA.

3. **Imaging**:

    a. **Chest X-ray**: To identify lung abnormalities consistent with TB.

    b. **CT Scan**: For detailed imaging, especially in extrapulmonary TB.

4. **Tuberculin Skin Test (TST)** and **Interferon-Gamma Release Assays (IGRAs)**: Used to detect latent TB infection.

**Treatment**

1. **First-line Anti-TB Drugs**: Standard regimen includes a combination of:

    a. **Isoniazid (INH)**

    b. **Rifampicin (RIF)**

    c. **Pyrazinamide (PZA)**

    d. **Ethambutol (EMB)**

    e. Initial intensive phase (2 months) followed by a continuation phase (4 months) with INH and RIF.

2. **Drug-Resistant TB**:

a. **Multidrug-Resistant TB (MDR-TB)**: Resistant to at least INH and RIF, requiring second-line drugs like fluoroquinolones and injectable agents.

b. **Extensively Drug-Resistant TB (XDR-TB)**: Resistant to first-line and several second-line drugs, needing more complex and prolonged treatment regimens.

3. **Supportive Care**: Nutritional support, management of side effects, and treatment of comorbid conditions.

**Complications**

1. **Chronic Pulmonary TB**: Leading to extensive lung damage, fibrosis, and respiratory failure.

2. **Relapse**: Recurrence of TB after successful treatment, often due to incomplete treatment or drug resistance.

3. **Disseminated TB**: Spread of TB to multiple organs, causing systemic illness.

4. **Social and Economic Impact**: Stigma, loss of productivity, and financial burden on patients and their families.

**Prevention**

1. **BCG Vaccination**: Bacille Calmette-Guérin (BCG) vaccine provides some protection against TB, especially severe forms in children.

2. **Infection Control Measures**:

a. **Early Detection and Treatment**: Prompt identification and treatment of active TB cases to reduce transmission.

b. **Isolation of Infectious Patients**: In healthcare settings and at home to prevent spread.

c. **Use of Personal Protective Equipment (PPE)**: For healthcare workers and caregivers.

3. **Public Health Education**: Raising awareness about TB transmission, symptoms, and the importance of completing treatment.

4. **Screening and Prophylaxis**:

   a. **Latent TB Infection**: Screening high-risk individuals (e.g., HIV-infected, close contacts of TB patients) and providing prophylactic treatment to prevent progression to active disease.

## URINARY TRACT INFECTIONS

### Introduction

Urinary tract infections (UTIs) are infections that affect any part of the urinary system, including the kidneys, ureters, bladder, and urethra. Most UTIs involve the lower urinary tract—the bladder and the urethra. UTIs are more common in women than men and can range from asymptomatic bacteriuria to severe kidney infections.

### Pathophysiology

1. **Entry and Colonization**: Pathogens typically enter the urinary tract through the urethra and begin to multiply in the bladder. The most common causative organism is *Escherichia coli* (E. coli), which is part of the normal gastrointestinal flora.

2. **Ascending Infection**: The bacteria can ascend from the bladder to the kidneys, causing pyelonephritis, a more severe infection.

3. **Host Defense Mechanisms**: The body has several defense mechanisms, including the flow of urine, the urinary tract's mucosal lining, and the immune response to prevent infections. When these defenses are compromised, UTIs are more likely to occur.

### Epidemiology

1. **Incidence**: UTIs are one of the most common infections, particularly among women. It is estimated that nearly 50-60% of women will experience a UTI at some point in their lives.

2. **Risk Factors**: Sexual activity, certain types of birth control (such as diaphragms), menopause, urinary tract abnormalities, blockages in the

urinary tract, a suppressed immune system, catheter use, and recent urinary procedures.

**Symptoms and Complications**

1. **Lower UTI (Cystitis)**:
    a. **Symptoms**: Dysuria (painful urination), frequent urination, urgency, cloudy or strong-smelling urine, hematuria (blood in the urine), and lower abdominal discomfort.

2. **Upper UTI (Pyelonephritis)**:
    a. **Symptoms**: Fever, chills, flank pain, nausea, vomiting, and severe cases can include signs of sepsis.

3. **Complications**:
    a. **Recurrent Infections**: Multiple UTIs, particularly in women.
    b. **Chronic Kidney Disease**: Repeated or severe kidney infections can lead to permanent kidney damage.
    c. **Sepsis**: A severe and potentially life-threatening response to infection.
    d. **Pregnancy Complications**: Increased risk of delivering low birth weight or premature infants.

**Diagnosis**

1. **Clinical Evaluation**: Assessment of symptoms and medical history.
2. **Urine Tests**:
    a. **Urinalysis**: Detection of pyuria (white blood cells in the urine), bacteriuria, hematuria, and nitrites.
    b. **Urine Culture**: Identifies the specific causative organism and its antibiotic sensitivities.
3. **Imaging**:
    a. **Ultrasound or CT Scan**: Used in complicated UTIs to assess for structural abnormalities, obstructions, or abscesses.
4. **Special Tests**:

a. **Cystoscopy**: In cases of recurrent UTIs to visualize the bladder and urethra.

**Treatment**

1. **Antibiotic Therapy**:
    a. **Uncomplicated UTIs**: Short-course antibiotics such as trimethoprim/sulfamethoxazole, nitrofurantoin, or fosfomycin.
    b. **Complicated UTIs**: Longer courses and possibly intravenous antibiotics, depending on the severity and the patient's health status.
    c. **Pyelonephritis**: Requires longer courses of antibiotics, often starting with intravenous therapy followed by oral antibiotics.
2. **Supportive Care**:
    a. **Hydration**: Encouraging fluid intake to help flush the urinary system.
    b. **Pain Relief**: Analgesics such as phenazopyridine can help relieve pain and discomfort.
3. **Treatment of Underlying Conditions**: Addressing any structural abnormalities or other risk factors contributing to recurrent infections.

**Complications**

1. **Recurrent Infections**: Frequent UTIs may lead to a cycle of reinfection.
2. **Kidney Damage**: Chronic or severe infections can cause permanent kidney damage.
3. **Urethral Stricture**: Scarring and narrowing of the urethra.
4. **Sepsis**: Particularly in the case of pyelonephritis, untreated UTIs can lead to systemic infection and sepsis, a life-threatening condition.

**Prevention**

1. **Hydration**: Drinking plenty of fluids, especially water, to help flush out bacteria from the urinary tract.
2. **Hygiene Practices**: Wiping from front to back after urination and bowel movements to prevent bacteria from the anus from entering the urethra.

3. **Urination Habits**: Urinating frequently and not holding urine for extended periods; urinating immediately after sexual intercourse to help clear bacteria.

4. **Avoiding Irritants**: Avoiding the use of potentially irritating feminine products such as deodorant sprays, douches, and powders.

5. **Prophylactic Antibiotics**: In certain cases of recurrent UTIs, low-dose antibiotics may be prescribed for a period of time.

6. **Cranberry Products**: Some studies suggest that cranberry juice or supplements may help reduce the risk of recurrent UTIs, although evidence is mixed.

**SEXUALLY TRANSMITTED DISEASES**

**AIDS**

**Introduction**

Acquired Immunodeficiency Syndrome (AIDS) is the final and most severe stage of infection caused by the Human Immunodeficiency Virus (HIV). HIV attacks and weakens the immune system by destroying CD4+ T cells, leaving the body vulnerable to opportunistic infections and certain cancers. Without treatment, most individuals with HIV will develop AIDS.

**Pathophysiology**

1. **HIV Infection**: HIV primarily targets CD4+ T cells, a type of white blood cell crucial for immune function. The virus binds to CD4 receptors and co-receptors (CCR5 or CXCR4) on the cell surface, allowing it to enter the cell.

2. **Viral Replication**: Once inside, HIV uses reverse transcriptase to convert its RNA into DNA, which is then integrated into the host cell's genome by the enzyme integrase. The virus hijacks the host cell's machinery to produce new viral particles.

3. **Immune System Decline**: Over time, the continuous destruction of CD4+ T cells leads to a gradual decline in immune function. When CD4+ T cell counts drop below 200 cells per microliter or when certain opportunistic infections or cancers develop, the condition progresses to AIDS.

**Epidemiology**

1. **Global Distribution**: AIDS is a global epidemic, with the highest prevalence in sub-Saharan Africa. Significant numbers of cases are also found in Asia, Latin America, Eastern Europe, and parts of North America.

2. **Incidence and Prevalence**: According to the World Health Organization (WHO) and UNAIDS, there were approximately 38 million people living with HIV/AIDS worldwide in 2019. Despite advances in treatment, millions of new infections and AIDS-related deaths occur each year.

3. **Risk Factors**: Major risk factors include unprotected sexual intercourse, sharing of contaminated needles, transfusion of infected blood products, and from mother to child during childbirth or breastfeeding.

**Symptoms and Complications**

1. **Acute HIV Infection**:
   a. **Symptoms**: Flu-like symptoms (fever, sore throat, rash, muscle aches) occurring 2-4 weeks after infection.

2. **Clinical Latency Stage**:
   a. **Symptoms**: The virus is active but reproduces at low levels. Most people do not exhibit symptoms, although some may experience generalized lymphadenopathy (swollen lymph nodes).

3. **AIDS**:
   a. **Symptoms**: Severe immune deficiency leading to opportunistic infections (e.g., Pneumocystis pneumonia, tuberculosis, candidiasis), cancers (e.g., Kaposi's sarcoma, lymphomas), wasting syndrome, and neurological complications (e.g., HIV-associated dementia).

**Diagnosis**

1. **HIV Testing**:
   a. **Antibody Tests**: Detect antibodies to HIV in blood or oral fluid, typically becoming positive within 3-12 weeks after infection.

b. **Combination or 4th Generation Tests**: Detect both HIV antibodies and p24 antigen, reducing the window period to about 2-4 weeks after infection.

c. **Nucleic Acid Tests (NATs)**: Detect HIV RNA and can identify infection as early as 1-2 weeks post-exposure.

2. **CD4 Count**: Measures the number of CD4+ T cells in the blood. A count below 200 cells per microliter is indicative of AIDS.

3. **Viral Load Test**: Quantifies the amount of HIV RNA in the blood, guiding treatment decisions and monitoring therapy effectiveness.

**Treatment**

1. **Antiretroviral Therapy (ART)**: The standard treatment for HIV/AIDS, involving a combination of antiretroviral drugs to suppress viral replication, boost immune function, and prevent progression to AIDS. Common ART regimens include:

   a. **Nucleoside/Nucleotide Reverse Transcriptase Inhibitors (NRTIs)**: e.g., tenofovir, emtricitabine.

   b. **Non-Nucleoside Reverse Transcriptase Inhibitors (NNRTIs)**: e.g., efavirenz, rilpivirine.

   c. **Protease Inhibitors (PIs)**: e.g., atazanavir, darunavir.

   d. **Integrase Strand Transfer Inhibitors (INSTIs)**: e.g., dolutegravir, bictegravir.

   e. **Entry Inhibitors**: e.g., maraviroc (CCR5 antagonist), enfuvirtide (fusion inhibitor).

2. **Prophylaxis and Treatment of Opportunistic Infections**: Medications such as trimethoprim-sulfamethoxazole for Pneumocystis pneumonia, and antifungals for candidiasis.

3. **Regular Monitoring**: Regular follow-up visits to monitor CD4 counts, viral load, and potential drug side effects.

**Complications**

1. **Opportunistic Infections**: Increased susceptibility to infections like tuberculosis, Pneumocystis pneumonia, and cytomegalovirus.
2. **Cancers**: Higher risk of cancers such as Kaposi's sarcoma, non-Hodgkin lymphoma, and invasive cervical cancer.
3. **Neurological Complications**: HIV-associated neurocognitive disorders, including dementia and peripheral neuropathy.
4. **Cardiovascular Disease**: Increased risk of cardiovascular complications due to chronic inflammation and ART side effects.

**Prevention**

1. **Safe Sex Practices**: Using condoms consistently and correctly, reducing the number of sexual partners, and knowing the HIV status of partners.
2. **Pre-Exposure Prophylaxis (PrEP)**: Daily medication for HIV-negative individuals at high risk of infection.
3. **Post-Exposure Prophylaxis (PEP)**: Emergency treatment started within 72 hours after potential exposure to HIV.
4. **Needle Exchange Programs**: Providing clean needles to reduce the risk of HIV transmission among people who inject drugs.
5. **Mother-to-Child Transmission Prevention**: ART for HIV-positive pregnant women, safe delivery practices, and avoiding breastfeeding when alternatives are available.
6. **Regular Testing and Early Treatment**: Routine HIV testing for early detection and prompt initiation of ART to reduce transmission and improve outcomes.
7. **Public Health Education**: Increasing awareness about HIV transmission, testing, and prevention strategies.

## SYPHILIS

**Introduction**

Syphilis is a sexually transmitted infection (STI) caused by the bacterium *Treponema pallidum*. It is a chronic disease with stages that can span many years, and if left untreated, it can cause serious health problems, including damage to the heart, brain, and other organs.

**Pathophysiology**

1. **Infection and Initial Spread**: Syphilis is primarily spread through direct contact with syphilitic sores (chancres) during sexual activity. The bacteria enter the body through mucous membranes or broken skin.

2. **Stages of Disease**:
    a. **Primary Syphilis**: Characterized by a single sore (chancre) at the site of infection. The chancre is typically painless and heals within a few weeks, but the bacteria remain in the body.
    b. **Secondary Syphilis**: Occurs weeks to months after the initial infection. The bacteria spread throughout the body, causing a widespread rash, often on the palms and soles, along with systemic symptoms.
    c. **Latent Syphilis**: A period with no symptoms. The infection can remain latent for years. During early latency, the infection can still be transmitted; late latent syphilis is not infectious.
    d. **Tertiary Syphilis**: Develops in about 30% of untreated cases years after the initial infection, leading to severe medical problems affecting the heart, brain, and other organs.

**Epidemiology**

1. **Global Distribution**: Syphilis is a global health issue, with higher prevalence in certain regions, including sub-Saharan Africa, Southeast Asia, and parts of Latin America.

2. **Incidence**: According to the World Health Organization (WHO), there are millions of new syphilis cases each year. The incidence has been rising in many countries, including high-income nations.

3. **Risk Factors**: Unprotected sexual intercourse, multiple sexual partners, men who have sex with men (MSM), HIV infection, and co-infection with other STIs.

**Symptoms and Complications**

1. **Primary Syphilis**:

    a. **Symptoms**: A single chancre, which is usually firm, round, and painless, appearing at the site where *Treponema pallidum* entered the body. The chancre heals spontaneously within 3-6 weeks.

2. **Secondary Syphilis**:

    a. **Symptoms**: Skin rash, often on the palms of the hands and soles of the feet; mucous membrane lesions; fever; sore throat; lymphadenopathy; patchy hair loss; headaches; weight loss; muscle aches; and fatigue.

3. **Latent Syphilis**: No visible symptoms, but serological tests for syphilis are positive.

4. **Tertiary Syphilis**:

    a. **Symptoms**: Severe medical problems, including gummas (soft, non-cancerous growths), cardiovascular syphilis (e.g., aortic aneurysm), and neurosyphilis (e.g., meningitis, dementia, tabes dorsalis).

**Diagnosis**

1. **Clinical Evaluation**: Based on history, physical examination, and the presence of characteristic signs and symptoms.

2. **Serological Tests**:

    a. **Non-Treponemal Tests**: Rapid Plasma Reagin (RPR) and Venereal Disease Research Laboratory (VDRL) tests, which detect antibodies produced in response to cellular damage caused by the infection.

    b. **Treponemal Tests**: Fluorescent Treponemal Antibody Absorption (FTA-ABS) and Treponema pallidum Particle Agglutination (TPPA), which detect antibodies specific to *Treponema pallidum*.

3. **Darkfield Microscopy**: Used to visualize *Treponema pallidum* from chancres or lesions.

4. **Direct Fluorescent Antibody Test**: Used to detect the presence of *Treponema pallidum* in lesion exudate or tissue.

**Treatment**

1. **Antibiotic Therapy**:
    a. **Primary and Secondary Syphilis**: Single intramuscular injection of benzathine penicillin G. For penicillin-allergic patients, doxycycline or tetracycline may be used.
    b. **Latent Syphilis**: Three weekly injections of benzathine penicillin G for late latent syphilis or syphilis of unknown duration.
    c. **Neurosyphilis**: Intravenous penicillin G for 10-14 days.

2. **Monitoring and Follow-up**: Serological testing at 6, 12, and 24 months after treatment to ensure the effectiveness of therapy and monitor for reinfection.

**Complications**

1. **Neurological Complications**: Neurosyphilis, which can cause meningitis, stroke, dementia, and sensory deficits.

2. **Cardiovascular Complications**: Aortitis, aortic aneurysm, and aortic valve insufficiency.

3. **Gummatous Syphilis**: Formation of gummas, which are destructive lesions that can affect skin, bone, and other organs.

4. **Congenital Syphilis**: Occurs when a pregnant woman with syphilis transmits the infection to her unborn child, leading to severe complications or fetal death.

**Prevention**

1. **Safe Sexual Practices**: Using condoms consistently and correctly, reducing the number of sexual partners, and engaging in mutually monogamous relationships with partners who have tested negative for STIs.

2. **Regular Screening and Early Detection**: Routine syphilis screening for high-risk populations, including pregnant women, MSM, and individuals with HIV.

3. **Treatment of Sexual Partners**: Ensuring that sexual partners of infected individuals are tested and treated to prevent reinfection and further spread of the disease.

4. **Public Health Education**: Raising awareness about syphilis transmission, symptoms, and the importance of early detection and treatment.

5. **Prenatal Care**: Routine syphilis screening for all pregnant women to prevent congenital syphilis.

## GONORRHEA

**Introduction:**

Gonorrhea is a common sexually transmitted infection (STI) caused by the bacterium *Neisseria gonorrhoeae*. It primarily affects the mucous membranes of the urogenital tract but can also infect the rectum, throat, and eyes. Gonorrhea is known for its potential to cause serious reproductive and other health problems if left untreated.

**Pathophysiology:**

**1. Infection Mechanism**

a. **Entry and Adherence**: *Neisseria gonorrhoeae*, the causative bacterium of gonorrhea, enters the body through mucous membranes during sexual contact. This typically involves the urethra in men and the endocervix in women, but it can also infect the rectum, throat, and eyes. The bacteria adhere to epithelial cells using pili (fimbriae) and other surface structures like outer membrane proteins, which interact with host cell receptors.

b. **Invasion and Colonization**: After adherence, the bacteria invade the epithelial cells and penetrate the underlying mucosal layers. The bacteria replicate within the epithelial cells and can cause local tissue damage.

This invasion is facilitated by bacterial surface structures that help resist host immune responses.

## 2. Immune Response and Inflammation

a. **Local Inflammatory Response**: The body's immune response to *N. gonorrhoeae* involves the recruitment of neutrophils (a type of white blood cell) to the site of infection. These neutrophils attempt to engulf and kill the bacteria. This response results in the characteristic purulent discharge associated with gonorrhea due to the accumulation of dead bacteria, neutrophils, and cellular debris.

b. **Evasion of the Immune System**: *N. gonorrhoeae* has several mechanisms to evade the host immune system, including:

   i. **Antigenic Variation**: The bacteria frequently change their surface proteins to avoid detection by the immune system.

   ii. **Phase Variation**: Alteration of the expression of surface molecules like pili to escape immune recognition.

   iii. **Resistance to Phagocytosis**: The bacteria produce substances that inhibit phagocytosis and damage immune cells.

## 3. Dissemination

a. **Local Spread**: Initially, the infection is localized to the mucosal surface, but the bacteria can spread to adjacent tissues, causing complications like pelvic inflammatory disease (PID) in women or epididymitis in men.

b. **Systemic Infection**: In some cases, *N. gonorrhoeae* can enter the bloodstream, leading to disseminated gonococcal infection (DGI). This condition can cause systemic symptoms and affect various organs. DGI is characterized by:

   i. **Septic Arthritis**: Infection of the joints, often presenting with joint pain, swelling, and inflammation.

   ii. **Dermatitis**: Skin lesions that may be pustular or papular.

   iii. **Endocarditis**: Infection of the heart valves, although less common.

**4. Complications and Long-Term Effects**

a. **Reproductive Health Issues**:

i. **Pelvic Inflammatory Disease (PID)**: In women, untreated gonorrhea can ascend to the upper reproductive tract, causing PID. PID can lead to chronic pelvic pain, infertility, and ectopic pregnancy.

ii. **Epididymitis**: In men, gonorrhea can cause inflammation of the epididymis, potentially leading to infertility.

b. **Increased Risk of HIV**: Gonorrhea infection increases susceptibility to HIV due to inflammation and mucosal damage, which can facilitate HIV transmission and acquisition.

c. **Neonatal Complications**: Infected mothers can transmit gonorrhea to their newborns during childbirth, potentially causing neonatal conjunctivitis (ophthalmia neonatorum), which can lead to blindness if not treated.

**5. Pathogen Characteristics**

a. **Bacterial Structure**: *N. gonorrhoeae* is a Gram-negative diplococcus with a distinctive kidney-bean shape. Its cell wall structure, which includes lipooligosaccharides (LOS) rather than lipopolysaccharides (LPS), plays a role in immune evasion and pathogenicity.

b. **Virulence Factors**:

i. **Pili (Fimbriae)**: Enhance adherence to epithelial cells and help in establishing infection.

ii. **Outer Membrane Proteins**: Contribute to adherence and immune evasion.

iii. **Peptidoglycan Layer**: Contributes to the bacteria's ability to resist phagocytosis and survive within host tissues.

**Epidemiology:**

**1. Global Prevalence**

b. **Global Burden**: Gonorrhea is a widespread sexually transmitted infection (STI) with an estimated 87 million new cases globally each year, according to the World Health Organization (WHO). The prevalence varies significantly across different regions and populations.

c. **Regional Variations**:
   i. **Sub-Saharan Africa**: High rates of gonorrhea are reported, with significant public health impacts.
   ii. **Southeast Asia**: Moderate to high prevalence, often exacerbated by factors like high-risk sexual behavior and limited access to healthcare.
   iii. **Western Countries**: Gonorrhea rates have seen fluctuations; recent years have shown increases in cases, often due to antibiotic resistance and changes in sexual behavior.

**2. Incidence and Prevalence Rates**

a. **Incidence Rates**: Vary by region, age group, and sexual behavior. In high-income countries, gonorrhea incidence is rising in certain populations, such as men who have sex with men (MSM) and young adults.

b. **Prevalence Rates**:
   i. **United States**: High prevalence, with over 600,000 reported cases annually. The rates are particularly high among adolescents and young adults, as well as among MSM.
   ii. **United Kingdom**: Increasing incidence, particularly in urban areas and among younger populations.

**3. Demographic Factors**

a. **Age**: Gonorrhea is most common among young adults aged 15-24 years. This age group is at higher risk due to higher rates of sexual activity and multiple partners.

b. **Gender**: While gonorrhea can affect both men and women, prevalence rates can differ. Women are often more symptomatic and have higher rates of complications such as pelvic inflammatory disease (PID), but men are more likely to present with symptomatic infection.

c. **Sexual Orientation**: Higher prevalence is observed among MSM, partly due to higher rates of multiple partners and unprotected sex.

## 4. Risk Factors

a. **Unprotected Sexual Intercourse**: Lack of condom use increases the risk of gonorrhea transmission.

b. **Multiple Sexual Partners**: Higher numbers of sexual partners increase the likelihood of exposure to gonorrhea.

c. **Sexually Transmitted Infections (STIs)**: Co-infection with other STIs, such as chlamydia, can increase the risk of gonorrhea. Additionally, gonorrhea itself increases susceptibility to HIV.

d. **Drug Use**: Injecting drug use is associated with higher rates of STI transmission due to risky sexual behaviors often associated with drug use.

e. **Socioeconomic Factors**: Lower socioeconomic status is linked to higher prevalence due to factors like limited access to healthcare, education, and preventive services.

## 5. Geographic Distribution

a. **Urban vs. Rural Areas**: Gonorrhea is generally more prevalent in urban areas compared to rural regions, due to higher population density and potentially higher rates of risky sexual behavior.

b. **Developed vs. Developing Countries**: Higher prevalence and incidence in developing countries often due to lower healthcare access, higher rates of high-risk sexual behavior, and less effective public health interventions.

## 6. Trends and Changes

a. **Antibiotic Resistance**: There has been an increase in antibiotic-resistant strains of *Neisseria gonorrhoeae*, particularly to commonly used treatments like penicillin and tetracyclines. This has led to changes in treatment guidelines and an increase in the need for more effective antibiotics.

b. **Public Health Responses**: Increased screening and public health campaigns in many countries aim to reduce gonorrhea rates and improve treatment outcomes. However, gaps remain in coverage and effectiveness, particularly in underserved populations.

c. **Impact of COVID-19**: The COVID-19 pandemic has affected STI testing and treatment services, potentially leading to delays in diagnosis and increased transmission rates.

## 7. Surveillance and Monitoring

a. **Public Health Agencies**: Organizations like the Centers for Disease Control and Prevention (CDC) and the World Health Organization (WHO) monitor gonorrhea rates and provide guidelines for prevention, diagnosis, and treatment.

b. **Screening Programs**: Many countries have screening programs targeting high-risk populations, such as sexually active adolescents, MSM, and pregnant women, to detect and manage gonorrhea early.

**Symptoms and Complications:**

## 1. Symptoms

**In Men:**

a. **Urethritis**: The most common symptom, characterized by a purulent, yellowish-green discharge from the urethra. Men often experience dysuria (painful urination) and increased frequency of urination.

b. **Epididymitis**: Inflammation of the epididymis, presenting as scrotal pain and swelling. This can lead to discomfort and potentially affect fertility if left untreated.

c. **Pharyngitis**: When gonorrhea infects the throat, it can cause a sore throat, although many infections in this area are asymptomatic.

d. **Proctitis**: Rectal infection can cause discomfort, rectal bleeding, and mucopurulent discharge. This is more common in individuals engaging in receptive anal intercourse.

**In Women:**

a. **Endocervicitis**: The most common presentation, involving abnormal vaginal discharge, which may be thick, yellow, or green, and may be accompanied by dysuria and intermenstrual bleeding (spotting between periods).

b. **Pelvic Inflammatory Disease (PID)**: Untreated gonorrhea can ascend to the uterus and fallopian tubes, causing PID. Symptoms include lower abdominal pain, fever, abnormal vaginal discharge, and pain during intercourse. PID can lead to serious reproductive complications.

c. **Vaginitis**: Inflammation of the vagina, often causing itching, soreness, and abnormal discharge.

d. **Pharyngitis**: Throat infection can occur but is usually asymptomatic.

e. **Proctitis**: Symptoms include anal itching, rectal bleeding, and pain during bowel movements, especially if the infection is acquired through anal intercourse.

**In Both Genders:**

a. **Disseminated Gonococcal Infection (DGI)**: When the infection spreads from the primary site to other areas of the body, it can cause systemic symptoms such as fever, rash, and arthritis. DGI can present as:

   i. **Arthritis**: Joint pain, swelling, and inflammation.

   ii. **Dermatitis**: Skin rash, often appearing as pustules or papules.

   iii. **Tenosynovitis**: Inflammation of the tendons and their sheaths, leading to pain and swelling.

   iv. **Endocarditis**: Infection of the heart valves, though this is less common.

**Neonates:**

a. **Ophthalmia Neonatorum**: Newborns exposed to gonorrhea during childbirth may develop conjunctivitis, which can lead to severe complications like blindness if untreated.

## 2. Complications

**In Men:**

a. **Infertility**: Chronic infection or complications like epididymitis can lead to scarring and obstruction, potentially causing infertility.

b. **Chronic Urethritis**: Persistent infection can result in ongoing urethral discomfort and discharge.

c. **Recurrent Gonorrhea**: Re-infection is possible if sexual partners are not treated simultaneously.

**In Women:**

a. **Infertility**: PID can cause scarring of the fallopian tubes and other reproductive organs, increasing the risk of infertility.

b. **Ectopic Pregnancy**: PID increases the risk of ectopic pregnancy, where the embryo implants outside the uterus, usually in the fallopian tubes.

c. **Chronic Pelvic Pain**: PID and other complications can lead to ongoing pelvic pain.

**In Both Genders:**

a. **Disseminated Gonococcal Infection (DGI)**: As mentioned, this systemic spread can lead to severe joint, skin, and systemic symptoms. DGI can be life-threatening if not treated promptly.

b. **Increased Risk of HIV**: Gonorrhea can cause mucosal inflammation, increasing susceptibility to HIV transmission and acquisition.

c. **Complications of Ocular Infection**: In neonates, untreated ophthalmia neonatorum can lead to severe vision impairment or blindness.

**Management and Monitoring**

1. **Antibiotic Treatment**: Effective treatment with antibiotics is crucial to resolving symptoms and preventing complications. Dual therapy with ceftriaxone and azithromycin is typically recommended.

2. **Follow-Up**: Patients should be re-evaluated to ensure that the infection has been eradicated and to assess for any potential complications.

3. **Partner Treatment**: Sexual partners should be tested and treated to prevent reinfection and further spread of the disease.

4. **Regular Screening**: Routine screening for individuals at high risk of gonorrhea can help detect and treat the infection early, reducing the risk of complications.

**Diagnosis:**

**1. Clinical Evaluation**

a. **History and Symptoms**: Diagnosis often starts with a detailed patient history and symptom assessment. Common symptoms include urethral discharge in men, abnormal vaginal discharge in women, and dysuria. For rectal or pharyngeal infections, symptoms might include anal itching, sore throat, or rectal bleeding.

b. **Physical Examination**: A physical examination can provide clues to the presence of gonorrhea, especially in symptomatic cases. This may involve examining the genital area for discharge, tenderness, or other signs of infection. For women, a pelvic examination may be necessary to assess for signs of pelvic inflammatory disease (PID).

**2. Laboratory Tests**

a. **Nucleic Acid Amplification Tests (NAATs):**

    i. **Description**: NAATs are the most sensitive and specific tests for detecting *Neisseria gonorrhoeae*. They detect bacterial DNA or RNA in various samples.

    ii. **Types of Samples**: NAATs can be performed on urine samples, urethral swabs (for men), endocervical swabs (for women), vaginal swabs, and pharyngeal and rectal swabs if infection in these sites is suspected.

    iii. **Advantages**: High sensitivity and specificity, ability to detect asymptomatic infections, and suitability for a variety of specimen types.

b. **Culture:**

    i. **Description**: Culturing *N. gonorrhoeae* from clinical specimens allows for isolation and identification of the bacteria.

    ii. **Types of Samples**: Urethral swabs (men), endocervical swabs (women), and samples from other sites such as the rectum and throat.

    iii. **Advantages**: Useful for confirming diagnosis, performing antibiotic susceptibility testing to guide treatment in case of resistance, and detecting antibiotic-resistant strains.

c. **Gram Stain:**

    i. **Description**: A Gram stain of a urethral discharge in symptomatic men can show Gram-negative diplococci within polymorphonuclear leukocytes (PMNs).

ii. **Advantages**: Provides rapid results and is particularly useful in diagnosing symptomatic men.

iii. **Limitations**: Less reliable in women, and less sensitive in pharyngeal and rectal infections.

d. **Rapid Antigen Tests**:

i. **Description**: These tests detect gonococcal antigens in samples.

ii. **Advantages**: Provide quick results.

iii. **Limitations**: Generally less sensitive and specific compared to NAATs and cultures, and are not widely used.

## 3. Screening and Testing

a. **Routine Screening**:

i. **High-Risk Populations**: Regular screening is recommended for sexually active individuals at higher risk, such as adolescents, young adults, MSM, and those with multiple sexual partners.

ii. **Pregnant Women**: Screening for gonorrhea is recommended during pregnancy to prevent transmission to the neonate.

b. **Partner Testing**:

i. **Importance**: All sexual partners of individuals diagnosed with gonorrhea should be tested and treated to prevent reinfection and further spread of the disease.

## 4. Diagnostic Considerations

a. **Coinfections**: Gonorrhea is often tested for alongside other STIs, such as chlamydia, due to the high likelihood of co-infection. Dual infection can complicate diagnosis and treatment, so testing for both is essential.

b. **Complications and Dissemination**: In cases of suspected disseminated gonococcal infection (DGI) or complicated infections, additional tests such as blood cultures or imaging studies may be required to assess systemic involvement and guide treatment.

**5. Diagnostic Algorithm**

    a. **Symptomatic Individuals**: For individuals presenting with symptoms of gonorrhea, NAATs are typically the first-line diagnostic test. If NAATs are unavailable or if there are symptoms at multiple sites, cultures may also be performed.

    b. **Asymptomatic Individuals**: For screening purposes, NAATs on urine samples or self-collected swabs are commonly used. In high-risk groups, regular screening can detect asymptomatic infections before they lead to complications.

    c. **Follow-Up**: In cases of persistent symptoms or suspected treatment failure, repeat testing, including NAATs or cultures, may be necessary to confirm diagnosis and ensure resolution of the infection.

Accurate and timely diagnosis of gonorrhea is crucial for effective treatment and prevention of complications. Utilizing a combination of clinical evaluation and laboratory tests helps ensure a comprehensive approach to managing this STI.

**Treatment:**

**1.Recommended Antibiotic Therapy**

    a. **First-Line Treatment**: Current guidelines from the Centers for Disease Control and Prevention (CDC) and other health organizations recommend dual therapy for gonorrhea to ensure effective treatment and reduce the risk of resistance. The standard regimen includes:

        1. **Ceftriaxone**:

            i. **Dosage**: 500 mg administered intramuscularly (IM) as a single dose.

            ii. **Role**: Ceftriaxone is a broad-spectrum cephalosporin antibiotic effective against *Neisseria gonorrhoeae* and is used as the primary treatment due to its efficacy and low resistance rates.

2. **Azithromycin**:
   i. **Dosage**: 1 g orally as a single dose.
   ii. **Role**: Azithromycin is a macrolide antibiotic that covers *N. gonorrhoeae* and is included to address potential co-infection with *Chlamydia trachomatis* and to reduce the likelihood of resistance.

b. **Alternative Treatment**: In cases where dual therapy is not possible or if there are contraindications to azithromycin, alternatives include:
   1. **Doxycycline**:
      i. **Dosage**: 100 mg orally twice daily for 7 days.
      ii. **Role**: Doxycycline is used when azithromycin cannot be used but is less preferred due to lower efficacy against *N. gonorrhoeae* compared to azithromycin.
   2. **Cefixime**:
      i. **Dosage**: 400 mg orally as a single dose.
      ii. **Role**: Cefixime is another cephalosporin alternative but is less commonly used due to concerns about resistance.

## 2. Special Populations

a. **Pregnant Women**:
   i. **Preferred Regimen**: Ceftriaxone (500 mg IM) plus azithromycin (1 g orally) is generally recommended. This regimen is effective and safe during pregnancy.
   ii. **Avoiding Tetracyclines**: Tetracyclines like doxycycline should be avoided in pregnant women due to potential harm to the fetus.

b. **Allergic Reactions**:
   i. **Penicillin Allergy**: For individuals with a history of severe penicillin allergy, alternative treatments such as ceftriaxone with azithromycin should still be considered unless contraindicated. Testing and desensitization might be an option in some cases.

ii. **Macrolide Allergy**: If allergic to azithromycin, alternative regimens such as doxycycline with ceftriaxone or other suitable antibiotics may be used.

c. **Disseminated Gonococcal Infection (DGI)**:

i. **Treatment**: Ceftriaxone (1 g IM or IV) every 24 hours for 7 days is recommended. Adjustments may be made based on clinical response and severity.

## 3. Management of Complications

a. **Pelvic Inflammatory Disease (PID)**:

i. **Treatment**: A combination of ceftriaxone (500 mg IM) plus doxycycline (100 mg orally twice daily for 14 days) is often used to cover *N. gonorrhoeae* and other potential pathogens.

b. **Epididymitis**:

i. **Treatment**: Ceftriaxone (500 mg IM) plus doxycycline (100 mg orally twice daily for 10 days) or other appropriate regimens may be used based on clinical presentation.

## 4. Follow-Up and Re-testing

a. **Re-testing**:

i. **Timing**: Patients should be re-tested for gonorrhea approximately 1 week after treatment if symptoms persist or if there is concern about treatment failure. This is particularly important if symptoms do not resolve or if there is ongoing risk of exposure.

ii. **Partner Testing**: Sexual partners should be tested and treated to prevent reinfection. It is crucial that all partners from the past 60 days or since the last sexual contact are notified, tested, and treated as necessary.

b. **Resistance Monitoring**: Surveillance for antibiotic resistance patterns is important to adapt treatment guidelines and ensure the use of effective therapies.

## 5. Prevention and Counseling

a. **Education**: Patients should be educated about safe sex practices, including the use of condoms, to reduce the risk of transmission and reinfection.

b. **Partner Notification**: Ensuring that all recent sexual partners are notified and treated helps prevent the spread of gonorrhea and other STIs.

c. **Regular Screening**: Individuals at high risk should undergo regular STI screenings to detect and treat infections early.

Effective management of gonorrhea involves appropriate antibiotic therapy, careful follow-up, and preventive measures to reduce transmission and complications. Adhering to updated treatment guidelines and ensuring partner treatment are essential components of comprehensive care.

## Complications:

Gonorrhea, if left untreated, can lead to a range of complications affecting various body systems. These complications can have serious health implications and often require prompt and effective management.

## 1. Complications in Men

a. **Epididymitis**:

   i. **Description**: Inflammation of the epididymis, the coiled tube at the back of the testicle that stores and carries sperm.

   ii. **Symptoms**: Pain, swelling, and tenderness in the scrotum, potentially accompanied by fever and chills.

   iii. **Outcome**: Can lead to chronic pain and, in severe cases, infertility.

b. **Urethral Stricture**:

   i. **Description**: Narrowing of the urethra due to scar tissue from chronic inflammation.

   ii. **Symptoms**: Difficulty urinating, reduced urine stream, and urinary obstruction.

   iii. **Outcome**: May require surgical intervention to correct.

c. **Prostatitis**:

    i. **Description**: Inflammation of the prostate gland.

    ii. **Symptoms**: Painful urination, pelvic pain, and discomfort during ejaculation.

    iii. **Outcome**: Can lead to chronic pelvic pain and sexual dysfunction.

d. **Disseminated Gonococcal Infection (DGI)**:

    i. **Description**: Systemic spread of gonococcal bacteria leading to infection in other parts of the body.

    ii. **Symptoms**: Fever, rash, arthritis, tenosynovitis (inflammation of the tendons), and endocarditis.

    iii. **Outcome**: Requires more intensive treatment and can lead to severe joint damage or systemic complications.

## 2. Complications in Women

a. **Pelvic Inflammatory Disease (PID)**:

    i. **Description**: Infection of the reproductive organs, including the uterus, fallopian tubes, and ovaries.

    ii. **Symptoms**: Lower abdominal pain, abnormal vaginal discharge, fever, and pain during intercourse.

    iii. **Outcome**: Can lead to chronic pelvic pain, infertility, and ectopic pregnancy. PID increases the risk of infertility due to scarring of the fallopian tubes.

b. **Cervicitis**:

    i. **Description**: Inflammation of the cervix.

    ii. **Symptoms**: Abnormal vaginal discharge, bleeding between periods, and pain during intercourse.

    iii. **Outcome**: Persistent cervicitis can lead to chronic pelvic pain and an increased risk of PID.

c. **Vulvovaginitis**:

    i. **Description**: Inflammation of the vulva and vagina.

ii. **Symptoms**: Itching, burning, and abnormal discharge.

iii. **Outcome**: May contribute to chronic discomfort and increase susceptibility to other infections.

d. **Disseminated Gonococcal Infection (DGI)**:

i. **Description**: Systemic infection with gonococcal bacteria.

ii. **Symptoms**: Similar to those in men, including arthritis, skin rashes, and systemic symptoms like fever.

iii. **Outcome**: Can be severe and requires prompt and effective treatment.

## 3. Complications in Both Genders

a. **Increased Risk of HIV**:

i. **Description**: Gonorrhea can cause mucosal inflammation and damage, increasing susceptibility to HIV transmission.

ii. **Outcome**: Individuals with gonorrhea are at a higher risk of acquiring and transmitting HIV.

b. **Ophthalmia Neonatorum**:

i. **Description**: Neonatal conjunctivitis caused by gonococcal infection acquired during childbirth.

ii. **Symptoms**: Severe eye infection in the newborn, characterized by redness, swelling, and purulent discharge.

iii. **Outcome**: Without treatment, can lead to blindness. Prophylactic treatment for newborns is essential.

c. **Systemic Complications**:

i. **Description**: Gonorrhea can lead to systemic infections affecting multiple organs.

ii. **Symptoms**: Fever, rash, arthritis, and in severe cases, endocarditis and meningitis.

iii. **Outcome**: Requires aggressive treatment and can lead to long-term health issues.

**4. Complications of Untreated Gonorrhea**

    a. **Chronic Health Issues**:

        i. **Chronic Pain**: Ongoing pelvic pain or scrotal pain due to complications such as PID or epididymitis.

        ii. **Reproductive Health Impact**: Infertility due to scarring of reproductive organs or fallopian tubes.

    b. **Antibiotic Resistance**:

        i. **Description**: Emergence of antibiotic-resistant strains of *N. gonorrhoeae* can complicate treatment and increase the risk of treatment failure.

        ii. **Outcome**: Requires the use of alternative antibiotics and more intensive surveillance and management.

**5. Prevention of Complications**

    a. **Early Detection and Treatment**: Prompt diagnosis and treatment of gonorrhea can prevent the development of complications. Regular screening in high-risk populations helps in early identification.

    b. **Partner Management**: Ensuring that all sexual partners are tested and treated helps prevent reinfection and the spread of the disease.

    c. **Education**: Educating individuals about safe sex practices, including the use of condoms, can reduce the risk of gonorrhea and its complications.

**Prevention:**

Preventing gonorrhea involves a combination of strategies aimed at reducing the risk of infection, promoting safe sexual practices, and ensuring effective treatment and management. Here's a detailed look at the various approaches to prevent gonorrhea:

**1. Safe Sex Practices**

    a. **Condom Use**:

i. **Description**: Consistent and correct use of condoms during vaginal, anal, and oral sex significantly reduces the risk of gonorrhea and other sexually transmitted infections (STIs).

ii. **Effectiveness**: Condoms act as a barrier that prevents direct contact with potentially infected bodily fluids and mucosal surfaces.

b. **Dental Dams**:

i. **Description**: Use of dental dams during oral sex can reduce the risk of transmission of gonorrhea and other STIs.

ii. **Effectiveness**: Provides a barrier between the mouth and genital or anal areas, reducing the risk of infection.

c. **Mutual Monogamy**:

i. **Description**: Engaging in a mutually monogamous relationship where both partners have been tested for STIs and are exclusively sexual partners.

ii. **Effectiveness**: Reduces the number of sexual partners, thereby decreasing the risk of STI exposure.

## 2. Regular STI Testing and Screening

a. **Routine Screening**:

i. **Description**: Regular screening for gonorrhea and other STIs, especially in high-risk populations, is crucial for early detection and treatment.

ii. **Recommendations**:

1. **Adolescents and Young Adults**: Screen annually, particularly if sexually active with multiple partners or if they have a history of STIs.

2. **Pregnant Women**: Screen for gonorrhea during pregnancy to prevent transmission to the neonate.

b. **High-Risk Populations**:

i. **Description**: Individuals at higher risk, such as those with multiple sexual partners, men who have sex with men (MSM), and individuals with a history of STIs, should be screened more frequently.

## 3. Partner Management and Notification

### a. Partner Testing and Treatment:

i. **Description**: Ensure that all sexual partners of individuals diagnosed with gonorrhea are tested and treated.

ii. **Effectiveness**: Prevents reinfection and further spread of the disease. It is crucial that partners are informed and treated simultaneously to reduce the risk of recurrence.

### b. Partner Services:

i. **Description**: Public health services may provide partner notification services to help individuals inform their sexual partners about potential exposure.

ii. **Effectiveness**: Facilitates timely testing and treatment of partners, reducing transmission rates.

## 4. Education and Awareness

### a. Sexual Health Education:

i. **Description**: Providing education on safe sex practices, the importance of STI testing, and the risks associated with gonorrhea.

ii. **Effectiveness**: Increases awareness and encourages individuals to adopt preventive measures and seek medical advice.

### b. Prevention Campaigns:

i. **Description**: Public health campaigns that promote condom use, regular testing, and safe sexual practices.

ii. **Effectiveness**: Raises awareness and encourages behavior changes that reduce the risk of gonorrhea and other STIs.

## 5. Vaccination

  a. **Current Status**:

    i.  **Description**: There is no vaccine currently available for gonorrhea.

    ii.  **Research**: Ongoing research aims to develop a vaccine, but until then, other preventive measures remain essential.

## 6. Prompt Diagnosis and Treatment

  a. **Early Treatment**:

    i.  **Description**: Early diagnosis and treatment of gonorrhea prevent complications and the spread of the infection.

    ii.  **Effectiveness**: Prompt treatment with appropriate antibiotics resolves the infection and reduces the risk of long-term health issues.

  b. **Treatment Adherence**:

    i.  **Description**: Ensuring that individuals complete their prescribed antibiotic regimen to fully eradicate the infection.

    ii.  **Effectiveness**: Prevents the development of antibiotic resistance and recurrence of the infection.

## 7. Regular Health Check-Ups

  a. **Comprehensive STI Testing**:

    i.  **Description**: Regular health check-ups that include STI testing as part of routine sexual health care.

    ii.  **Effectiveness**: Allows for early detection of gonorrhea and other STIs, ensuring timely treatment and prevention of complications.

## 8. Reducing Risky Behaviors

  a. **Limiting Number of Sexual Partners**:

    i.  **Description**: Reducing the number of sexual partners to lower the risk of exposure to STIs.

    ii.  **Effectiveness**: Decreases the likelihood of encountering partners who may have STIs.

b. **Avoiding High-Risk Sexual Practices**:

  i. **Description**: Avoiding practices that increase the risk of STI transmission, such as unprotected sex and sharing sex toys without proper cleaning.

  ii. **Effectiveness**: Reduces the risk of infection by minimizing exposure to potentially infected bodily fluids.

Preventing gonorrhea involves a multi-faceted approach that combines safe sex practices, regular screening, partner management, and education. By implementing these strategies, individuals can significantly reduce their risk of contracting and spreading gonorrhea and other STIs.

**Multiple-Choice Questions (Objective)**

1. What is the primary cause of meningitis?

    a) Virus

    b) Bacteria

    c) Fungus

    d) All of the above

2. Which pathogen is most commonly associated with bacterial meningitis?

    a) Streptococcus pneumoniae

    b) Enterovirus

    c) Cryptococcus neoformans

    d) Naegleria fowleri

3. What is the primary diagnostic method for meningitis?

    a) Blood test

    b) Lumbar puncture (spinal tap)

    c) Urine test

    d) Skin biopsy

4. Which type of medication is used to treat bacterial meningitis?

    a) Antivirals

b) Antibiotics

c) Antifungals

d) Antiparasitics

5. What is the main route of transmission for typhoid fever?

   a) Airborne droplets

   b) Contaminated food and water

   c) Direct contact

   d) Vector-borne

6. Which test is most definitive for diagnosing typhoid fever?

   a) Urine culture

   b) Blood culture

   c) Stool test

   d) Serological test

7. What is the primary treatment for typhoid fever?

   a) Antivirals

   b) Antibiotics

   c) Vaccination

   d) Supportive care

8. Which organism causes leprosy?

   a) Mycobacterium leprae

   b) Mycobacterium tuberculosis

   c) Streptococcus pneumoniae

   d) Neisseria gonorrhoeae

9. What is a major complication of untreated leprosy?

   a) Blindness

   b) Joint pain

   c) Skin rash

   d) Neuropathy

10. How is urinary tract infection (UTI) most commonly diagnosed?

    a) Blood test

    b) Urinalysis

    c) Stool test

    d) Skin biopsy

11. What is the most common causative organism of UTIs?

    a) Escherichia coli (E. coli)

    b) Staphylococcus aureus

    c) Streptococcus pneumoniae

    d) Candida albicans

12. Which symptom is most characteristic of cystitis?

    a) Fever

    b) Painful urination (dysuria)

    c) Nausea

    d) Headache

13. What is the primary treatment for uncomplicated UTIs?

    a) Antivirals

    b) Antibiotics

    c) Antifungals

    d) Pain relievers

14. What is the causative agent of AIDS?

    a) Human Immunodeficiency Virus (HIV)

    b) Hepatitis B virus

    c) Herpes Simplex Virus

    d) Human Papillomavirus (HPV)

15. Which test is used to measure the number of CD4+ T cells in the blood?

    a) Urinalysis

    b) Complete blood count (CBC)

    c) CD4 count

d) Liver function test

16. What is the recommended treatment for HIV/AIDS?

    a) Antibiotics

    b) Antiretroviral therapy (ART)

    c) Vaccination

    d) Surgery

17. Which stage of syphilis is characterized by a painless sore (chancre)?

    a) Primary syphilis

    b) Secondary syphilis

    c) Latent syphilis

    d) Tertiary syphilis

18. What is the primary treatment for syphilis?

    a) Antivirals

    b) Antibiotics

    c) Antifungals

    d) Pain relievers

19. What is the most common symptom of gonorrhea in men?

    a) Joint pain

    b) Skin rash

    c) Urethral discharge

    d) Headache

20. Which diagnostic test is most sensitive for detecting gonorrhea?

    a) Blood culture

    b) Gram stain

    c) Nucleic Acid Amplification Tests (NAATs)

    d) Urinalysis

**Short Answer Type Questions (Subjective)**

1. Describe the pathophysiology of bacterial meningitis.

2. What are the common symptoms of viral meningitis?

3. Explain the mechanism of infection in typhoid fever.

4. What are the risk factors for developing urinary tract infections (UTIs)?

5. Describe the diagnostic process for HIV/AIDS.

6. What are the main symptoms of primary syphilis?

7. How is gonorrhea transmitted?

8. What are the complications of untreated syphilis?

9. Describe the treatment regimen for typhoid fever.

10. What preventive measures can reduce the incidence of UTIs?

11. Explain the role of antiretroviral therapy in the management of HIV/AIDS.

12. What are the symptoms of disseminated gonococcal infection (DGI)?

13. How is leprosy diagnosed?

14. What are the symptoms and complications of pelvic inflammatory disease (PID) caused by gonorrhea?

15. Describe the pathogenesis of AIDS.

16. What are the common diagnostic tests for syphilis?

17. How can sexually transmitted infections (STIs) be prevented?

18. What are the key features of fungal meningitis?

19. Describe the epidemiology of typhoid fever.

20. What are the potential complications of untreated UTIs?

**Long Answer Type Questions (Subjective)**

1. Discuss the pathophysiology, symptoms, diagnosis, treatment, and prevention of meningitis.

2. Explain the epidemiology, pathophysiology, diagnosis, treatment, and complications of typhoid fever.

3. Describe the pathogenesis, symptoms, diagnosis, and treatment of HIV/AIDS.

4. Discuss the stages, symptoms, diagnosis, treatment, and complications of syphilis.

5. Explain the pathophysiology, symptoms, diagnosis, treatment, and prevention of urinary tract infections (UTIs).

6. Describe the epidemiology, pathogenesis, symptoms, diagnosis, treatment, and complications of gonorrhea.

7. Discuss the pathophysiology, symptoms, diagnosis, treatment, and complications of leprosy.

8. Explain the prevention, diagnosis, and treatment of sexually transmitted infections (STIs).

9. Describe the impact of HIV/AIDS on public health and the strategies to control its spread.

10. Discuss the diagnostic and treatment challenges associated with antibiotic-resistant gonorrhea.

**Answer Key for MCQ Questions**

1. d) All of the above
2. a) Streptococcus pneumoniae
3. b) Lumbar puncture (spinal tap)
4. b) Antibiotics
5. b) Contaminated food and water
6. b) Blood culture
7. b) Antibiotics
8. a) Mycobacterium leprae
9. d) Neuropathy
10. b) Urinalysis
11. a) Escherichia coli (E. coli)
12. b) Painful urination (dysuria)
13. b) Antibiotics

14.a) Human Immunodeficiency Virus (HIV)

15.c) CD4 count

16.b) Antiretroviral therapy (ART)

17.a) Primary syphilis: "Primary Syphilis

18.b) Antibiotics

19.c) Urethral discharge

20.c) Nucleic Acid Amplification Tests (NAATs)